W9-BLZ-065

THE TAX REVOLT

THE TAX

REVOLT

Alvin Rabushka

Pauline Ryan

HOOVER INSTITUTION
Stanford University, Stanford, California 94305

The Hoover Institution on War, Revolution and Peace, founded at
Stanford University in 1919 by the late President Herbert Hoover, is
an interdisciplinary research center for advanced study on domestic
and international affairs in the twentieth century. The views
expressed in its publications are entirely those of the authors and do
not necessarily reflect the views of the staff, officers, or Board of
Overseers of the Hoover Institution.

Acknowledgment is made to the following for permission to reprint the cartoons:
    Opposite title page: Reprinted by permission, Lee Judge/*Sacramento Union**
    Opposite Ch. 1: Reprinted by permission, Lee Judge/*Sacramento Union**
    Opposite Ch. 2: Reprinted by permission, Lee Judge/*Sacramento Union**
    Opposite Ch. 3: Reprinted by permission, *California Journal*
    Opposite Ch. 4: Lou Grant, © *Oakland Tribune/L.A. Times Syndicate*
    Opposite Ch. 5: Bob Englehart, *Journal Herald*, Dayton, Ohio
    Opposite Ch. 6: Reprinted by permission of the *Chicago Tribune–New York News
        Syndicate, Inc.*
    Opposite Ch. 7: Lou Grant, © *Oakland Tribune/L.A. Times Syndicate*
    Opposite Ch. 8: Dennis Renault, *Sacramento Bee*
    Opposite Ch. 9: Steve Greenberg, *Daily News*, Los Angeles
    Opposite Ch. 10: Doug Marlette, *The Charlotte Observer*
    Dust Jacket: Lou Grant, © *Oakland Tribune/L.A. Times Syndicate*
*These were redrawn by Lee Judge from the originals specifically for use in *The Tax Revolt*.

Hoover Press Publication 270

Library of Congress Cataloging in Publication Data

Rabushka, Alvin.
   The tax revolt.

   Bibliography: p. 239
   Includes index.
   Appendixes (p. 213): Text of Article XIII A (Proposition 13) —
Text of Article XIII B (Proposition 4) — Text of Proposition 9.
   1. Real property tax — California.   2. Tax and expenditure
limitations — California.   I. Ryan, Pauline.
II. Title.
HJ4121.C22R3   336.22'09794   81-84219
ISBN 0-8179-7701-5   AACR2

CONTENTS

FIGURES

TABLES

PREFACE

This is a book about Proposition 13 and the tax revolt. Throughout the 1970s public discontent over the tax burden rose almost as
fast as taxes themselves. On June 6, 1978, Californians proclaimed
that they had had enough. On that day, by a resounding two-to-
one margin, they approved Proposition 13, feisty curmudgeon
Howard Jarvis's proposal to slash property taxes.

Commentators greeted its passage with rhetoric reminiscent of
the Revolutionary War. To the *New York Times*, it was "a modern Boston Tea Party." To Nobel laureate Milton Friedman, it was
"heard throughout the land." Indeed, Proposition 13 ignited a political movement that seemed destined to reconstitute government as radically as had the American Revolution.

Almost two years later, Californians again sent a signal to the
nation. This time, however, Cornwallis won at Yorktown. California's overwhelming rejection of Jarvis's proposal to halve state income taxes marked the end of the tax revolt.

What happened in those two years to convert public sentiment so dramatically? Had those voters who expected Proposition
13 to lead to more responsive government changed their views on
the effects of tax cuts? Or had events proven correct the predictions of opponents that Proposition 13 would lead to disaster?

Proposition 13 and similar movements in other states raised
fundamental questions about the American polity and brought to
the fore a conflict between basic political forces. Behind these

questions lie important issues of concern to all citizens—the effects of taxes on the economy, the financing of government services, the role of public opinion in politics, and, most important, popular control over government.

Many of the present work's findings rest on statistics, and a few words on working with statistics on state and local government finances are necessary. A unified source on state and local government finance is available in the annual Governmental Finances series issued by the Bureau of the Census, U.S. Department of Commerce. As of January 1982, these reports were available through the 1979–80 fiscal year. For more recent information, there is no single source. Statistics on revenues and expenditures are prepared periodically by different branches of state and local government. To aggregate the overall figures on state and local government finances requires separate statistics from the state government in Sacramento and the 6,000-odd units of local government throughout the state. The most accurate accounting of public finances appears in the State Controller's Annual Reports, which are issued separately for the state, for counties, for cities, for school districts, and for special districts. The fiscal year ends on June 30, and the controller's reports are typically released after April of the following year. As this book went to press, the reports were available only for the first two fiscal years following Proposition 13; for financial information about the 1980–81 fiscal year, we used estimates prepared by other government agencies, such as the Assembly Office of Research, the legislative analyst, the State Department of Finance, and by private banks.

The State Controller's Annual Reports on local governments are extracted from reports prepared by city, county, school district, and special district fiscal officers. In most instances, these reports are not subject to audit by the controller. Moreover, accounting methods and practices vary among cities and among special districts, which makes comparisons within these units of government of questionable validity. Still, it is widely acknowledged that the controller's reports are the most valid and reliable sources of evidence on actual revenues and expenditures, and they were a primary source of financial information.

Over the past four years a large number of people contributed their assistance to this study, and we take this opportunity to thank them. In Sacramento, the list includes William B. Hamm, the legislative analyst; Bill Lawson of the State Department of Employment Development; Kevin M. Bacon and Arthur Packenham of the Assembly Office of Research; Lewis Watkins, chief of the Bureau of Special Districts in the State Controller's Office; and Bernard Donnelly, Roger Anderman, and James Apps in the State Department of Finance. We also received assistance from the Criminal Justice Council, the Chancellor's Office of the California Community Colleges, the California School Boards Association, the governor's Office of Planning and Research, the Department of Education, and the Business and Transportation Agency.

We relied heavily on the publications and staff of the California Taxpayers' Association, a nonprofit organization located in Sacramento. Kirk West, Loren Kaye, Maureen Fitzgerald, John Sullivan, and Pam McNally were especially helpful. We also tapped the resources of other organizations, including SRI, International; League of California Cities; County Supervisors Association; Rand Corporation; Security Pacific National Bank; Bank of America; and the National Center for Disease Control in Atlanta.

The police departments of Atherton, Redwood City, Mountain View, Menlo Park, Palo Alto, and San Jose answered our queries on the initial impact of Proposition 13 on their programs during 1978–79. The fire departments in the mid-peninsula segment of the Bay Area were equally helpful.

Our colleague, William Schneider, helped us acquire three important polls from the *Los Angeles Times.* John Foley and Susan Pinkus at the *Times* gave us copies of the survey responses, for which we thank the *Los Angeles Times.* Charles Moore ably performed the computer analysis of these three surveys. Christina Peck executed the computer plots on which the figures that appear in the book were based.

Critical readings of the manuscript were given by several colleagues at the Hoover Institution: John Bunzel, Roger A. Freeman, Robert Hessen, Thomas Gale Moore, and Dan Throop Smith. Gerald Dorfman of Iowa State University, Aaron Wildavsky at the University of California-Berkeley, and Richard P. Brady of Hughes, Heiss and Associates all supplied valuable comments.

We thank all the cartoonists and publications that granted permission to reproduce these charming, sometimes biting, commentaries of Proposition 13 and its dramatis personae.

Ilse Dignam did a superb job of multiple typings of the manuscript, at times having to bully the word processor to disgorge the printed record. Phyllis Cairns and her capable staff at the Hoover Press saw the book to speedy publication.

Financial support was provided by the Domestic Studies Program of the Hoover Institution.

We gratefully acknowledge the help from all these sources, who are, of course, not responsible for any errors the book may contain.

one

DON'T MAKE ME USE THIS! GIVE ME ALL YOUR PROPERTY TAX RELIEF!

PRELUDE

On June 6, 1978, California voters approved Proposition 13 by a two-to-one margin and thrust cosponsor Howard Jarvis into the national limelight. Jarvis and Paul Gann's proposition slashed property taxes for the coming year by 57 percent and rolled tax rates back to 1 percent of a property's market value, based on its 1975–76 assessment. Once set, this value may be raised only by a maximum of 2 percent a year. However, when a property is sold, it may be reassessed at its current market value. Under this measure, which amended the state's constitution, a two-thirds vote of the state legislature is now required to increase state taxes. Local governments may impose special taxes only if two-thirds of a jurisdiction's voters approve.

Heralded as the start of a modern tax revolt, Proposition 13 triggered the approval of tax and spending limits in more than a dozen states during 1978 and 1979. It also helped to spur a variety of movements that proposed constitutional amendments to set federal spending limits, require a balanced federal budget, or index tax brackets. During the 1978 and 1979 legislative sessions, 37 states reduced property taxes, 28 states cut income taxes, and 13 states restricted sales tax collections; income and sales tax cuts alone surpassed $4 billion.[1] In early 1978 the nation's state and local governments enjoyed a net surplus of revenues over expenditures of $7.9 billion, not counting previously accumulated reserves. By fall 1979, after more than a year of tax-cutting fever, state and local governments slipped into the red by $6 billion.[2]

Newsweek
2 Per AP 2 N6772

Meanwhile, tax and spending limits qualified for the 1980 ballot in another dozen states.[3]

Media analysts and scholars quickly noted the historic importance of Proposition 13. The *New York Times* (June 12, 1978) wrote that "when California voters approved Proposition 13, the blockbuster initiative that mandates sweeping reductions in property taxes, it was interpreted around the nation as the beginning of a tax revolt—a modern Boston Tea Party." Nobel laureate Milton Friedman, in his *Newsweek* column of June 19, 1978, proclaimed that "the sweeping victory of Proposition 13 will be heard throughout the land. The 'brewing' tax revolt is no longer brewing. It is boiling over . . . California may be the leading edge, but the tax revolt is nationwide."

Newsweek and *Time* each ran cover stories on "the big tax revolt." The *Newsweek* account stressed the national significance of Howard Jarvis's sweeping victory:

Opening Quotes?

> Every once in a while, something happens in America that galvanizes the citizenry and shakes up the country. California erupted last week with just such a seismic outburst. Defying the counsel of politicians, labor leaders and economists, a damn-it-all 65 percent of the voters backed a proposal to slash their own property taxes—and made the tax revolt the new gut issue in American politics . . .
>
> To the backers and beneficiaries of Jarvis-Gann, the stunning yes vote meant several joyous things at once—a genuine and effective revolt against spiraling taxes and profligate spending . . .
>
> What seemed undeniable, however, was that the California tax revolt had raced the middle-class pulse of the country as feverishly as anything since the invention of the station wagon . . . In Idaho, in Utah—in fact in many of the 23 states that provide for ballot initiatives—the California vote proved an instantaneous shot in the arm for groups seeking to get their own Jarvis-type propositions on the November ballot.[4]

All of a sudden, the movement to cut taxes had become irresistible.

Time was no less graphic:

> That sound roaring out of the West—what was it? A California earthquake? A Pacific tidal wave threatening to sweep across the

country? Literally, it was neither; figuratively, it was both. That angry noise was the sound of a middle class tax revolt erupting, and its tremors are shaking public officials from Sacramento to Washington, D.C. Suddenly all kinds of candidates in election year 1978 are joining the chorus of seductive antitax sentiment, assailing high taxes, inflation and government spending.[5]

Journalistic proclamation of a national tax revolt was echoed in the statements of more dispassionate academic observers. John Petersen and Marcia Claxton, for example, argued that passage of Proposition 13 "brought national attention to what had been termed a taxpayer revolt. Although the revolt had surfaced many times before, calling for limits on spending or rollbacks of taxes, it seldom enjoyed much success. However, conditions in California seemed to augur a momentous happening as the referendum drew closer."[6] Somewhat more colorful was Barry Siegel, who anticipated that "June 6, 1978, may go down in history as Black Tuesday for government . . . the tax cutting fever has spread to many parts of the country . . . The November 1978 elections brought fiscal conservatives to office in such unlikely places as Minnesota and Massachusetts . . . the revolt is not likely to go away."[7]

These paragraphs represent a small sample from a blizzard of printed stories on Proposition 13, which some now call the process of "fiscal containment."[8] Passage of Proposition 13 and its contagious effects mean that government at all levels—state, local, and federal—will now have to make do with tighter budgets, smaller staffs, and fewer new programs than in past years. Polls taken in California through 1979 and early 1980 showed both steady and widespread support for Proposition 13. Passage of Gann's statewide spending limit initiative (Proposition 4) in November 1979 by an overwhelming three-to-one majority showed that the steam had not gone out of the taxpayers' revolt. In 1980, Howard Jarvis's subsequent initiative (Proposition 9), which proposed a halving of state personal income tax rates, initially met with equally enthusiastic support. A January 30, 1980, story in the *Wall Street Journal,* for example, was headlined "California Voters Appear Sure to Approve Proposition to Slash Personal Income Tax."

On June 3, 1980, California voters went to the polls once again, but this time the turnout was the lowest since 1960. In a complete volte-face, voters rejected Jarvis's Proposition 9 (dubbed "Jaws II" by critics) by a lopsided 61–39 percent margin. Almost instantly, in some quarters this stunning defeat signified the death of the tax revolt. The *Times* of London (June 6, 1980) remarked that "just as the success of Proposition Thirteen heralded the nation-wide movement for tax-cutting, so it is possible that the defeat of Proposition Nine might mark its general decline." The *Washington Post* used more forceful language:

> Following the overwhelming triumph of his Proposition 13 two years ago, Howard Jarvis emerged as an instant celebrity, widely acknowledged as the father of a "tax revolt" said to be sweeping the nation.
>
> Today, in the wake of Tuesday's 5-to-3 defeat of Proposition 9, his proposal to cut state income taxes in half, Jarvis appears to be returning to political oblivion. The same politicians and pundits who once sought his favor now are beginning to forget him like a bad dream.[9]

Just before the primary election, columnists Rowland Evans and Robert Novak acknowledged that "defeat of Proposition 9 Tuesday will be interpreted nationally as a dying tax revolt."[10]

Unlike Proposition 13, Proposition 9 did not dominate public debate in California. It appeared on the same ballot with two even more controversial measures: rent control and a tax on oil company profits. But even in a presidential primary year, all three measures together could not inspire a voter turnout anywhere near Proposition 13 levels. Voters had simply lost interest. The turnout of 59 percent was the lowest in a presidential primary election in more than twenty years, and Jarvis himself, rather than the tax cuts he championed, often became the issue. Did his rapid fall from grace signal defeat for tax cutters everywhere? Or were Californians acting uniquely "crazy," "faddish," and "flaky?"

For two years, Californians had voted for tax-cutting experiments. The June 1980 election marked the conclusion of this period of taxpayers' revolt—and provides a convenient date from which to evaluate both the impact and meaning of the experiment.

THINKING ABOUT THE TAX REVOLT

Tax revolts rarely happen in American history. The War of American Independence was partly fought to ensure "no taxation without representation," and for the first 150 years following independence, taxation remained relatively moderate, save in times of war. The growth of the welfare state since the Great Depression and the development of a massive array of nondefense government spending programs over the past three decades has brought overall taxation to about 40 percent of personal income. Since 1929 taxation has nearly quadrupled as a share of personal income.

The tax revolt must be viewed in the context of the steady, inexorable rise in the growth of government and taxation in the twentieth century. Some saw in Proposition 13 a reversal of this trend. Others saw only an outcry specifically directed against the property tax. Still others saw a selfish act by hedonistic, middle-class Californians lashing out against the poorer segments of the community who were heavily dependent on government programs. Proposition 13 and the tax revolt it spawned raise a number of interesting questions.

1. Which events precipitated the tax revolt in California? Why did that state's voters wholeheartedly adopt Proposition 13 in June 1978 after rejecting several similar measures during the previous ten years?

2. Why did the revolt focus on property taxes? Were other proposals to cut taxes or limit overall public spending less attractive to voters? Or were conditions so ripe that any tax cutting measure, regardless of its form, would have won overwhelming voter approval in 1978?

3. What kind of message were voters trying to send to state and local governments? What changes did they hope or expect would occur in Sacramento and throughout the counties and cities of California?

4. Did Proposition 13 help or hinder the state's economy?

What happened to employment? How have public servants coped with changing fiscal circumstances? What has happened to taxing and spending trends in the years immediately following 13? How have the quality and quantity of public services changed? Which services have borne the brunt of government decisions to reallocate spending priorities? Why?

5. What have been the unintended consequences of Proposition 13? Are such trends as the movement toward rent control, greater reliance on fees and charges for public services, and increasing state control of formerly local government finances harbingers of permanent change?

6. Why did Proposition 13 touch off so many similar measures in other states and even influence politics in Washington, D.C.? What will be its permanent effect on state and local government financial issues?

7. What are the merits and faults of Proposition 13 as a tax limitation measure? What pitfalls may arise in the future? Will it survive intact or fall prey to amendments or substitute measures as its full effects materialize? If we could start from scratch, what kind of measure should we draft?

8. What is the role of public opinion on tax cuts, given the public's simultaneous commitment to government services that are part of mainstream American social and political values? Does the tax revolt in any way fundamentally threaten these values?

9. Why did the tax revolt dissipate in just two years? How did events and political actors relieve the pressures that fostered the revolt and encouraged its spread? Are those pressures likely to return in the near future? What has the tax revolt revealed about the political motives and behavior of our elected officials?

In the following chapters we propose to answer these questions, using all the available evidence on the effects of Proposition 13 in the three years following its passage. Answers to long-term effects must remain a subject for continuous study throughout the 1980s, but we will attempt to sketch a number of possible changes.

BACKGROUND TO THE TAX REVOLT

Analysts of Proposition 13 suggest that the seeds of the tax revolt were a number of trends that sprouted on June 6, 1978. Some of these trends were economic and political; some national, others purely local; some could be related to pocketbook issues and others to changes in public attitudes. Taken together, they helped set the stage for the approval of Howard Jarvis's measure. The success of this measure represented the culmination of Jarvis's fifteen-year campaign to limit property taxes. On June 6, 1978, the time was ripe at last. Why should this be so?

Inflation. From the close of the Korean War until 1965, Americans enjoyed virtual price stability. All through the Eisenhower years, inflation averaged about 1.5 percent each year. From 1960 through 1965, inflation fell to an even lower average annual rate of 1.3 percent, but the advent of both the Vietnam war and Great Society social programs at home brought this twelve-year period of stable prices to an end. Between 1965 and 1970, prices increased 4.2 percent per year. Inflation worsened during the 1970s. Although the annual increase in the Consumer Price Index ranged from a low of 3.3 percent in 1972 to a high of 11 percent in 1974, the average rate between 1970 and 1978 stood at 6.7 percent.[11] By 1978 all public opinion polls revealed that the public viewed controlling inflation as the number-one national priority.[12]

Rising Taxes. Californians pay federal and state personal income taxes. As incomes rise, so do tax rates. California state income taxes range from a low of 1 percent of taxable income (after exemptions and credits) for single earners in the $2,000 or under bracket to 11 percent of taxable income over $14,000. Until the 1981 tax reforms, federal income taxes ranged from a minimum rate of 14 percent on the first $500 of taxable income over $3,200 for single persons and $5,200 for joint returns to a maximum rate of 70 percent on taxable income exceeding $100,000 for single taxpayers and $200,000 for joint returns.

Statistics support the impact of such progressivity. In 1978 the upper 10 percent of income earners in America paid 49.7 percent of all federal personal income taxes, up from 47.5 percent in 1973. In contrast, the lowest 25 percent of income earners paid only 0.4 percent of all federal income taxes in 1978, down from 0.6 percent in 1973.[13] About half of all California personal income taxes are also paid by the upper 10 percent of income earners in the state.

When real income rises (that is, after taking inflation into account), progressivity increases government's share of national income, but individuals still typically experience an increase in real take-home pay. However, when a taxpayer's income increases solely due to inflation, the effects are quite different.

Inflation places taxpayers into higher tax brackets without increasing their real aftertax income. This phenomenon is known as "bracket creep."[14] Inflation interacts with progressivity in two ways that increase real tax burdens. First, if a taxpayer's income increases at the same rate as inflation, the share of income paid as tax rises because the increase is taxed at a higher rate. Inflation simultaneously erodes the purchasing power of all remaining take-home dollars. Second, the set personal exemptions do not rise in value to keep pace with inflation. The net effect is that real purchasing power may not increase—or may even decline—despite an apparent increase in salary that keeps pace with inflation. Bracket creep thus raises taxes without direct increases in the tax rate schedules. The higher the rate of inflation, the more rapidly tax revenues grow in relation to personal income. This in turn generates a larger public sector. Until 1965, inflation played little part in raising tax burdens, which were mainly due to increases in real income. Since 1965, a significantly greater share of the rise in tax burdens has been due solely to the effects of inflation.

Californians, in particular, were hit doubly hard. As inflation escalated after 1965, the state government raised income tax rates, rather than lowering them to offset the bracket-creep effects of inflation. Before 1967, the state imposed a maximum rate of 7 percent on taxable incomes exceeding $15,000. In 1967 it raised this rate to 10 percent on taxable incomes exceeding $14,000 and in 1971 increased the maximum rate to 11 percent. Increasing the progressivity of the state's personal income tax made bracket creep even more costly for taxpayers. In the decade preceding Proposition 13, each 1 percent inflation-induced growth in personal income raised state income tax collections by 1.7 percent—a bonus of 0.7 percent for the state.[15] An inflation rate of 7 to 8 percent, with private incomes keeping pace, means a *real* increase of 5 percent in state income tax revenues and a decline in private purchasing power.

Other taxes have also risen since 1965. The state hiked the sales tax from 3 to 4 percent in 1967 and again to 4.75 percent in 1972. (The balance of the sales tax is collected on behalf of local governments.) In total, the percentage of personal income paid as state and local taxes grew from just over 8 percent in 1953 to between 15 and 16 percent by 1977. Thus as a share of personal income, state and local taxes doubled for Californians in the quarter century ending in 1977.[16] In money terms, total state and local government tax revenue (exclusive of federal transfers) rose from $414 per capita in 1966 to $1,233 by 1977. This increase in taxes was 25 percent higher than the increase in per capita personal income over the same period, reflecting the combined effects of tax rate increases and bracket creep.[17]

State and local taxes as a share of personal income also rose in the other 49 states, but at a slower rate, during this same period. For example, in 1962 California taxpayers paid about 10.5 percent of their personal income in state and local taxes compared with 9.3 percent in other states, a difference of 1.2 percent. By the 1977–78 fiscal year, Californians paid almost 16 percent in state and local taxes compared to just over 12 percent for non-Californians. Put another way, on the eve of Proposition 13, residents of the Golden State were paying one-third more in state and local taxes as a share of personal income than were the residents of the other 49 states.[18] During the 1970s, California fell increasingly out of step with the rest of the country. (The gap closed to about 0.7 percent after passage of Proposition 13.)

It is interesting to note the difference between the dramatic increase in personal dollar income in California during the past few decades and the actual increase in aftertax, after-inflation purchasing power that remains for each person to spend as he likes. The former has grown by leaps and bounds, while the latter has remained level or somewhat declined. In 1967, disposable per capita income in California was $3,199. (Disposable income is computed by subtracting federal and state income taxes, but not sales and property taxes, from total personal income.) In the eleven-year period from 1967 through 1977, per capita disposable income rose more than 116 percent, from $3,199 to $6,913 per year. But these figures do not take inflation into account. Corrected for inflation by expressing all amounts in 1967 dollars, the actual rise in per capita disposable income is on the order of 20 percent, from $3,199 to $3,836, an annual increase of 1.5 percent.[19] Twenty percent is a far cry from 116 percent.

One of the clues to the eruption of the tax revolt in 1978 can be seen in the trend of changes in real purchasing power. Between 1948 and 1975, real disposable per capita income increased on average slightly more than 2 percent per year. But during the 1970s, the labor force grew dramatically as greater percentages of women went to work. Thus, while real disposable per capita income rose at an annual average of 2.8 percent between 1976 and 1978, this was due solely to higher rates of labor force participation.

Corrected for the increase in the size of the work force, real disposable income per worker actually fell in 1976, 1977, and 1978. Thus, the bulk of economic growth that occurred in California after 1975 found its way through taxes into government hands for government spending.[20] Rising taxes and falling real incomes are not a popular combination with the public.

Rising Property Taxes.   Inflation was a major contributor to the rising tide of property taxes. These comprised about two-fifths of all state and local tax revenue in California before Proposition 13. Indeed, by 1978, property taxes in California per $1,000 of personal income had risen to a level nearly 50 percent above the national norm.

After 1972, home values in California climbed especially rapidly, well outpacing the general rate of inflation. For example, in 1972, single-family homes increased in value 6.1 percent, but overall prices rose 3.3 percent. In 1974, the comparable figures were 14.3 and 11 percent, respectively. By 1976, this gap had widened to 23.7 and 5.8 percent, and, in 1977, remained far apart at 24.6 and 6.5 percent. In some instances, home values doubled and tripled in the short span of five years. Consequently, property taxes also doubled and tripled.[21] Although the effective tax rate, as a percentage of home values, remained relatively stable at about 2.5 percent, an efficient, computerized system of property assessment quickly converted astronomic increases in home values into equally astronomic increases in property taxes.

Several factors worked to push California housing prices up faster than the overall inflation index (for example, no-growth policies, scarcity of land).[22] It is true that homeowners as a class were made better off because of the large capital gains in the value of their homes. But although homeowners were now worth more, they had no more spendable income than they did in the previous decade unless they elected to remortgage part of this gain in housing value and were able to afford the higher monthly payments or moved to a less expensive house to realize the capital gain. However, those on small or fixed incomes, such as the elderly, are less able to refinance than are middle-aged professionals whose annual incomes keep pace with or surpass inflation rates. As a result of escalating property taxes, there were numerous cases of higher property taxes forcing elderly homeowners to sell their homes. Public pressure for property tax relief continued to mount, and Howard Jarvis was able to capitalize on this discontent.

Sharp property tax increases provide especially good fuel for a taxpayers' revolt. Increases in property taxes are more readily felt and publicly criticized than similar increases in personal income taxes. The reason is that personal income taxes are withheld on a weekly, biweekly, or monthly basis and any increase is divided into 12, 24, or 52 separate portions. In the case of property taxes, however, taxpayers receive an annual notice of their new assessment and typically pay the tax in one or two installments. Any sharp rise is instantly apparent.

Cost of Government Services. Elections and polls in America during the 1970s showed a pronounced swing in political orientation as increasing numbers of Americans identified themselves as conservatives rather than liberals. Even college students shifted from their left of center views. Distrust of government had been building since the Vietnam war. Most Americans saw government as wasteful and inefficient: the percentage of people who said that the government wastes much of our tax money rose substantially, from 48 percent in 1964 to 74 percent in 1978.[23] Many believed that government workers were overpaid: in the 1970s the salaries of public employees rose more rapidly than those of private sector employees.[24] "Bloated bureaucrats" became the watchword of 1978.

Although federal employment has remained relatively stable over the past three decades, state, local, and municipal employment rose from just over four million workers in 1949 to nearly thirteen million by 1978.[25] (Overall, the government's share of the labor force rose from 14 to 20 percent in the post–World War II era.) Since the majority of state and local government outlays go for salaries, the increasingly rapid growth of the public sector entailed ever increasing tax demands on the private taxpayer, a trend that could not continue indefinitely without sooner or later encountering taxpayer resistance.

By 1978, a majority of California taxpayers had come to believe that rising taxes were no longer accompanied by a corresponding increase in services, that in some instances they were receiving fewer services. Revelations of massive waste and fraud in welfare and other redistributive programs helped to reinforce middle-class objections to a shift of emphasis by state and local governments from provision of essential services to welfare, health care, and special education programs for low-income, non-taxpaying groups. Public opinion polls revealed that supporters of Proposition 13 most wanted cuts in welfare spending.[26]

Not only had the emphasis in public services shifted from the provision of basic services for all community residents to programs specifically for lower-income persons, but, at the same time, the quality of the essential services had declined. In public education, for example, objective test scores steadily fell year-in and year-out, and even though enrollment declined, pupil-teacher ratios increased and per pupil expenditures rose in real terms.[27] Nor did significant increases in police budgets reduce crime rates. In short, taxpayers paid more every year and often got less.

The Initiative Process   Representative government is sometimes slow to respond to the wishes of the majority; sometimes it fails to respond altogether. But when a state legislature fails to act, America has a political system that often allows individuals and groups to take matters into their own hands. Twenty-three states provide their inhabitants with a means of affecting their own government—ballot initiatives. Given America's federal form of government, with its division of power between the federal government and the several states, a tax revolt need not mean a frontal assault on the national center of power in Washington, D.C. Instead, it can be specifically directed against capitals in those states whose citizens feel themselves overtaxed and are willing to collect enough signatures to qualify an initiative petition for the ballot.

Californians have been accused of overusing the initiative process in areas that range from taxation and smoking to rent control.[28] Since 1970, Jarvis himself had tried but failed to qualify four different property tax relief measures; others had qualified relief measures only to have them voted down on election day. While the initiative may be much used and abused, in the past only a small minority of the measures that qualified were approved. Still, the initiative process provides an outlet for frustrated and outraged electors to try to directly convert public sentiment into a law or a constitutional amendment.

During the 1960s and most of the 1970s, voters turned down a number of ballot measures that would have cut property taxes or limited government spending. So long as real disposable income grew, the taxpayers were prepared to tolerate even more rapid growth in the public sector. But as the growth of real aftertax purchasing power waned, toleration of higher taxes and bigger government was tested to the extreme. On June 6, 1978, it finally broke. The tax revolt was under way, and the nation had a new folk hero—Howard Jarvis.

ERUPTION

The Jarvis-Gann initiative, Proposition 13, was a great personal victory for Howard Jarvis. His fifth attempt since 1968 to amend the state constitution to limit property taxes, it was the first time he obtained enough signatures to qualify his property tax measure as a ballot proposition. In 1968, his first attempt missed by some 400,000 signatures (about half a million valid signatures of registered voters are required to qualify an amendment initiative). Three years later Jarvis came within 100,000 signatures of the magic number. His third (1976) and fourth (1977) tries missed by successively smaller margins of 10,000 and 1,400. His fifth try was a triumph. Proposition 13 garnered a record 1.2 million signatures by the filing deadline; another 300,000 poured in later. Howard Jarvis's persistence had finally paid off. Proposition 13 and the tax revolt are partly his story.

Jarvis was one of many who took the initiative route. Between 1960 and 1978, California's secretary of state authorized the collection of signatures for 188 statewide initiatives, but only 30 obtained the requisite number of names. Of these, the voters approved only 9. Included among these 30 were several other property tax or general spending limit measures, all of which failed.[1]

A convenient point to begin the tale of Proposition 13 is with a series of stories by the *San Francisco Chronicle* (beginning on July 23, 1965) concerning the bribery of property tax assessors across the state.[2] Some tax assessors—elected officers in California—reportedly received campaign contributions in exchange for favorable assessments on business properties.

In California, the "assessed valuation" of each piece of property is supposed to equal 25 percent of the market value of that property. The various political entities empowered to levy property taxes—city councils, county boards of supervisors, hospital, water, and other districts—independently set a tax rate on property within their jurisdiction. Multiplying the assessed valuation by the tax rate determines annual tax payments. Taxes rise whenever assessed valuations rise or tax rates on property are increased. A fall in one can offset, in part or in whole, a rise in the other. But jurisdictions dependent on property taxes can collect more revenues each year without increasing tax rates as long as assessed valuations continue to rise.

The *Chronicle*'s accusations implied that assessments on some business properties had been set below 25 percent of market value.[3] This scandal instantly prompted a previously indifferent legislature to adopt a strong reform bill (the Petris-Knox bill) requiring county assessors to reassess all categories of property at 25 percent of market value within a three-year period and to make frequent reassessments to ensure that valuations remained correct.

Before this reform, assessments varied widely. Single-family homes in San Francisco were assessed, on average, at about 9 percent of market value; across the bay, in Alameda county, the average was 22 percent. Rates on commercial buildings ran as high as 35 percent in San Francisco. Imposition of a uniform 25 percent assessment ratio rapidly increased some homeowner assessments (such as those in San Francisco). Since the increases were not offset by reductions in property tax rates, property taxes correspondingly rose. Although local governments have the legal power to reduce tax rates on residential property, they are required by the state constitution to tax *all* property at the same rate. It was impossible to lower the tax rate on single-family homes without giving up some tax revenues from commercial properties as well, which local governments were loathe to do. Failure to cut rates allowed spiraling assessments to fuel spiraling property taxes. In all, local governments lowered the average tax rate for a California homeowner about 5 percent from 1974 to 1978, but this modest reduction barely offset the doubling or even tripling of assessments over the same period.

In the wake of this reform and the subsequent unintentional rise in homeowners' tax bills came the first attempt to limit or restrict property taxes by the initiative process. In 1968, on his initial drive to limit taxes, Howard Jarvis failed dismally, garnering only 100,000 signatures. He then channeled his support to an initiative authored by Phillip Watson, county assessor of Los Angeles. Proposition 9, as it was labeled on the November 1968 ballot, proposed a separation of property tax revenues into two classes: those allocated to "people-related services" (for example, education and welfare) and those for "property-related services" (public safety, streets, parks). Each year property-tax revenues for people-related services would be reduced by 20 percent of their 1969–1970 levels, until their complete elimination in 1973. Tax collections for property-related services would be limited to 1 percent of a property's market value.

Watson's initiative would have transferred the funding of people-related services from property to general state revenues and perhaps have required increases in the state's income or sales tax levies, although Watson did not specify or suggest where replacement revenues were to be found. The legislature countered Watson with California's first homeowner's property-tax exemption bill. The first $750 of assessed value of an owner-occupied home was to be exempt from property taxation, with the state reimbursing local governments for lost revenues. The legislature placed this measure on the ballot alongside the Watson initiative and sold it to the voter as "responsible" tax relief.

The legislature won round one. Proposition 9 lost by a 68 to 32 percent margin (4.6 million no votes against 2.1 million yes votes). In contrast, the homeowner's bill won 54 percent of the vote. This moderate margin of victory for a modest measure of relief signified that property taxes did not unduly trouble voters. One reason was that in the late 1960s real income in California grew vigorously. The post-WWII boom was in full steam, and Californians were optimistic about their economic future.

Jarvis next tried to qualify a property tax limit measure in 1971. A direct forerunner of Proposition 13, it limited taxes to 1 percent of market value and prohibited special assessments of real property in order to restrict a growing trend toward bonded indebt-edness that had resulted in rising tax levies. It also required a two-thirds vote of the legislature to exempt any category of property, such as churches or private schools, from taxation. This clause immediately drew the ire of religious, charitable, and educational institutions, which enjoyed a tax advantage. The campaign failed by 100,000 signatures. Jarvis did not make this mistake again.

Despite Jarvis's failure, Watson managed to qualify a second initiative, known as Watson II, for the November 1972 ballot. This measure (officially titled Proposition 14) proposed explicit in-creases in sales and business taxes, along with higher taxation on liquor and tobacco, to replace some $2 billion in property tax re-ductions. Watson inserted these explicit tax increases to forestall charges leveled during the debate on Proposition 9 in 1968 that he had failed to devise an alternative source of funding to maintain services charged to the property tax. The voters were hardly more responsive the second time around. Watson II lost by 66 to 34 percent (5.2 million no votes versus 2.7 million yes votes).

Governor Reagan's Spending Limit Interlude. In contrast to Democrats, Republicans traditionally advocate limited govern-ment and low taxes. But in eight years as governor of California, Ronald Reagan raised both sales and personal income tax rates to their highest levels in the state's history. Both rose more than 50 percent. Receipts from these two taxes correspondingly escalated and fueled an increase in state government spending.

In 1973, to counteract the trend of increased state spending, funded in part by these tax rate hikes, Governor Reagan proposed a ballot measure to limit spending. Proposition 1 proposed that state spending be limited to 8.3 percent of personal income in the state and that overall spending be reduced by 0.1 percent a year until it reached a maximum of 7 percent. At 5,700 words, Proposi-tion 1 was both complex and lengthy, but it came much closer to adoption than any of the previous measures proposed by Watson and Jarvis. It lost by 54 to 46 percent (2.3 million no votes against 1.9 million yes votes).

Property Tax Reform Revisited. In 1973, housing prices in Cal-ifornia took off. The state's reformed system of periodic, computerized assessments automatically converted gains in housing values into equally impressive leaps in property taxes, making property tax relief a potentially explosive issue throughout the 1970s.

On election as governor in 1974, Jerry Brown became the fiscal beneficiary of Reagan's tax increases. Governor Brown reaped a steadily growing harvest of tax receipts, without having to raise any of the state's tax rates. Inflation pushed collections from the sales, income, and property taxes to record levels each year.

During the first half of 1976, Howard Jarvis undertook his third petition drive. It missed qualifying for the ballot by a 2 percent margin of 10,000 votes. Watson fared no better. He failed to qualify a 1.5 percent limit measure.

In the second half of 1976, Jarvis picked up exactly where he had left off. His fourth petition drive missed the magic mark by a scant 1,400 signatures. In four unsuccessful petition drives, Jarvis had closed the gap from 400,000 to 1,400, presaging victory in the near future. All through the 1970s the rumbling to limit taxes or spending grew louder.

On July 6, 1977, Howard Jarvis, now on his fifth campaign, teamed up with Paul Gann to file a property tax limitation initiative, the famous Proposition 13. As before, this measure limited property taxes to 1 percent of market value (compared with the existing rate of about 2.5 percent), but this time Jarvis introduced a new feature. Any future increase in taxes or tax rates (excluding property taxes, which could not be raised) would require a two-thirds vote of the state legislature or a vote of two-thirds of the electors in any given local jurisdiction. Proposition 13 did not touch upon the issue of removing exemptions on religious and educational properties, a fatal flaw in the 1971 measure. (For complete text, see Appendix A.)

Jarvis easily met the signature requirements: his organization obtained over a million signatures in southern California, while Gann obtained 158,000 in the northern half of the state. For the first time in the state's history, all 58 counties provided signatures. By the December 2, 1977, deadline, some 1.2 million signatures had been counted. Another 300,000 arrived too late to be included. The overall return of 1.5 million signatures doubled the highest existing record in the state's history. Jarvis and his organization spent a grand total of $28,500 in cash, and an army of eager volunteers donated countless hours of time.

Legislative recalcitrance should get some of the credit (or blame) for the overwhelming success of Jarvis's fifth petition drive. Throughout the 1977 session, the legislature had dallied with three measures to grant property tax relief. California law requires that any appropriations bill pass each house by a two-thirds vote. A compromise plan to grant some $4.7 billion in tax relief over a five-year period fell apart during the summer of 1977, and all subsequent attempts failed. The legislature adjourned in the summer of 1977 without passing a bill. But 1977 was not an election year, and the legislators could safely defer consideration of tax relief until January 1978. This legislative inaction on an increasingly urgent issue sparked Jarvis's campaign and was partly responsible for the record number of signatures. When the legislature reconvened in Sacramento in January, it faced a ballot measure with the most widespread support of any tax limitation measure in the state's history.

THE CAMPAIGN FOR PROPOSITION 13

Having garnered 1.5 million signatures, Howard Jarvis and Paul Gann were off to a running start. A million and a half registered voters by themselves make up 10 percent of all Californians eligible to register to vote (about 15 million), an even larger 15 percent of those actually registered to vote (10 million), and somewhere between 20 and 25 percent of the likely turnout (6.0–6.5 million). The first poll taken on Proposition 13, the Field organization's California Poll of mid- to late February, showed precisely this configuration of support: 20 percent said they would vote for Proposition 13. Victory required only another 1.5 million or so registered voters.

Both the California Poll and the *Los Angeles Times* Poll monitored the shifting trends in public support for Proposition 13. Between mid-February and the end of May, in four separate surveys Field asked registered voters how they would vote on Proposition 13. The results showed an even race throughout the spring, culminating in a dramatic upswing in favor of Proposition 13 in the week immediately preceding the election.[4] By the last three days of May, both a large number of undecided voters and many former opponents of Proposition 13 had become supporters. The dramatic nature of this shift makes an interesting story. (See Tables 2.1 and 2.2.)

The *Los Angeles Times* Poll did not solicit a precise expression of the vote but sought, instead, a more general impression of how the public viewed Proposition 13.[5] Unlike the California Poll, which showed the measure in doubt until late May, the *Times* Poll revealed public support growing in strength with each passing month. The issue was not really settled until sometime in May, when large blocs of undecided or unsure voters joined the Jarvis-Gann bandwagon.

Financial Contributions. Turnout for the June 1978 election was the highest for any nonpresidential primary in over twenty years, due entirely to the controversy sparked by Proposition 13. The two sides in this bitter election together spent some $3 million in an effort to entice or intimidate voters. Opponents outspent sup-

TABLE 2.1

CALIFORNIA POLLS: VOTING TRENDS
(percentage)

If voting now on Proposition 13, would vote:	February 11–23	March 27– April 3	May 1–8	May 29–31
Yes	20	27	42	57
No	10	25	39	34
Undecided/unaware	70	48	19	9

TABLE 2.2

LOS ANGELES TIMES POLLS: IMPRESSION OF PROPOSITION 13
(percentage)

	March	April	May	June
Favorable	39	41	52	56
Unfavorable	31	34	35	36
Unsure	30	25	13	8

porters $1.6 million to $1.4 million, but the sources of financial support are much more interesting than the dollar amounts.

David indeed fought and slew Goliath. The largest donation, $16,000, to the Yes on 13 campaign came from an apartment owners' association with which Howard Jarvis was affiliated. Apart from that one five-figure sum, only two sizable corporations supported the initiative with substantial donations: Host International, Inc., of Santa Monica gave $5,000, and Lassen Land Company in Chico gave $2,500. No other large corporation or brokerage house made any contribution exceeding $200. Instead, the names of thousands of individual donors, most of whom gave between $10 and $100, filled a book some two and a half inches thick.[6]

Goliath was backed by a less numerous, but fatter, group of organizations and individuals, led by public employee and teacher organizations. The California Teachers Association, which contributed through several organizations, gave more than $225,000 to the No on 13 campaign, while various arms of the California State Employees Association added another $100,000. A group of fifteen brokerage firms that sell municipal bonds contributed $125,000. California firemen put in $52,000. Seventeen firms—corporations, banks, insurance companies, utilities—each contributed $10,000 or more; five gave $25,000 each. Another twelve contributed $5,000 or more, with 23 donating between $1,000 and $4,000. The list is a who's who of firms important in California, including major oil companies, utilities, banks, department stores, high-technology industries, hotels, and manufacturers.[7] Businesses evidently feared that property tax cuts might be offset with new taxes on them. Big business liked the status quo.

Supporters and Opponents. Endorsements paralleled the pattern of financial contributions. Prominent proponents were few and far between; the opposition comprised virtually the state's political, business, labor, and educational establishments. Yes on 13 endorsements came from a handful of economists, including Milton Friedman, Arthur Laffer, and Neil Jacoby, who wrote, spoke, and testified on behalf of Proposition 13 and the boost its passage would give the state's economy. Twenty-four economists ran a full-page advertisement endorsing Proposition 13 in the *Wall*

Street Journal. The California Republican party did not take a stand on 13, but two of the four Republican candidates for governor, Evelle Younger and Ed Davis, belatedly endorsed Proposition 13 (and finished one-two in the primary).

Opposition to Proposition 13 came from labor, business, and education circles, the press, and politicians themselves. A partial list of naysayers included, among labor, the AFL-CIO, the California Teachers Association, the American Federation of Teachers, the California State Employees Association, and the American Federation of State, County and Municipal Employees; among business, Bank of America, Atlantic Richfield, and Standard Oil; among political groups, Common Cause, the League of Women Voters, the California PTA, the League of California Cities, and the Democratic party; among the press, every major paper except the *Los Angeles Herald Examiner*; and among politicians, the vast majority of members of the state legislature, the 58 county boards of supervisors, most city councillors, school board members, special district directors, Governor Jerry Brown, and two Republican candidates for governor, Pete Wilson and Ken Maddy.

Radio advertisements repeated that seven past presidents of the American Economics Association and 450 economists teaching in California's universities and state and community colleges opposed 13 on the grounds that removing $7 billion in property taxes from government revenues would severely disrupt the state's economy and vital public services. Full-page newspaper advertisements appeared throughout the state listing the names of thousands of educators opposed to 13. These were men and women of integrity, but the vast majority worked in state-financed institutions.

The Legislature's Belated Response. During the 1977 session, the legislature had failed to agree on a tax relief measure. Things were different in January 1978; every senator and assemblyman was well aware that Proposition 13 had qualified for the ballot. Still, the legislature squabbled for nearly two months before enacting a $1.6 billion property tax relief measure (compared with $7 billion under Proposition 13). SB 1, known as the "Behr bill" after its chief sponsor, Senator Peter Behr, established separate tax rates on residential and commercial construction. Since all property had to be treated equally under the state constitution, SB 1 required a constitutional amendment to split the tax rolls. The amendment was listed as Proposition 8 on the June ballot. For the measure to take effect, voters had to both approve Proposition 8 and reject Proposition 13. If both passed, 13 would supersede 8.

Governor Brown signed SB 1 on March 3, 1978. Altogether, it was calculated to provide $1.4 billion in homeowner and renter relief in fiscal 1978–79. For homeowners, the bill reduced property taxes in the coming year by 30 percent, while maintaining the homeowner exemption (at that point, $7,000). For renters, SB 1 increased the state income tax credit from $37 to $75 and allowed welfare recipients to qualify for the credit. Senior citizens with income below $13,000 were granted additional relief. A complicated provision limited revenues accruing to local governments, and a state revenue limit restricted future state revenue growth to 1.2 times the annual percentage growth in state personal income. For 1978–79, the average homeowner would have received a property tax cut of $366 from SB 1 if Proposition 8 had passed and 13 failed. Kirk West, executive vice-president of the California Taxpayers' Association, championed SB 1, calling it "a massive, bold program with a huge relief structure for homeowners and renters. It contains local revenue limits which go even beyond the property tax."[8]

In contrast to Proposition 13, which was simple in wording and effects, 8 was complex (especially the section distinguishing business property from owner-occupied residential property). Furthermore, the controls in 8 were not as firm as those in 13. Although the Behr plan might have lowered tax rates, future assessment increases could still have increased property taxes. Future tax rate reductions under 8 need have occurred only when assessed values exceeded the complicated local government revenue limit. Under 13, assessment increases were limited to 2 percent per year so long as a house was not sold. Thirteen offered much greater assurance to property owners about their future property taxes.

Virtually the entire legislature championed 8 over 13.

A Campaign of Fear.   One had to be living in California to fully experience the degree to which the voters were warned, intimidated, threatened, or bribed by the ever shriller hysteria, dishonesty, and hypocrisy of 13's opponents. Teachers told their students that classrooms would be eliminated and playgrounds closed. Governor Brown told business firms that he would abolish the business inventory tax, but only if Proposition 13 were defeated. Various lawmakers suggested that the legislature should punish or reward California cities depending on how their residents voted. The elderly were sent a message from the senior citizens division of the Franchise Tax Board implying that they might lose certain tax benefits if 13 passed.

Doomsaying reached record levels in the No on 13 campaign. Black spokesmen warned of a slowdown in affirmative action gains. Clyde Rainwater, director of special programs for Sacramento county, said that 13 would adversely affect the Comprehensive Employment and Training Act (CETA) program, threatening future minority group gains. Former Sacramento Councilwoman Callie Carney claimed that programs for the poor, aged, and ethnic minorities would be threatened. Sacramento county welfare director William Redmond predicted high staff layoffs and costly errors in the administration of welfare programs: he threatened staff cutbacks of up to 50 percent of his 1,250 employees.[9]

The 35,000-member California Federation of Teachers recommended that public schools be closed when the money ran out, if need be in midyear, should Proposition 13 pass. Evonne Braithwaite, a Democratic candidate for attorney general, predicted that passage of 13 would devastate not only schools but all municipal services in California.[10]

Governor Jerry Brown actively campaigned against 13. He warned that local revenue losses due to Proposition 13 would cause major cuts in police and fire services and that state aid to replace local revenues would first have to pay for such legally mandated programs as welfare. Virtually all of the 50 fire chiefs meeting with Brown and his aides agreed that massive cutbacks in fire services would occur if the Jarvis-Gann initiative were approved. In some fire districts, up to half of the fire stations might be closed due to a lack of funds, they claimed. Assembly Speaker Leo T. McCarthy (Democrat–San Francisco) told reporters that most of the estimated $3 billion state budget surplus (a questionable figure, as shown below) would be used to meet federal pro-gram–financing requirements. The money would not even come close, said McCarthy, to covering the revenue losses that schools, community colleges, and other local services would experience if Proposition 13 passed.[11]

Perhaps the most repeated statistic throughout the campaign was produced by a team of econometric forecasters at UCLA's Graduate School of Management. Robert M. Williams, director of the business-forecasting project, and Larry J. Kimbell, director of forecasting models, produce a quarterly business forecast, available to the public, projecting future economic conditions both in Cal-ifornia and throughout the nation. Kimbell and Williams plugged the possible approval of Proposition 13 into their complex model in order to estimate its impact. Their first results in May 1978 predicted a reduction of 451,000 jobs (in both the public and pri-vate sectors) and a jump in the unemployment rate from 7.2 to 10 percent within one year. (These predictions were adjusted down-ward several times and even reversed, in the year following pas-sage of 13.)

Opponents of Proposition 13 chanted these findings with near religious conviction. Over and over again, they warned of massive layoffs and widespread chaos in the delivery of essential services. Using these figures, opponents of 13 gleefully shouted that the overwhelming majority of economics professors in and out of Cal-ifornia considered Proposition 13 irresponsible, if not downright dangerous.

The Surplus. Perhaps no issue more strained government's cred-ibility with the public than the state's volatile surplus. Estimates of its size swelled from about $1 billion in January 1977 to almost $6.8 billion shortly after the election. A $7 billion loss in property tax receipts for local governments, due to 13, implied serious cuts in spending and staffing (even though a leaner government might be a more efficient government), if voters accepted the claim that the state's surplus ranged between $2 billion and $3 billion. But a surplus of $6 billion or more allowed voters to cut property taxes by $7 billion and still maintain existing local government ser-vices, on the assumption that the state would offset most of the loss in property taxes from this surplus. It comes as no surprise that the huge swing to Proposition 13 came precisely at the time when official estimates of the surplus were perceived by voters as deliberate underestimates.

Five years earlier, in fiscal 1973–74, the state's budget surplus had stood at $180 million. ("Surplus" refers to uncommitted resources in the state's General Fund at the end of a fiscal year. The total consists of any accumulated leftovers from previous years plus new revenues minus expenditures.) From 1973 to 1978, the annual growth in revenues outpaced the growth in expenditures by several percentage points. Between fiscal years 1973–74 and 1977–78, revenues increased at an annual rate of 18.4 percent (due partly to bracket creep), while expenditures grew by only 12.5 percent per year. The year-end surplus grew from $555 million to $732 million to $1,713 million, and finally to $3,686 million. On June 30, 1978, the state's books showed an unrestricted surplus of $3.69 billion. Forecasts predicted a $6.8 billion surplus by June 30, 1979, in the absence of state tax relief or a local government assistance package.[12]

In January when state budgeteers presented the 1978–79 budget (to run from July 1, 1978 through June 30, 1979), they faced a major problem—explaining what would be done with the state's excess revenue before passing a property tax relief bill (SB 1 was enacted and signed by March 3). The solution was to estimate a $2.69 billion surplus *and* a $2 billion "reserve," with over $1 billion earmarked for property tax relief. The governor's budget submitted on January 10, 1978, estimated a year-end surplus of $2.69 billion, along with reserves of $2.02 billion that would adequately accommodate any property tax relief measure the legislature might pass.

The State Department of Finance's revised budget of May 1978 included the impact of SB 1, assuming passage of Proposition 8. It revised the estimated surplus from $2.69 billion to $3.58 billion, due largely to an economic boom that increased anticipated 1977–78 revenues by $350 million, with even larger increases in store for 1978–79. But if 8 lost (which seemed likely) and 13 won, the $1.6 billion of earmarked reserve funds would be returned to the general surplus, which would then exceed $5 billion. This announcement was reported in both the *Los Angeles Times* and the *Sacramento Bee* on May 26, 1978, just three days before the final *Los Angeles Times* Poll was taken. Thus two weeks before the election, voters had every reason to believe in a probable surplus exceeding $5 billion.

The surplus would, in fact, be at least $600 million higher if 13 passed because the state rebate for homeowner's property tax exemption reimbursements to local governments would be reduced. Also, deductions on state income tax returns for property taxes would fall, thus increasing state income tax collections in the coming year.

Moreover, the Department of Finance's estimates conflicted with the higher figures released by the state treasurer and the state controller, further weakening the No on 13 campaign. Members of the legislature who had campaigned on the basis of a $2.7 billion surplus now found a $6 billion surplus hard to explain. Indeed, without passage of Proposition 13, the state's cumulative surplus, which at the beginning of fiscal 1978–79 was estimated at $6.8 billion, would have grown to over $10 billion by late 1979–80.

In late July 1978, A. Alan Post, California's widely respected legislative analyst, reported to state lawmakers that the projected budget surplus available for fiscal 1978–79 was in the vicinity of $6.6 billion. How did the $2.7 billion surplus of January become the $6.6 billion of July? Governor Brown offered the following accounting: (1) $400 million from unanticipated tax revenues due to heightened economic activity; (2) $200 million from "tight management and savings of funds not spent"; (3) $800 million from projects eliminated from the budget; (4) $800 million from freezes on state employee pay increases; (5) $1.0 billion from the funds earmarked for property tax relief under Proposition 8; and (6) $700 million from reductions in state reimbursements to local governments to offset revenue losses and reductions in property tax deductions on state income taxes.[13] As it turned out, the legislative analyst's revised total projected surplus for 1978–79 came to $6.8 billion, an increase of over $200 million due to additional federal revenue-sharing funds.[14]

As an aside, Roy Bell lost his job as state director of finance. One year later, in light of the consistent mistakes of the State Department of Finance in estimating the surplus, the legislature created the Commission on State Finance to make quarterly forecasts of state revenues and expenditures. The new, independent entity is composed of four members of the legislature and three members of the executive branch.

The Final Days.   Equally as damaging as the magical growth of the state surplus was a widely reported episode involving the Los Angeles county assessor, Alexander Pope.[15] Appointed to replace Phillip Watson in February 1978, Pope had discovered that a third of Los Angeles county's parcels of property would be reassessed some 50 to 100 percent higher or even more. Since Pope was running for election in November, he did not want to keep the new assessments for 1978 secret until after the June vote and then catch the blame for the increases. In mid-May Pope opened all of his eighteen offices in Los Angeles county to taxpayers. Thousands lined up daily, and their stunned reactions to assessments that in some instances doubled or tripled were relayed on the nightly news and made front-page headlines in the morning papers. The Los Angeles County Board of Supervisors subsequently instructed Pope to mail assessment notices by June 1, but only to homeowners who were being reassessed. Pope refused. Then the board ordered Pope to rescind the increases on 500,000 homes and 200,000 commercial properties and restore their assessed valuations to the 1977 level. On Thursday, May 25, Pope canceled the increases. Governor Brown immediately asked assessors in the other 57 counties to freeze assessments at the current year's level, an action that State Board of Equalization member William Bennet said was illegal.

All along the opponents of 13 had said that government could not function without the property taxes. Now they were taking politically motivated action to stop increases in these "essential" revenues. Between the surplus and the Pope affair, Jarvis emerged as a champion of integrity and government officials as purveyors of dishonesty and hypocrisy.

JUNE 6, 1978: JARVIS DAY

On the thirty-fourth anniversary of D Day, California voters successfully assaulted the beachheads of Sacramento. On that day,

4,280,689 Californians voted to cut property taxes for the coming year by some 57 percent, or a total of about $7 billion. The margin of victory was overwhelming, a landslide 65 to 35 percent. Proposition 13 won a majority of the vote in 55 of the state's 58 counties, losing only in San Francisco, Kern (just barely), and Yolo counties. To make June 6 sweeter still for Howard Jarvis, voters rejected Proposition 8, the legislature's substitute relief measure, by 53 to 47 percent. The vote was a genuine expression of the people's will: the turnout of 65 percent was the highest for a non-presidential primary in twenty years.

It is difficult to overstate the importance of the huge margin of victory. A 51 to 49 percent outcome would not have signaled a tax revolt in California nor spread tax-cutting fever across state lines. But a two-thirds vote could not be ignored, not even in Washington, D.C. The tax revolt was the major economic story all throughout the second half of 1978 and all of 1979.

Both Mervin Field and the *Los Angeles Times* conducted intensive polls before, on, and after election day to discern the causes and meaning of the vote. Gallup, Roper, and Harris immediately conducted national polls on taxes to see if the West had begun a truly national uprising. Analyses and reanalyses of these state and national surveys reveal that the old political divisions—rich versus poor, black versus white, urban against rural, Democrat versus Republican—gave way to a general rebellion against overtaxation and unresponsive government that encompassed all classes of voters.

The California Poll. Two months after the election, pollster Mervin Field summarized his interpretation of the vote, its causes, and consequences.[16] A California Poll conducted the first week in May had found that an unprecedented 94 percent of the voting public was already aware of Proposition 13 and that the unusually intense public debate had generated strong feelings on both sides. Supporters of 13 had already narrowed in on two main objectives: 51 percent said that "taxes are too high" and 46 percent said "the time has come to cut government costs, waste and inefficiency." Opponents reflected a more diffuse range of concerns, with none of them dominant. Twenty-seven percent worried about "school cutbacks," 20 percent feared "cuts in needed services," 19 percent did not want to "put public servants out of jobs," 17 percent thought "other taxes would increase," and 17 percent opposed "windfalls to landlords and business."

In early May, one month before the June 6 election, the Chicken Little syndrome had already worn thin among voters. Among those polled, 73 percent agreed that "local governments can get by on a lot less money" and 47 percent rejected the claim that "Proposition 13 would seriously impair police and fire protecton and the local school system." Whether voters believed that Proposition 13 was the most appropriate way to reduce and reform taxes, seven out of ten concurred that "Proposition 13 is the only way to send a strong message to government that people are fed up with high taxes and too much government spending."

In Field's last pre-election survey, taken May 29–31, the twin themes of high taxes and government waste prevailed. Nearly three-fourths of those sampled rated state government "ineffi-cient," and majorities thought county and city governments and school boards wasteful. About five out of nine thought that state and local governments could provide the same level of services with a 10 percent cutback in funds. Even with a 30 percent cut-back in funds, over 40 percent did not fear service cuts.

The public was quite specific about the areas in which it wanted spending cuts. Welfare occupied first place (62 percent), with public housing in second (41 percent). In most other service areas, voters wanted to retain current levels of spending or in-crease budgets.

Field concluded that "levels of support for Proposition 13 among various demographic and social groups that did go to the polls appeared to hold up remarkably well across partisan, ideolog-ical and social class levels that one might have expected to show marked differences."[17] For example, even a majority of Democrats and Latinos supported the measure.

The Los Angeles Times Poll.　The *Los Angeles Times,* in conjunc-tion with a local TV station, questioned nearly 2,500 voters as they left polling booths on June 6. In a column written for the *Times,* political consultant William Schneider highlighted two di-mensions of the vote: self-interest and ideology.[18]

Schneider reported that only 28 percent of voters living in

rental housing with at least one member of the household a public employee said yes to 13. But this group comprised only 8 percent of the sample. At the other extreme, 81 percent of those
living in their own homes and privately employed voted for the
proposition. This group alone is a majority of the electorate.

The exit poll also elicited a self-definition of ideology: liberal,
moderate, or conservative. For these three groups, the respective
vote for Proposition 13 was 45 percent, 65 percent, and 82 percent.
Support for 13 was so strong that even 45 percent of all self-de-
fined liberals voted for tax relief. "When one takes both interest
and ideology into account, the vote on Proposition 13 has largely
been explained."

For voters, Propositions 8 and 13 were mutually exclusive.
Only 20 percent of those who voted for 13 also voted for 8, while
91 percent who voted against 13 supported 8. Among conservatives, only 2 percent favored 8, compared with 63 percent of the
liberals. Voters saw Proposition 8 as the liberal alternative to 13.

Expectations about local services and possible new taxes dis-
tinguished yes and no voters on 13 even more sharply than homeownership, public employment, and ideology. When asked, "Do
you think local services will be reduced if Proposition 13 passes?"
74 percent of the yes-on-13 voters said no. Conversely, 85 percent
of the naysayers predicted service cuts. The same pattern surfaced
when voters were asked to agree or disagree with the statement "If
Proposition 13 passes, other taxes will be increased." Supporters of
13 disagreed by 52 percent to 37 percent; opponents agreed 82 to 6.

In a nutshell, the two-thirds of the electorate joining the Jarvis
crusade calculated, correctly as events showed, that the massive
state surplus would postpone cuts in local services and obviate any
need to impose new taxes (which the two-thirds vote requirement
of Proposition 13 makes more difficult). Opponents of Jarvis feared
either service cuts, new taxes, or both, but in any event they represented only one-third of the electorate.

Three weeks after the election, between June 26 and June 29,
the *Los Angeles Times* conducted a follow-up poll of 1,083 Californians on Proposition 13, of whom 685 had voted for or against the
measure. In these intervening weeks, Governor Brown and the
legislature had successfully fashioned a $4 billion state aid package

to local governments to replace much of the lost property tax receipts.

A more comprehensive analysis of the *Times* follow-up poll than that reported on July 10 and 11 illustrates how completely the old political coalitions had been overwhelmed by the new wave of tax cutting, which united heretofore disparate groups in the common conviction that taxation had become excessive and could be cut back with little risk to essential public services.[19]

The *Los Angeles Times* Poll of late June elicited basic background information about respondents and their expectations about the impact of Proposition 13 on the state's economy and local government services. Since demographic differences are often used to explain voting patterns, the *Times* Poll assembled facts about each respondent's age, sex, income, employment status, housing situation, political party identification, race or ethnic origin, county of residence, and if he or she worked for the government. Expectations and attitudes also mold the voter's choice, so the *Times* Poll asked each respondent to predict the political and economic impact of Proposition 13. This information affords a detailed look at each voter's characteristics, values, and beliefs, allowing one to discover the reasons for Proposition 13's victory and what voters were trying to say. (The following paragraphs consider only those who said they voted for or against Proposition 13. Those not registered or who failed to vote are excluded.)

A first glance at the survey results suggests that Schneider's explanation—self-interest and ideology—was on the right track. Of those who lived in their own homes, 71 percent voted for Proposition 13. In contrast, only 45 percent of renters endorsed the measure. The same pattern held for those who felt their jobs might be at risk: 67 percent of those with safe jobs supported Jarvis; only 41 percent of those who feared loss of employment followed suit. But there was no difference at all between those employed and those out of work: in each instance, 61 percent voted for 13.

Differences occurred along other lines as well. Among Republicans, 72 percent said yes, compared with 54 percent of Democrats. Still, a majority of Democrats voted for the initiative, which shows the breadth of its appeal. Jarvis drew support uniformly across the state, save in San Francisco, where only 47 percent joined the bandwagon. Sixty-five percent of whites, 49 percent of Chicanos, and 30 percent of blacks said yes. But since the two minority groups comprised only 14 percent of the voting population, the ethnic factor bore weakly on the final results. Finally, the better-educated were most opposed to Proposition 13. The percentage supporting 13 fell from 67 percent among those with some high school education to 58 percent among college graduates to only 40 percent among those with postgraduate education.

To summarize these preliminary findings, Republicans, whites, homeowners, and those in secure jobs voted overwhelmingly for Proposition 13. Democrats (though only a bare minority), ethnic groups, the exceptionally highly educated, renters, San Franciscans, and those fearful of losing their jobs voted against it. These results are entirely plausible; yet, as we will see, they are also misleading and mask the real determinants of Proposition 13's landslide victory.

In an early review of the election, Mervin Field correctly concluded that levels of support for Proposition 13 cut across partisan, ideological, and social class lines that usually show marked differences in these respects. Professor Richard A. Brody of Stanford echoed these findings. Using counties as the basis of his analysis, Brody compared size of a county's school age population, average personal income and its rate of change between 1970 and 1978, liberal or conservative ideology as seen in support for previous marijuana and death penalty initiatives, political party registration, property tax levels, homeownership, or growth in per capita county taxes. He, too, could find little to distinguish yes from no voters: "Enthusiasm for the Prop. 13 approach to property tax relief was widespread and did not reflect merely the vote of special interests. All of the state's geographical, political, ideological, and economic divisions came out strongly for the measure."[20]

Why was this so? The main reason was that each voter's perception of the effects of Proposition 13 was more important in shaping his vote than was political belief or socioeconomic status. Throughout the campaign, opponents threatened the voting public with severe disruptions in services, especially police, fire, and education. Proponents promised that 13 would eliminate waste in government and stimulate the economy. Voter evaluation of these claims did not fall into traditional social, economic, or political packages. Rather, voters from all social backgrounds shared common beliefs about the future.[21]

Seventy-five percent of those who voted on June 6 rejected the prediction that "public safety will be endangered because of fewer police and firemen" and 63 percent did not agree that "education will deteriorate with lower school budgets" because Proposition 13 had passed. Between two-thirds and three-quarters of the voters were deaf to the Chicken Little syndrome. In other words, only one-quarter to one-third of the electorate feared decay in either police and fire protection or public education.

To look more closely at the relationship between expectations about public services and the vote on Proposition 13, 62 percent of those who feared a decline in public safety and 70 percent of those who feared a decline in education voted no. But of those who rejected the doomsaying, the percentages who foresaw no decline in safety and education were 70 and 79, respectively. To simplify somewhat, those fearing cuts in local services voted no. Those without such fears voted yes. And the overwhelming majority of all classes of people were not fearful.

Proponents of 13 promised two benefits: "The economy will be stimulated because people will have more money to spend" and "wasteful government programs will be eliminated." Among all voters, 40 percent agreed with the first statement and 66 percent with the second. In turn, of those who agreed, 81 percent and 71 percent, respectively, voted for 13. Of those who rejected both claims, 54 percent and 56 percent voted no. In sum, the optimists endorsed the measure by overwhelming majorities; the pessimists split just about even.

A last issue was the way Proposition 13 would distribute tax relief. Fifty-seven percent of those who voted believed the rich would benefit most. Of those people, some 57 percent in turn voted against 13. However, among the 43 percent who disagreed with the statement, a huge 81 percent voted themselves a tax cut.

Overall, supporters of Howard Jarvis felt strongly about Proposition 13 and its potential benefits to both the economy and government of California. In contrast, skeptics split almost evenly. The outcome, rather unconventional in democratic societies, reflected the wishes of an intense majority over a moderate-to-indifferent minority.

Was there any systematic relationship among economic, political, and social class characteristics of the voters and their expectations about local services or economic stimulation? The answer is *no*. Neither race, income, party registration, area of residence, homeownership, nor other demographic elements separated those who feared declines in services from those who did not.[22]

And there is good reason for these findings. Each respondent was asked to predict the one, final, lasting result of Proposition 13 from among the following choices: "Government services will be cut back permanently; other taxes will be raised to make up the difference; the gap will be closed by cutting out waste and inefficiency; or none of these will happen—they'll find the money somewhere else." Only 8 percent of all respondents said that government services would be cut back permanently; of those who had favored Proposition 13 only 5 percent selected that result. Of those who had voted for 13, a robust 43 percent said that waste and inefficiency would be cut and 18 percent believed that money would be found elsewhere (no doubt the state's large surplus). Some 26 percent feared new taxes, but had voted for Proposition 13 anyway. But for a majority of voters, the expected gains from cutting waste and inefficiency coupled with the massive state surplus had meant that passage of Proposition 13 was virtually risk-free.

Voters had few doubts about where the ax should fall. Welfare was the majority's first choice (some 54 percent) for reductions in service. Parks and libraries came in second (26 percent) and third (25 percent). When people were asked which two or three services they were least willing to see cut, the answers were police (75 percent), fire (56 percent), and schools (52 percent). A majority wanted to spare these three "essential" services. Field's election-day California Poll revealed the same feelings: 62 percent favored spending cuts in welfare and public assistance programs, 41 percent in public housing projects, but only 8 percent sought cuts in police and 6 percent in fire services. The voters wanted selective, not wholesale, reductions in government services.

Was it irrational that welfare programs were overwhelmingly the first choice for spending cuts since these expenditures are, by and large, mandated by state and federal laws and are unlikely to be pruned? No. The electorate's answer was not so much a guide to likely reductions in government spending as a statement about the relationship between tax burdens and tax benefits.

Taxpayers support and use such locally provided services as police, fire, and schools. Here, the relationship between property taxes and property-related services is clear. To stretch the point, voters can appreciate a general tie between paying taxes and getting in return police, fire, schools, and other local services. Not so for welfare. Welfare recipients and property-tax payers are mutually exclusive classes. One class (property owners) is taxed to support the other (welfare recipients). Since the taxpayer in general does not benefit directly from welfare payments, they are, therefore, most expendable. In this regard, Proposition 13 was a middle-class revolt against taxation for purposes of redistribution of wealth and income by government. Voters were seeking not to dismantle the whole framework of government but to reduce the scope of its activities to link a reasonable level of taxation with essential services.

A NATIONAL REFERENDUM ON PROPOSITION 13

Within a month, Proposition 13 and the tax revolt became the favorite subject of public opinion pollsters. *Newsweek* released a Gallup Poll on June 19; the CBS/*New York Times* Poll was aired on June 27; and the Harris Survey followed on June 29. Taken together, these surveys confirmed suspicions that Jarvis had indeed touched off a potential national tax revolt.

Newsweek was first off the press with a freshly commissioned Gallup Poll of 750 Americans to determine the nationwide extent of the tax revolt.[23] The first question tested support for Proposition 13: "Would you favor or oppose a proposal in your state to cut or limit property taxes—even if it means a reduction in certain local services, or an increase in other forms of tax?" To this question, 57 percent replied "favor" and only 30 percent "oppose." Voters across the country favored a Jarvis-type property tax limit by almost two to one. One in four said that property taxes could be cut 20 percent with no serious reduction in local services. And, as in

California, voters most resented excessive spending on such social services as welfare, counseling, and mental health. The most cited reasons for the rapid increase in local taxes in recent years were that "too much money is spent on overhead and administration" and that "money is often spent on programs and services that are really not needed."

The CBS/*New York Times* Poll interviewed 1,527 adults between June 19 and 23, of whom 434 were a special sample of Californians to see if Californians differed from other Americans.[24] In the sample of 1,093 Americans of voting age outside California, 51 percent supported a Proposition 13 measure for their local communities, 24 percent were opposed, and the others were undecided—a two-to-one ratio among those with an opinion. The corresponding California percentages were 53 and 34. If anything, support was stronger outside the state.

The findings signaled widespread concern over wasteful, inefficient government. Seventy-eight percent of those polled felt that government squandered "a lot of the money we pay in taxes" and overwhelmingly identified welfare and other social services as their preferred target for spending cuts. A considerable minority, 31 percent, agreed that "almost all welfare services paid for by the government could be eliminated." Few recommended cuts in schools, police, and fire, the "essential" services.

Belief in government waste has steadily increased in the past few decades, rising from 47 percent in 1964, to 66 percent in 1972, to an all-time high of 78 percent in this June 1978 survey. Fully three in four supported a law requiring a balanced federal budget.

The CBS/*New York Times* Poll statistical breakdown of the support for 13 showed solid nationwide approval. Respondents supported the measure in roughly equal proportions regardless of race, income, age, political ideology, political party affiliation, and homeownership/renter status.

The Harris Survey, released in June, reported that Americans favored a Proposition 13–type measure for their own states by more than a two-to-one margin.[25] By 89 to 5 percent, this survey of 1,500 adults found that Americans interpreted the vote for Proposition 13 as "a strong protest that people running government will have to respond by trimming a lot of waste from government spending." By a margin of 68 to 26 percent, Americans believed that taxpayers did not get good value for their state tax dollars; for local government, the margin was an equally damning 63 to 34 percent.

Between mid-May, the turning point in the campaign that made Proposition 13 inevitable, and the end of June, Howard Jarvis had transformed the entire national landscape. A nationwide tax revolt was in full swing. Americans across the land would watch with interest how Jerry Brown and the state would cope with the Great California Taxquake of 1978.

three EVERYONE

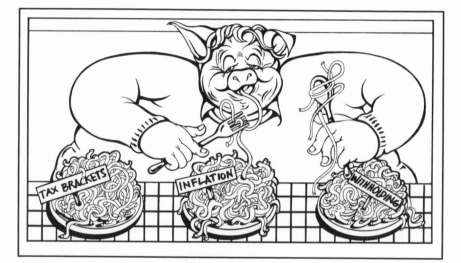

the 'obscene' surplus

SCRAMBLES

THE CONVERSION OF JERRY BROWN

To understand Governor Jerry Brown's changing political stances on Proposition 13 requires consideration of his political ambitions for the 1980 presidential primaries. These ambitions led him first to oppose 13 and later to become its total devotee, as he strove to be in the vanguard of public opinion.

Initially, Brown vigorously championed the legislature's alternative, Proposition 8, on the grounds that it was a far more moderate and preferable way to grant property tax relief. In his ardent support of 8, Brown labeled 13 "a ripoff" and warned voters that "we're looking at the biggest can of worms that has ever been presented to government anywhere . . . There's been nothing like this since the Depression."[1] He stressed that passage of 13 would replace "one monster with another," with "disastrous implications." But when the polls began showing in May that 13 would win, Brown softened his rhetoric and prepared contingency plans. On June 6, Brown was among the first to proclaim the victory, as if it were his own. He pledged to the people that he would implement the new measure immediately "in the most humane, sensitive way I can." He also pledged that no new state taxes would be passed to make up for the lost property tax revenues. "The people want a tax cut, not a shell game," he said.[2] His sensitivity to public opinion and his reassuring speeches and actions after 13's passage induced a large share of the public to forget that the governor had recently been its most vocal critic. The post-13 polls showed a truly remarkable turnaround. More people thought it was Brown who had supported the measure rather than Evelle Younger, the Republican candidate for governor in November, who in fact had supported it all along.

Brown's overnight change of opinion might have been difficult to explain in ordinary circumstances, but these were no ordinary times. This was a year of major political importance. Brown was an aspiring candidate for re-election to the governorship and selection as the Democratic nominee for president in 1980.

In addition, Brown was no stranger to the art of the political flip-flop; it had been his stock-in-trade throughout his career. By the time of his election to the governorship in 1974, Brown had already acquired a reputation for evanescent political stances on major issues, so much so that he had acquired the pejorative nickname "the spirit." Originally, as part of his campaign for governor, Brown had tagged himself a "new spirit," who would drive out the evil ghosts left in Sacramento by former Governor Reagan. Later the name came to be used against Brown and to represent all that was bad about his airy political stances and his disinclination to be pinned down to concrete facts and issues.

As soon as Proposition 13 was seen to presage a national trend, Brown quickly maneuvered from a position of opposition to one of leadership on the themes of tax limitation and smaller government, even supporting the national movement to balance the federal budget with a constitutional amendment. But why initially did he so misjudge public opinion when he chose to support 8 over 13? Various reasons have been suggested to account for this mistake, among them: (1) Gray Davis, the governor's chief aide, wrongly advised him to oppose the measure; (2) Since the measure was initially opposed by Democrats and favored by Republicans, Brown, as leader of his party, was expected to battle the proposition; and (3) Brown felt pressure from big corporations, such as the Bank of America, to oppose 13 as disruptive to California's economy, the more so since he had supported the "California Means Business" campaign to boost industry in the state. Whatever the reasons, Brown never verbally assassinated Howard Jarvis, thus leaving the door open to rapprochement. As Mike Qualls of the Los Angeles Herald Examiner put it: Brown "was always careful not to criticize Jarvis himself . . . He was beating the hell out of 13 on the one hand and praising Jarvis on the other . . . Jarvis and Brown [had] a mutual stroking society."[3]

Brown's philosophy had always been stated as one of economic conservation. As far back as 1974, before property tax limitation had become the spearhead of the taxpayers' revolt, Brown's ticket to office had been as the innovator of an "era of limits." He claimed an awareness of growing public discontent with waste, extravagance, and inefficiency in government. In 1975, he stated that "an honest government is not enough. We also have to be effective . . . Restoring the legitimacy of government requires that public officials act like servants to the people, not like kings."[4]

Yet, despite his promises and exhortations to limit spending, state and local governments continued to increase spending, and property taxes on owner-occupied dwellings escalated at an alarming rate between 1975 and 1978. Moreover, Brown sat on a "contingency cushion" in the form of the state surplus. A small bequest from Reagan, Brown had carefully and vigilantly conserved and built it up to provide for his own political needs. By exercising tight control over this nest egg, Brown knew that he could cut taxes in 1977 or 1978 to ensure both a good showing for his first term as governor and re-election for a second.

In spite of the surplus, Brown warned Californians in 1975 that "avoiding a general tax increase will not be easy . . . but I'm determined to see this year through without asking the people for a further sacrifice in the form of new taxes. And this means that every branch and department of government must reexamine itself with a view toward eliminating expenditures not absolutely essential to the well-being of the people . . . The uncertainty of the economy . . . make[s] it imperative to keep state expenditures well within credit revenues."[5]

In his first budget in January 1975, Brown stressed the need to conserve funds in an "era of limits" and called his budget—personally written—a "no-nonsense budget." He emphasized that "the first test of all of us is to live within realistic limits."[6] By July 1975, the state anticipated a year-end reserve of $313 million, yet the budget was enacted with grave warnings of potential fiscal difficulty. Only a few days after Brown signed this budget into law, he sent a memorandum to the appropriate agency department heads on the 1976–77 budget, warning them that he intended to "take every step possible to avoid a general tax increase in the fiscal year 1976–77. Accordingly, new programs which cost money require corresponding reductions in other programs."

When January 1976 arrived, Brown was able to fulfill his intention of not increasing taxes. The 1976–77 budget left a surplus exceeding $510 million. But Brown had been talking so long about his efforts to prevent a tax increase in this "era of limits" that the public had reason to believe that the state was running low on funds. Brown continually stressed impending hard times not only to the public but also to the legislature, warning them, "Do not lull yourselves into thinking that hard times are over or ignore the lessons of other states which have raised taxes and cut vital services . . . we must be prepared to weather cyclical economic reverses that may be just around the corner."[7] Due to his constant vigilance, the state treasury had amassed a huge surplus of about $2.7 billion by January 1978, later revised upward to $6.8 billion, the largest state budget surplus in the nation's history. Meanwhile Brown was pleading for conservation in the face of shrinking government funds.

Thus when Proposition 13 passed by landslide proportions, Brown quickly revived his old themes. "We have our marching orders from the people," he announced. "This is the strongest expression of the democratic process in a decade." Proposition 13 "reaffirms my era of limits," he declared. Brown then proceeded to demonstrate this by freezing all salaries of state employees and setting aside funds for the emergency bailout of local governments and schools newly deprived of their tax base.

In answer to critics' labels of "Jerry Jarvis" and "political opportunist," Brown responded that his political conversion to 13 was not unusual, but in fact quite in line with his "era of limits" philosophy. He admitted having made mistakes and changing his mind but stressed that he would do everything he could to implement Proposition 13 humanely and sensitively. In explaining his new position, he said: "I opposed [13] because I thought there were problems. I think they're still there . . . But, nevertheless, that [Proposition 13] is the mood. It's an opportunity as well as a problem. And I've tried to fix it . . . People say, 'Well, isn't that a change of mind?' When 65% of the people tell you something, you're a darn fool if you don't listen. You shouldn't be there if you don't want to listen."[8] Major attempts to implement 13 included the state pay freeze, over $4 billion in bailouts to local governments from the surplus, significant cuts in the state budget, and the establishment of the Post Commission to examine local government and suggest formulas for cost-saving and streamlining local services.

Brown's embrace of 13—sincere, realistic, or opportunistic— served his political fortunes well. Even before passage of 13, Brown's Republican opponent, Evelle Younger, had supported the measure, and polls taken at the time of the primary showed Brown and Younger almost even in the race for governor. Younger celebrated his Republican primary victory with a week in Hawaii and then entered the hospital for surgery. But, after the primary and the passage of 13, polls showed Brown running way ahead and predicted him the winner by a landslide. When Younger finally emerged from the hospital, Brown enjoyed great popularity and an unassailable lead in the polls, subsequently confirmed by his re-election to the governorship.

When challenged on his particular brand of politics and affiliation during the campaign, Jerry told the Catholic Labor Institute: "People say, 'What are you? Are you a liberal or are you a conservative?' I think you can be both." He had, he said, come to Sacramento as a fiscal conservative, became corrupted somewhat by the political process, and then become a "born again" tax cutter.[9] In effect, Brown turned what might have been a personal political disaster into a campaign triumph.

During Brown's conservative resurrection, Younger was caught napping. Before the race had officially begun, Brown had effectively sewn up his re-election. Had Younger had his surgery before taking his vacation, he might have been able to offer some challenge to the incumbent. But, then, all along Brown was thinking in a larger political framework than Younger, and the lure of the White House beckoned for 1980. Winning the governorship by a large margin in California virtually assured Brown of a place in the presidential race, and given his presidential aspirations, this was Brown's apparent intention. According to Brown's personal philosophy, there was nothing inconsistent in the way he implemented his political ambition either pre- or post-13. As he quite clearly stated on separate occasions, "When I see a good idea, I'm prepared to steal it. In politics, we don't have any laws against plagiarism."[10] "Now, occasionally, I've changed my mind—Proposition 13. I found out I was wrong and I was ready, at least to try to make it work . . . Once the people make the choice, we make it work. And that's really what you ask from a leader."[11] And a leader was exactly what Brown intended to be— first the governor for a second term and then the presidential candidate for 1980, and perhaps 1984, if the first run was promising.

THE BAILOUT: FAST, FAST RELIEF

Following passage of 13 on June 6, the legislature and local governments had three weeks to survey the damage and develop workable plans for the new fiscal year, which began July 1. Suddenly bereft of billions in property tax receipts, local governments turned to the legislature for assistance. Fortunately, the $6.8 billion state surplus was available to tide local agencies over until long-term solutions could be found. However, despite this massive surplus, both time restrictions and the need to devise plans for equitable distribution of these funds imposed a difficult task on the legislature.

Yet, in spite of great pressure, "a harried, almost terrorized legislature managed to produce a workable distribution of $5 billion to school districts, counties, cities and special taxing districts a full week before the July 1 deadline imposed by the referendum."[12] In all, the occasion provided evidence that governments have a remarkable ability to legislate with speed when circumstances demand. As a member of Brown's administration summed up the event, "Everyone showed extraordinary self-discipline. There was just no room to fiddle."[13]

The first bill produced by the legislature, popularly termed "Bailout I," more technically SB 154 (shortly followed by SB 2212), was drafted during one of the most chaotic periods in the state's political history. "Within three weeks more funds . . . were distributed than had ever been allocated in one action by any state legislature, while the most urgent particular needs were also met."[14]

In the scramble for funds, cities, counties, schools, and special districts fought each other, each demanding that the legislature provide it with the revenues necessary for its survival. Representatives of various interest groups crowded the halls of the capitol during the deliberations. Representing the various major interest groups were (1) for the schools: Wilson Riles, state superintendent of public instruction, together with representatives of the California Teachers Association and the California School Boards Association; (2) for the counties: representatives of the County Supervisors Association of California; (3) for the cities: representatives of the League of California Cities; (4) for children: representatives of the children's lobby; and (5) for the special districts: since special districts offered such a great variety of services and "had difficulty coming up with hard data to justify their fiscal needs,"[15] only the firefighters' lobby was thought to be effective. Furthermore, although fire and police services were to remain at the levels provided in 1977-78, thus limiting the competition for funds somewhat, the various units of government nevertheless still jockeyed with one another for state support.

One of the major problems caused by the bill involved "reserves." Bailout I provided that cities, special districts, and counties with substantial reserves received less state aid than others. Those who had conserved were penalized and forced to spend their savings. As one firefighter from northern California explained, "Fire districts often keep what may look like reserves to purchase equipment. We're scheduled for our next purchase—of a fire truck—in 1980 . . . We have what looks like substantial reserves but [these] are already allocated."[16]

Due largely to the machinations of partisan politics, police and fire services emerged with full funding.[17] Most state legislators, in both political parties, were shocked by 13's passage. Few had supported it, and most were stunned by its margin of victory. Although angry with the electorate, legislators could vent their hostilities only on each other. Initially Republicans and Democrats deadlocked. Newly convinced that the tax cuts would lead to economic expansion, Republicans, led by Assembly Minority Leader Paul Priolo, announced their support for allocating the surplus to local governments with "no strings attached" and no new taxes. However, on June 16, 1978, when the Joint Conference

Committee, composed of members from both parties, concluded its work on the exact details on the fiscal relief package, Priolo, together with Senate Republican leader William Campbell, revealed his own program for state fund allocation. Priolo called for "full funding of police and fire services," thereby reversing his previous position. It was not entirely coincidental that this proposal closely followed an announcement that a thousand Los Angeles policemen were facing layoffs due to anticipated Proposition 13 budget cuts. The Republican proposals received widespread publicity in the news media and were the subject of partisan negotiating during the subsequent week. The Republicans, in their battle against the state buyout of health and welfare programs, cited public opinion polls to support their position and showed that the public did not want cuts in police or fire protection. In response, Democrats accused Republicans of advocating "government by polling"; attempting "to fashion the California legislature into a California City Council" that would override local priorities; and pushing the state toward bankruptcy (the cost of full state funding of local police and fire services was estimated at $2 billion).

Finally, Democrats conceded priority funding to police and fire as part of a compromise to win Republican support for Democratic fiscal relief suggestions. However, this concession stopped short of guaranteeing a specified amount for police and fire services; rather, it permitted wide local discretion in setting priorities.

The two major police law enforcement lobbies strongly supported the idea of priority funding for police services, but their political influence was not the determining factor in fashioning the bailout—rather partisan political jousting resulted in the compromise package that finally emerged from the legislature. The lobbies did, however, solidify support among already sympathetic politicians for funding priority. The prime impetus for police and fire protection priorities among Republicans was their fear of a "spite syndrome"; that is, local officials might attempt to cut essential services as a demonstration of their post-13 sentiments. In the end, Democrats and the governor accepted "priority funding," primarily because of polls showing high voter support for police and fire services.

In the area of education, the formula funding fight was equally fierce, but one of the schools' main lobbyists, Superintendent of Public Instruction Wilson Riles, presented an excellently prepared case to the government. Due to the superiority of his data, unlike those prepared by representatives of other special interests, "he was able to set a state-aid target (restoring school districts to 90 percent of formerly projected levels) and then prepare computer runs demonstrating the effects on each (school) district of various methods of attaining that statewide average."[18]

"In contrast with education, the State knew relatively little about city budgets, and next to nothing that was current about special districts. There was a widespread feeling in Sacramento that State aid should be allocated according to damages caused by Proposition 13 to 'vital' local services, but lack of data made it impossible to translate that belief into finely grained formulas."[19]

In the end, the legislators used historical shares of property tax receipts as a base to determine city bailout allocations, as well as the nonwelfare and Medi-Cal (California's medical insurance program) component of county allocations. However, the city formula was "insensitive to patterns of spending on types of services; each jurisdiction simply got an amount based upon former shares of property-tax revenues . . . Without knowing how this would affect other vital local services, policymakers assumed that cuts in other services would be more tolerable than police or fire cuts."[20] Adoption of a pro rata formula helped solve the immediate crisis, but only postponed squabbles over long-term funding.

Special districts were least able to lobby for their share of funds, partly due to the diversity of their needs. For example, according to the *Sonora Daily Union Democrat* (July 28, 1978), "only local fire districts are expected to get 'bailout funds' from the state . . . Representatives of special districts other than fire departments were told . . . that they will probably not get any of the funds . . . Park, cemetery, water and sanitary districts will have to come up with the money from somewhere else." But another state requirement upset district representatives even more. Money saved for improvement projects, such as equipment purchases, new park restrooms, new fire trucks, had to be used to make up the deficits.

When the legislature gave each county total control over the distribution of the surplus allocated to special districts within its borders, the autonomy of this class of administrative units was further eroded. However, as Humboldt County Supervisor Erv Renner put it, "distributing the surplus funds will put the board in a powerful position. But it is a power the board never wanted . . . We never had done it before and it is like making a cake without a recipe."[21] "We're going to attempt to distribute [the bailout money] fairly as we go. That's as far as our responsibility goes."[22]

Before reaching agreement on the final wording of Bailout I, the legislature considered and rejected a number of plans. Among these, the legislature had considered giving additional funds to those cities that had a pre-13 tax rate of $1.50 or more per $100 assessed valuation. However, this plan was abandoned as impractical since it unfairly rewarded the high-tax, big-spending cities. Under this plan, the city of Los Angeles would have ended up with almost half the relief set aside for cities while San Diego would have received nothing. Another abandoned proposal based relief to cities and counties on current tax rates, which would have unduly penalized fiscally conservative cities that had kept tax rates down. Eventually, the legislature fashioned a program that held revenue losses of local governments to about 10 percent of their pre-13 budgets for 1978–79.

The rescue bill itself (SB 154) was written by Senator Albert S. Rodda (Democrat–Sacramento). This twenty-page bill specified that surplus state funds were to be distributed directly to counties, cities, and school districts, but the funds for the special districts were to be given to the various county boards of supervisors to allot as they wished.

School districts were to receive roughly $2.2 billion, the counties $1.48 billion, the cities $250 million, and the special districts $125 million. In addition, $900 million was set aside for short-term loans to local governments "so that vital services are not interrupted." (The final loan fund turned out to be $870 million, but local governments drew only $28 million of this. The remaining $842 million stayed in Sacramento and was carried over as surplus into the next fiscal year.)[23] The funds were to be distributed by both the state and the county boards of supervisors. The state agreed to fund health and welfare programs that, hitherto, had been paid for mainly by the counties. The bill also provided for a freeze on state-paid employee salaries.

In school district financing, the state bailout was based on the wealth of each district. Those who spent most per student lost up to 15 percent of their proposed budgets for 1978–79 (not actual 1977–78 spending), while the poorer districts lost, on average, about 9 percent.

Despite the apparent advantages to the majority of cities, several rejected the state aid offer and went it alone. National City, in Los Angeles county, was the first to officially refuse the aid. City leaders felt that the redistribution of the surplus was "detrimental to the interests of National City and its people" because it (1) shifted major local decisions to the state level; (2) encouraged increased local spending to qualify for a share of the state surplus in "clear violation of the mandate of the people as expressed in the adoption of Proposition 13"; and (3) violated the basic principle of home rule by regulating such local issues as employee salary levels, local governmental service and manning levels, and the amount and use of local reserve funds. Furthermore, by advocating the use of local reserve funds, the bill contributed to inflation and contravened "principles of prudent fiscal planning."[24]

Others soon followed National City's lead, but the specific reasons for declining the funds varied from one local unit to the next. Some cited "principle"—they felt that they should be able to spend their money without state interference. Others believed that it was "an issue of integrity" or that the money they were getting was not worth the restraints that came with it. Among those who refused help, Alpine county had the most unique reason; namely, the funds were "unnecessary." "We're so small, it [Proposition 13] just didn't affect us the way it did others," said county accountant Susan Brooker. "We are very self-sufficient this year. We didn't need it."

Only Alpine, among the counties, declined its allocation. Of the state's 400-odd cities, 11 finally rejected bailout funds, ranging from a low of $2,000 for Monte Sereno to a high of $2 million for Garden Grove. Known city refusals totaled at least $3.5 million, a very small fraction of the $250 million set aside for them.

The story was somewhat more complicated for special districts. Three categories of special districts—those entirely within cities, those entirely within one specific county, and those taking in portions of several counties—provide a myriad of unique services. These three groups were respectively allocated $2.1 million,

$110.1 million, and $12.7 million. Three special districts entirely within cities refused a total of $39,500 and ten multicounty districts declined their quota of $1,304,000. Since counties took over the distribution of funds for special districts within their boundaries, all $110.1 million was accepted. In total, less than 1 percent of the bailout funds was rejected.[25]

When the bill was finally completed, the various senators who had worked so hard to fashion it had mixed reactions. But overall, they felt it was as good as it could be, given the pressing circumstances of its composition, and the immediacy of its drafting. Senator Bob Wilson (Democrat–La Mesa) described his own feelings and those of the county delegations on the bill's shortcomings: "There's not time to make a perfect bill. There's a lot about it that I don't like. With time, next year, we can work out the problems and perfect the more subtle aspects."[26]

In explaining his decision to support the bill, Assemblyman Larry Kapiloff (Democrat–San Diego) said he would vote for it, "but I'm not proud of it." "The blind, the crippled children, the old folks and the totally disabled are not going to get cost of living increases to keep up with the inflated dollar. I'm voting for it only because of the urgency of the moment."[27]

Assemblyman Waddie Deddeh (Democrat–Chula Vista) described his feelings more graphically: "It's as if we had a drowning child in intensive care . . . All we did was get him breathing again. He's still in danger and a long way from recovery."[28]

The main stumbling blocks had been the delicate subject of state buyout and takeover of certain programs that local government could no longer afford to support. Chief among these were health and welfare programs, which had always been a bone of contention between the state and the counties. Well before the arrival of Proposition 13, county boards of supervisors had tried to persuade the state to assume the local share of welfare costs, which were too financially burdensome for most counties to support. However, once the state agreed to take over these costs, together with those of the schools, everyone was relatively pleased with the bill, despite its other shortcomings. But Senator Wilson voiced the opposition's viewpoint. He objected to the state takeover of all welfare and Medi-Cal costs because most of the money would go to counties with large numbers of welfare recipients. "I don't want the state to take over the two systems."[29] However, the author of the bill, Senator Rodda, proclaimed his bill to be nothing more than a stopgap. It was his feeling that passage of Proposition 13 had unearthed a number of problems. In his words, "We have fallen into a ditch—the fiscal ditch—and who knows how deep it will be."[30]

Having managed to save essential services for the immediate fiscal year, the state then faced the problem of long-term funding. The chief deputy legislative analyst, John Vicherman, did not see any easy solutions down the road. He pointed out to the Senate Finance Committee, which was dealing with long-term financing plans, that "unless things change dramatically in the next few months, it's going to be very hard for you to be generous with local governments."[31] All local agencies were duly forewarned that the bill was a one-year program and that they would have to gird themselves for continued cutbacks in the future.

The governor himself was equally insistent in pointing out that the surplus would not permanently solve the long-term financial problems of local governments. In campaigning against 13, Brown had warned that he wanted "people to be fully aware of the fact that the reduction in local government would in fact be a serious and substantial reduction . . . Year one, we have a very healthy surplus . . . Year two, we may have a similar amount. Year three, and then the economists begin to differ."[32]

In order to help solve the long-term needs of the local governments, Brown appointed a blue-ribbon commission composed of prominent individuals from both the government and the business sectors. As chairman, he selected ex–legislative analyst A. Alan Post, who brought many years of experience in government to this task. The commission met for several months in an attempt to work out how, given a permanent reduction in revenues, local governments could best reorganize and streamline their services.

An Interlude in Futility

The Post Commission, officially entitled "The Commission on Government Reform," consisted of fourteen members whose expertise in public affairs covered a wide field. Besides Post, the commission included Mayor Tom Bradley of Los Angeles; Helen

Copley, publisher of the *San Diego Union and Tribune;* Darlene
Daniel, member of the board of directors, California League of
Women Voters; John Henning, labor leader, the California Labor
Federation, AFL-CIO; Fred Heringer, president of the California
Farm Bureau Federation; Neil Jacoby, economist, UCLA; Clayton
Record, president of the County Supervisors Association of Cal-
ifornia; Cruz Reynoso, appellate justice and former director of Cal-
ifornia Rural Legal Assistance; Wilson Riles, state superintendent
of public instruction; William Matson Roth, businessman and a
1974 Brown gubernatorial opponent; Nathan Shapell, businessman and chairman of the Commission on Government Organization and Economy (the Little Hoover Commission); Rocco
Siciliano, business executive of Ticor, the parent corporation of
Title Insurance and Trust and other financial firms; and Caspar
Weinberger, former secretary of the U.S. Department of Health,
Education, and Welfare and former director of the California Department of Finance. In fulfilling their appointed task, the members sought advice from numerous representatives of local
government and public interest groups. By the end of July 1978,
they had prepared an ambitious 44-page outline of the tasks in
hand, focusing on four major areas: (1) state and local tax systems;
(2) state and local expenditures; (3) the organization of state and
local government; and (4) the effects and opportunities afforded by
Proposition 13.

Within each of these four areas, "57 separate study projects
were to be examined by volunteer task forces comprised of representatives from cities, counties, school boards, taxpayer associations, low-income advocate groups, private businesses and other
areas."[33] The commission took almost seven months to prepare its
117-page final report, which was submitted to the government on
February 5, 1979. Its major recommendations were threefold: permanent state takeover of more than $4 billion in local-govern-
ment costs for schools, health and welfare, and the courts; sharing
of state sales tax revenue on a permanent basis with local agencies;
and increased state taxes, if necessary, to maintain reasonable government service levels. The report concluded that significant program reductions and economies would eventually be required at
all levels of government.

Despite the initial enthusiasm of everyone involved and the

amount of time spent, their final product proved both controversial and disappointing. One observer suggested that the governor had balanced the commission so evenly between supporters and opponents of Proposition 13 that "the panel was unable to tackle the hard questions concerning the size, cost and scope of government." It was also noted that if "Brown had wanted the commission to succeed, he should have stacked it with Proposition 13 supporters."[34] Furthermore, Brown was accused of increasingly undermining the basic efficiency of the commission by not allotting it any funds for staff or even paper-copying costs. Instead, it was told by executive order that its report was due January 15, 1979, and that it was to use existing facilities and personnel.

Given these operational difficulties and time limits, it appears that the commission set up too ambitious a program. First, four committees had trouble producing reports. "A number of the task force reports contained good background analyses but few clear-cut findings and recommendations." Second, the commission tried but failed to deal with two basic questions; namely, "What was the Proposition 13 message?" and "Is Proposition 13 good or bad?" Last, the commission was unable to decide if its task was "to find replacement revenues for Proposition 13 losses or to identify major program cuts and other means of delivering the same programs at less cost."[35]

Yet, as Chairman Post himself noted at one of the meetings, "if the report was to be useful to the Governor and the Legislature, it must have clear-cut findings and recommendations."[36] But despite an awareness of its goal the commission failed almost totally in this respect.

For example, "the commission recommends that the state take over the major costs of schools, welfare, courts and county health expenditures on a permanent basis, but nowhere in the report are there any dollar figures attached to these recommendations, although the total cost is given as $4.1 billion." The report also failed to allocate dollar amounts to recommended reductions and economies. The sole reference to a figure appeared in Post's additional comments. "At the outside, by my own estimate, our recommended economies and specific cost reductions might reach upward of $1 billion." The report also did not tell the governor and the legislature that the "net effect of the state permanently assuming more than $4 billion in new obligations is an increase in state budget expenditures by about 25% above the pre–Proposition 13 budget levels" (from $15 to $19 billion).[37]

Furthermore, the commission also skirted the issue of economies in local government. Instead, it emphasized what the governor and legislature should do to fill the gap between local revenue and local needs. Despite its mandate, the commission spent most of its time dealing with the more philosophical aspects of the problems involved than with "the nuts and bolts of government." Part of the reason for this theoretical preoccupation lay in the opposing viewpoints of the individual members. For example, on the issue of cuts in local governments, the liberal members of the commission, such as William Matson Roth, John Henning, and Wilson Riles, held that local government was incapable of absorbing a $7 billion property tax cut without severely disrupting state and local services and programs. Consequently they preferred to emphasize replacement revenues rather than future cutbacks as a solution to funding problems.

The pro-13-ers, for their part, offered few concrete proposals on cuts in state and local government. Instead, they settled for an adversarial position, disagreeing with the opposition's viewpoint and making few suggestions.

Given all these problems, it was not surprising that the commission's report was a disappointment, pleasing no one and actively antagonizing some. Both Assembly Speaker Leo McCarthy and State Finance Director Richard T. Silberman personally disassociated themselves from the report's tax-increase recommendation since this directly contradicted the voters' mandate of Proposition 13. Both they and the governor again stressed that "state taxes will not be increased to cope with the consequences of 13." Similarly, other leaders in local and state government were equally disappointed to find no new ideas and suggestions in the report, and soon after its publication, the document became doomed to rest on "a dusty niche in a backroom shelf."[38]

Yet, despite its failure, the commission had served its purpose—saving the governor's political face. Creating the commission so soon after the landslide victory of 13 showed Brown to be both publicly responsible and sensitive to the voters' mandate. A blue-ribbon commission was exactly what he needed to show him the best way to meet this mandate. That the findings of the commission were not due until 1979, after his re-election, was perhaps less important than the public knowledge that the commissioners were pursuing their task at the governor's behest.

CHALLENGE IN THE COURTS

Landslide passage of Proposition 13 was a glorious victory for Howard Jarvis and his supporters, but its outspoken opponents did not accept defeat graciously. Instead, they filed numerous lawsuits challenging the legality of 13 and attempting to have it struck down. Gradually all levels of the California court system became embroiled in arguments over the legality of the measure. Finally the state Supreme Court itself resolved the issue in September 1978.

This was no ordinary trial, however. Emotions ran very high. Indeed, prior to the hearing, the high court justices had been threatened with recall. Both they and their families received anonymous threats of physical harm if they overturned the case. But Chief Justice Rose Bird stressed at the beginning of the hearing that those "who threatened us fail to recognize the proper role of the judge in our society." She also pointed out that "our oath of office does not ask us to make popular decisions but to have the courage to follow the law, obey our consciences and uphold the constitution." She vowed that "all the threats in the world will not deter us from the important task before us."[39]

Attorney General Evelle Younger charged that in attempting to strike down Proposition 13, its opponents were in fact attacking the initiative process itself, which, in his view, was "nothing less than the fundamental right of the people to control their government." He noted that the opponents of 13, having lost at the ballot box, had come before the Supreme Court "seeking to accomplish through judicial decision what they failed to do through the democratic process." It would be "tragic" for the court to overturn Proposition 13 because such a move "would represent nothing less than a statement by this court that the people of California have lost control of their government."[40]

The court quickly agreed in June to hear three lawsuits challenging the legality of Proposition 13: one filed by a group of school districts and educational associations, a second by several counties, and a third by the city of San Francisco. On August 11, the court listened to three hours of oral arguments in a courtroom jammed with spectators and reporters. Attorneys representing 27 school and community college districts, six Northern California counties, and the city of San Francisco argued that the measure was blatantly unconstitutional. Court members accorded the arguments great importance, allocating 90 minutes to each side to present its case instead of the usual 30.

The principal arguments against Proposition 13 were:

1. It was not a mere amendment to the state constitution, but rather a basic constitutional revision—something only a constitutional convention had power to engineer.

2. It covered more than one subject, which the California constitution says an initiative cannot do.

3. It violated 14th Amendment equal-protection guarantees because property owners whose assessments were frozen at the 1975–76 level would pay less in taxes than those who had bought property more recently.

4. Proposition 13 was vague and would be impossible to implement.

5. San Francisco argued that it was "contractually obligated" to pay retirement benefits to former city employees and must make contributions to employees' health plans. The attorney for the city argued that the U.S. Constitution prohibited passage of laws that could endanger the fulfillment of contracts.

In defending Proposition 13, Attorney General Evelle Younger and his assistant, John Klee, argued that:

1. A "revision" was something that affects the entire state constitution, which Proposition 13 did not.

2. The four tax-related sections of Proposition 13 did not cover more than one subject but were "fundamentally related in furtherance of a common underlying purpose."

3. The proposition was not vague because, among other

things, "the initiative [was] clearly more precise than the conflict-of-interest legislation upheld by [the Supreme] Court" four years earlier.

4. It did not violate equal-protection guarantees because the reduction and control of property taxes provided in Proposition 13 would tend to make the purchase of property more affordable for all.

5. As for San Francisco's contractual problem, Klee argued that the city was "far from any situation" of defaulting on its contracts.

The counsel for the school districts, Los Angeles lawyer William Norris, told the court that Proposition 13 had gone far beyond granting property tax relief. It had crippled local governments' taxing authority and had overturned the long-established constitutional guarantee of local home rule. In making such a drastic change, this measure had violated two constitutional provisions. First, an initiative may only amend, but not revise, the constitution; second, an initiative may address only one subject. Unfortunately, due to frequent questioning by Justices Frank Richardson and Mathew Tobriner, Norris ran out of time before he could argue this last key point. But the essence of his case was that the measure went far beyond just tax relief to make "sweeping changes" in the state constitution. In winding up his case, Norris conceded that since the proposition was already in effect, it would be extremely difficult to reverse the complex machinery and so he requested that any court ruling to overturn it should be "prospective" and not "retroactive."[41]

Assistant Attorney General John Klee hotly disputed this argument. He claimed that the cities, counties, and school districts "were at the sufferance of the state long before June 6" and that Proposition 13 had not, therefore, substantially revised the relationship between state and local government, as Norris had claimed. Klee did concede that Proposition 13 had had a varied effect on methods of taxation, but maintained that it did not violate the "one-subject rule" because its several provisions were related and had an "underlying purpose"—tax relief. "There is nothing in the one-subject rule that says you can't have different provisions that do different things as long as they are related."[42]

Alameda county's counsel, Richard J. Moore, argued that the proposition violated the equal-protection clause of the Constitution and pointed out that the disparity in taxation resulting from the measure's arbitrary 1975 cutoff would have a "chilling effect" on the buying and selling of houses. Justice Tobriner responded that "some date had to be fixed." Moreover, it was "not irrational" for people to be taxed at different rates; indeed, sales tax rates varied within the state. Tobriner asked Moore, "What's wrong with it?" Moore countered, "The mere fact that you know that you have to pay a higher valuation does not free a person from equal protection under the law."[43]

San Francisco Deputy City Attorney Burk E. Delventhal argued that the proposition could endanger a local government's ability to meet contractual obligations, for example, to a public retirement system, in violation of the provision in the U.S. Constitution prohibiting impairment of contracts. Delventhal told the justices that San Francisco feared that due to the loss of property tax moneys, the city would be prevented from fulfilling its contractual obligations to the city retirement system.

Justices Tobriner, Richardson, and Stanley Mosk questioned Delventhal sharply on the prematurity of his argument. Tobriner asked specifically, "Has any bondholder not received his interest?" Mosk asked if a city could never "cut back on its tax collections" because of contractual obligations. Delventhal responded, "That's exactly what I'm saying."[44] In replying to Delventhal's argument, Assistant Attorney General Klee noted that "Proposition 13 really is no mystery." There was neither evidence that people were being denied equal-protection rights nor that contracts were being endangered.

Attorney General Younger labeled the various petitioners' attempts to have the measure overturned as "technical arguments" designed to subvert democratic process and urged the court to overrule them. "In passing Proposition 13," said Younger, "the people did not vote to abolish government but simply to reduce taxes." Chief Justice Bird asked Younger whether he was questioning the petitioners' right to raise these constitutional issues. Younger denied that this was his intention, but pointed out that the petitioners were arguing that for the technical reasons they had presented, the people could not reduce their taxes. "If you follow [the petitioners'] argument to its logical conclusion, they're saying an initiative can't do more than change a comma ... Therefore they are doing more than challenging Proposition 13. They are challenging the fundamental principle that the people of California have a right to exercise control over their government through the initiative process."

All sides eagerly awaited the next stage of the court's deliberations. Usually the Supreme Court does not rule in haste, and an opinion takes six to eight months to appear. This would have meant a decision in Jaunary 1979, creating much uncertainty for school districts, cities, and counties in planning budgets for the coming fiscal year. However, in the case of Proposition 13, the ruling was surprising not by its actual terms, but by its speed.

A responsive court reached its decision by September 1978, two months ahead of the November state elections in which the voters had to confirm the gubernatorial appointment of four of the justices, Rose Bird, Wiley W. Manuel, Frank C. Newman, and Frank K. Richardson. In a unanimous opinion handed down on Friday, September 22, the justices ruled that Proposition 13—now officially Title XIII A of the California constitution— "survives each of the substantial challenges raised by the petitioners."[45] The justices ruled that:

1. Proposition 13 was not a revision of the constitution, but was instead "modest in both concept and effect."
2. The measure did not violate the equal-protection clause because the idea of differential taxation for identical property was not a new one in the tax scheme.
3. Contracts between public employers and their existing and retired employees are not violated because a case providing such violation has not been brought to the court's attention.

If courts follow election returns, the two-thirds vote for 13 had also brought forth a legal verdict upholding its constitutionality. But it is interesting to speculate how the court might have ruled had Proposition 13 passed by only a 51 to 49 percent margin.

Salary Freeze

After this landmark ruling on the constitutionality of Proposition 13, the Supreme Court was asked to adjudicate another volatile issue: the legality of the wage freeze for nearly 1.6 million government workers that the state had imposed under the terms of the bailout.

The case was brought to the Supreme Court by five public employee unions that filed lawsuits against the counties of Sonoma and Santa Clara, the cities of Monterey and Long Beach, and the state of California itself. The members of these unions had been scheduled to receive pay increases, but the bailout froze the salaries of state government employees and stipulated that local governments receiving aid must do likewise. Any local agency giving its employees pay raises larger than those given to state employees was ineligible for bailout funds. Prior to the bailout, state employees had been due for a cost-of-living increase. However, Governor Brown vetoed this raise, citing public economy and the need to conserve revenues.

In similar fashion, most local governments throughout the state withheld scheduled pay raises from their workers. This action led several local unions to ask the Supreme Court to reinstate the pay increases. They argued that the freeze violated the law of contract and that the state had acted illegally in mandating a pay freeze as a condition for obtaining bailout funds.

The public employee unions had been encouraged in their suit by the success of an earlier case. In that suit, filed by the Public Employees Association of Riverside, Superior Court Judge Ronald Deissler had ruled in favor of granting nurses at Riverside General Hospital scheduled pay increases. He declared that attempts to bar pay raises for local employees were "unconstitutional and void."

The Supreme Court convened for the hearing on February 15, 1979. The plaintiffs argued that according to the state constitution, the legislature could not pass any law nullifying contracts. The state defense attorneys argued that because of Proposition 13, the state was facing a fiscal crisis and, therefore, had no option but to cancel the planned pay raises. They contended that the state's action was legal because, according to the constitution, the legislature can act for "the general welfare of the state."

The State Assembly majority leader, Howard Berman, explained that the legislature felt that a general wage freeze was the fairest way of dealing with the problems posed by the bailout. Since state employees were denied a wage increase in order to conserve government funds and prevent layoffs, it would have been unfair to use these savings to boost the wages of local government employees.

The state attorney's argument that the law was a valid response to a "fiscal emergency" and the expected massive layoffs and cutbacks in public services was contested by the plaintiffs on the grounds that the surplus had forestalled any layoffs and cutbacks. The plaintiffs' attorneys argued that the U.S. Constitution allows no exceptions to the sanctity of contract.

The Supreme Court did not accept the state's argument and ruled (with the benefit of hindsight) that, in fact, there was no "fiscal crisis" to justify the abrogation of the pre-existing contracts. It noted that an analysis provided by the local governments in question, which showed an average 22 percent reduction in revenues resulting from the passage of Proposition 13, was actually written *before* the bailout provided approximately $4 billion in state aid.

Justice Stanley Mosk wrote in his opinion that "the asserted 'fiscal emergency' relied upon by respondents as justification for the salary limitation was largely alleviated by the very same bill which contains the limitation." He pointed out that the "bailout package brought local agency losses down to an average of 6 percent rather than the 22 percent upon which respondents' claim of emergency is based." "Respondents do not claim" he added, "that a 6 percent loss of revenue would justify the invalidation of wage increases."[46]

In addition to the "violation of contract" argument, the plaintiffs also argued that the state had violated a law mandating "home rule" for local government. On this issue, the court ruled that the legislature did not have the power to interfere with the salary–setting authority of local governments. "While the state may not have been under an obligation to distribute state funds to local agencies to assist them in resolving whatever problems were contemplated in the wake of Proposition 13, it could not require as a condition of granting those funds that the local agencies impair valid contracts to pay wage increases."[47] The court also extended its ruling to local entities other than cities and counties covered by the home-rule law, on the grounds that to do otherwise would be unfair to workers in general-law cities, counties, and school and other special districts.[48] "To deny them an increase because of these provisions would amount to a denial of due process and equal protection of the laws, and would be contrary to the Legislature's intent," wrote Justice Mosk. "We are persuaded by the claim that the Legislature intended to treat all local government employees and officers in a uniform manner."[49]

In an unanimous decision, the seven-member Supreme Court concluded that the actions of the legislature and Governor Brown had violated federal and state constitutional provisions that bar the legislature from impairing contractual agreements, as well as a California guarantee of home rule for local government. Local entities with pre-existing agreements were ordered to provide the pay increases retroactively to the date specified by contract. However, public employers did not have to pay interest on the outstanding increases. In making this point, the court recognized that these agencies had no choice but to deny contractually established increases to their employees in the face of the state's conditions for receiving funds (which most agencies desperately needed).

This decision affected about 1.1 million employees of cities, counties, schools, and special districts. It was estimated that the ruling could cost a total of $1 billion, but that figure was conjectural because it depended on the outcome of negotiations between employee organizations and government agencies.

Cleaning up the Measure

The constitutionality of 13 and the local government pay freeze, while perhaps the most important, were not the only issues to require court resolution. Other legal clarifications were sought in such areas as unsecured property assessments, user fees, retroactivity, pensions, and tuition.

The subject of unsecured property assessment promised substantial savings for both private individuals and corporations if the 1 percent limitation extended to unsecured as well as to real property. (Unsecured property is basically property that can be moved, such as boats, airplanes, supplies, equipment, and business machines.) An early and important case to determine the proper charges on the 1978–79 unsecured tax roll was filed in San Diego Superior Court by the San Diego Board of Supervisors against the county's tax collector, Gerald Lonergan, and its auditor, James E. Jones.

The plaintiffs requested the court to declare that the 1 percent rate limitation on property assessment under Article XIII A was equally applicable to personal property. Before the suit was filed, Lonergan and Jones had issued unsecured tax bills that reflected the 1977–78 secured tax rate. Some 800 of the county's 70,000 unsecured tax bills had been mailed when the Board of Supervisors filed its suit and obtained a temporary restraining order preventing the issuance of any more bills until the correct levy was judicially determined.

The Board of Supervisors argued that distinguishing between the two tax rolls for "unsecured" and "secured" property was unconstitutional because it violated the equal-protection law. The presiding judge, Jack R. Levitt, denied this contention. He cited the case of *Abrams* v. *San Francisco* (1941), which clearly defined the distinction between these two tax rolls as a "matter of collectability of taxes," not mere "administrative convenience," as the supervisors argued. "There is a natural, intrinsic and constitutional difference," ruled Judge Levitt, "between secured and unsecured taxes."[50] Even though he denied the plaintiffs' argument that the assessors' action had been unconstitutional, the judge ruled on January 8, 1980, in favor of the supervisors that unsecured property should receive the same tax reduction treatment under Proposition 13 as real property. This meant that the 1 percent rate limitation was equally applicable to personal property. His intent was "to preserve the taxpayer and voter confidence in our system of government."[51]

Other suits to force the equal treatment of unsecured and secured property were not so successful. Attorney General Younger had earlier filed suit in the Supreme Court to prevent 23 counties, including San Diego, from using the 1977–78 tax rates on the current unsecured tax rolls. On August 16, 1978, the court refused to issue a writ requiring the counties to apply the 1 percent rate to personal property. The case was denied without hearing. "In essence the court concluded that there was an adequate remedy at law: payment of tax and filing of a claim for refund."[52]

The Supreme Court finally settled the dispute over unsecured tax rates on August 14, 1980, when it allowed counties to collect $590 million in unsecured property taxes, thus overturning both the earlier San Diego Superior Court ruling and a related appellate court judgment issued in Los Angeles on January 24, 1980. Twenty-two counties had already collected $440 million on unsecured property in excess of Proposition 13 rates, and this ruling enabled the remaining 36 counties to collect another $150 million. The court found that Article XIII A, Section 12, requiring that taxes on unsecured property be levied at the tax rate for the preceding year, was "clear and unambiguous." Court members pointed out that the ballot pamphlet on Proposition 13 offered no convincing evidence that it was the intent of the initiative to apply the 1 percent limitation on real property taxes to unsecured property on the assessment roll for the 1978 tax year.

It is impossible to say if the court's ruling was influenced by Jarvis's stunning defeat on his June 1980 income tax–cutting initiative (see Chapter 8). State Senate Republicans tried, but failed, to place a constitutional amendment on the ballot to prevent counties from spending the money until the legislature could consider the question in 1981. The Assembly, with passage of AB 2196, forbade counties that had not yet collected the back tax from doing so and also prevented counties from spending the tax money they had collected until the legislature considered the subject in 1981. In June 1981, during passage of the budget, Democrats agreed with a Republican plan to refund taxpayers $125 million in payments of unsecured property taxes, allocating another $200 million to the state's General Fund. Under this agreement, counties would be allowed to keep 15 percent of the unsecured revenues and special districts $35 million, with the remainder going to the state through existing school finance mechanisms. As of September 1981, the specific tax bill implementing this agreement, AB 11, had not attained final approval in both houses of the legislature.

Another legal issue to be settled involved the 1975 rollback provision. Proposition 13 required that all county property valuations be rolled back to 1975 levels, but failed to mention assessments for public utilities and transportation companies, which are determined by the State Board of Equalization. After the passage of Proposition 13, the board updated valuations for these companies, ignoring the rollback clause. The public utilities felt that Jarvis-Gann meant to treat county- and state-assessed parcels of property alike for purposes of taxation and took their case to court, promising the public that all tax savings would be passed on in the form of lower bills. The difference in assessments came to $3.5 billion and the tax collected on this difference to $35 million.

The case was heard in San Francisco Superior Court by Judge Francis Mayer. The lawyers for the three utilities (Pacific Gas & Electric, Southern California Edison, and San Diego Gas & Electric) argued that Proposition 13 should apply to public utilities. Further, the State Board had misinterpreted Proposition 13 and thereby violated the state constitutional provision making state-assessed property "subject to taxation to the same extent and in the same manner as other property."[53] A PG&E staff lawyer, Richard Locke, pointed out that the board had begun working on 1978 assessments of utilities before Proposition 13 was approved and had since refused to roll these assessments back to 1975 levels in accordance with Section 2(a) of Proposition 13.

Deputy Attorney General Philip Griffin argued that the utility companies were wrong for two reasons. First, the state constitution forbade the filing of any lawsuit aimed at preventing the collection of a tax. The law required that a taxpayer first pay his money and then seek a refund. Second, the rollback clause of Proposition 13 did not apply to utility companies because it referred only to "county assessors," who were barred by the state constitution from assessing utilities. That job belonged exclusively to the Board of Equalization.[54]

The court ruled in favor of the Board of Equalization and decided that Article XIII A did not apply to state assessments. The plaintiffs naturally appealed that decision to the appellate court. On October 16, 1979, the Court of Appeals held that utility and transportation companies *were* covered by Article XIII A and their holdings had to be assessed like any other real property in California. The appellate court reasoned that "if the property of state assessees is given a current valuation and all other property is given a 1975–76 valuation, then the property of state assessees is not being taxed to the same extent and in the same manner as other property" (as required by Article XIII, Section 19). The court also pointed out that "had the drafters of Proposition 13 wished to make it inapplicable to State assessees, they could have easily so provided in language which would be readily understandable to all voters." But, despite this ruling, the board did not give up the fight. The Supreme Court agreed to consider its appeal and heard oral comments on May 5, 1980.

On June 5, 1980, the California Supreme Court unanimously ruled that the three utilities could not file a suit directly against the State Board of Equalization to have their tax assessments rolled back to 1975 levels. The correct procedure was for the utilities to pay the taxes and then file for a rollback in a single county. As matters stand now, until the utilities file as instructed in a single county and win their case, the State Board of Equalization may collect property taxes on utilities well in excess of the 1 percent limitation.

A final, but important, legal issue arising from Proposition 13 involved fee increases. User charges are fees and taxes "derived from or earmarked for specific services." They are not limited to special-fund revenues. Examples are the business license tax, hotel-motel tax, construction fees, and annual licenses. In fiscal 1967–68, total revenues from user charges amounted to $600 million; in 1976–77 the total was $1.84 billion. These user charges provided one-fifth of municipal revenues and 10 percent of county revenues in the fiscal year prior to Proposition 13, 1976–77.[55] Between passage of Proposition 13 on June 6, 1978, and its implementation on July 1, 1978, many cities, counties, and special districts rushed to raise fees and service charges and introduced new fees to boost their revenues. The legality of these actions was challenged in the courts.[56]

Paul Gann, in a lawsuit against the city of Arcadia, claimed that the proposition had stipulated July 1 because he and Howard Jarvis had assumed that local elections could not be held before that date. They had thought that city councils would not attempt to raise fees in the face of the tax revolt. In addition, the proposition also stated that "special taxes" could be levied only by a two-thirds vote of the electorate.

However, the legal problems and the lawsuits that followed arose from the initiative's failure to define "special tax." Given this ambiguity, the various cities, counties, and special districts had renamed a number of the new taxes "user fees."

A Trinity County Superior Court judge, Clyde Small, ruled that "fee increases imposed since the passage of Proposition 13 must be subjected to a two-thirds vote because they were 'special taxes.' " Moreover, "all money collected in post 13 fee increases must be returned." The fees in this case were increases in rezoning charges from $50 to $200 and parcel-map charges from $10 to $200. However, the county decided to appeal this ruling. The county lawyer, Ron Barbitoe, felt that fees and taxes were distinguishable: "If it flows to the general good, it's a tax. But we feel the subdivider who is gaining property value by filing a parcel map is benefiting monetarily and should pay a fee."[57]

Other counties, cities, and special districts were taken to court by concerned citizen groups in order to get a clear ruling on this important issue. For example, a Shasta County Superior Court judge ruled that the county could not impose a "residential fee" on a development company to finance new classroom construction on the grounds that it was a "special tax" and required prior voter approval. The school district appealed.

Not all courts that heard fee cases ruled in favor of the taxpayers. An appellate court in Fresno ruled that Proposition 13 did not prevent the imposition of special assessment fees to pay off street, sewer, and utility bonds. The panel of judges ruled that nothing in the Jarvis-Gann initiative limited "governments' ability to improve specified areas by assessing those property owners benefited by the installations. The court said that a special tax would be one that did not necessarily benefit the property being assessed."[58]

To remedy the ambiguities of 13, the legislature enacted a series of statutes in 1979 and 1980. Among other things, it authorized water districts to raise water charges to cover costs of district water supplies; county clerks to increase fees for various services; flood control and lighting districts to impose benefit assessments; local governments that provide fire and police protection services to impose benefit assessments and special taxes for fire or police protection services, subject to a two-thirds approval of the local electorate; and cities, counties, and special districts to impose special taxes on approval of a two-thirds vote of the local electorate.[59]

The fundamental principle underlying these statutes was that government can charge for the full cost of a specific service, but no more. The taxes or benefit assessments must fall within the definition of "reasonable cost of providing the service," and the costs must be related directly to the provision of the service for which the fee is charged and not to other services provided by a local agency. A special assessment made solely on the basis of benefits received is not considered a "tax" and can be validly imposed without a vote of the electorate. Similarly, service or regulatory fees limited to the cost of the service are not considered a tax. However, "excess" fees or charges are considered to be a tax and thus subject to voter control.

All in all, the three weeks encompassing election day and the fashioning of the state bailout of local government agencies were a harried, but exciting, period in the history of California government and politics. A governor who had bitterly fought Proposition 13 became its most ardent spokesman overnight. A legislature that had initially threatened and intimidated voters eventually acted effectively to sustain the entire panoply of local services with, in retrospect, almost no serious cuts in either quality or quantity. The majority of interest groups that had worried about economic chaos and service disruptions emerged from the June turmoil virtually unscathed. And most of all, Howard Jarvis became a new American folk hero and symbol of the national tax revolt that was to follow.

Three years have passed since that tumultuous period in California history. Yet, it is difficult to determine fully the long-range effects of 13 on government finance, provision of local services, the state's economy, and the character of political life in California. Only now are some of these consequences beginning to surface. Their total effect may not be fully felt until well into the mid-1980s. At this stage it is possible, however, to assess some of the likely outcomes and to project their consequences for the state of California.

four AN ECONOMIC

BOOM

Judging from the shrill cries of opponents to Proposition 13 predicting economic chaos and outright disaster, one might have expected the state of California to lapse into a severe recession within months of implementing the initiative. In addition to a breakdown in the delivery of vital services—education and police and fire protection—they also forecast growing unemployment for both the private and public sectors. Although the $6.8 billion surplus might postpone California's day of reckoning for the first year of life under Jarvis, pundits warned that the chickens would come home to roost in the second year (1979–80) and Californians would pay at last for their hedonism and selfishness. Serious observers shared these concerns for the future of local government financing. Legislative analyst William Hamm said that the surplus of 1978 provided a one-time solution for the first year, but would be inadequate for the second, third, or fourth years, when the true effects would be seen.[1] California Taxpayers' Association Executive Vice-President Kirk West concurred; the surplus would not be high enough to continue the bailout and the "real crunch" would come in the third and fourth years.[2] Newspaper and television accounts of post-13 cutbacks, such as reduced library hours, teacher layoffs, park closings, and other tales in the weeks and months immediately following passage were hailed as specific warnings of the worse fate to come. Reviewing the economic rather than human interest events of that period with the benefit of hindsight, one can make a more comprehensive review of 13's impact on the state, employment, investment, construction, and the delivery of local and state government services. This chapter examines the overall employment and economic picture; the next looks at government services.

WHAT HAPPENED TO THE LAYOFFS?

As soon as the Jarvis-Gann initiative qualified for the California ballot, its opponents in both government and business began using a number of scare tactics to frighten the electorate into a no vote. The major targets were jobs and local services. Voters were warned daily that a yes vote on 13 would translate into massive unemployment throughout the state, a major breakdown in the delivery of local services, the end of good public education and health and welfare programs, the eventual demise of the Golden State as they knew it.

From the governor down, opponents of 13 treated voters to a devastating scenario of the consequences of this proposition. Brown stated categorically that "if 13 passes we're looking at several hundred thousand job losses in the public and private sectors . . . Some of those who will be laid off will not be eligible for unemployment or it will not be adequate for them to live on."[3] He also warned fire chiefs that if 13 passed, local services might have to be drastically curtailed and that "affirmative action programs and lottery-style layoff systems might be imposed."[4] Business offered equally pessimistic predictions: "Chaos is not too strong a word for the disruptions we'd get." Even more moderate businessmen who did not disagree with taxpayer discontent "also fear[ed] that job loss, recession and social upheaval could result."[5]

The weight of government and business opinion was reinforced against 13 by the addition of academic prediction. Professors Robert M. Williams and Larry J. Kimbell of UCLA concluded that passage of 13 would cost 451,000 jobs and a jump in the unemployment rate from 7.2 to 10 percent within one year.

Not only jobs but also services would suffer drastically. One Sacramento city council member warned: "Most counties will face such drastic staff cutbacks that efficient administration of welfare programs at the local level will be impossible." As for welfare payments, always a touchy subject with voters, "errors in overpayments and payments to ineligible recipients already cost taxpayers about $80 million a year. That figure could conceivably rise to more than $200 million a year if the counties are forced to administer the program with inadequate staffs." Sacramento county welfare director William Redmond confirmed and echoed these predictions. If 13 passed, he would probably have to lay off up to 50 percent of his employees. "What this means," he said, "is a drastic reduction in programs."[6]

Watching the development of the doomsayers' campaign against 13, Paul Gann told a news conference in Sacramento a month or so before the polling day, "For the first time in history we have business, capital, labor and education all goose-stepping down life's highway together to defeat Proposition 13 ... This campaign has degenerated into a fight between the people and the bureaucrats with vested interests."[7]

When the fight was over on June 6, 1978, and the people had won, everyone waited for the sky to fall. They waited and waited, but "nearly two weeks after Jarvis-Gann took effect California was still in one piece and the state's estimate of the number of bodies caught under the Proposition 13 bulldozer had been sharply reduced to 9,617—or a few more workers than the 8,400 workers laid off in Southern California when the U.S.'s B-1 bomber program was cancelled last year." As the county administrator for Napa, Albert Haberger, expressed it, "In all my years I have never been so embarrassed as by such scare tactics [as those used against Proposition 13]. They were blatant and dishonest. We never did envision any great problems and had faith the state would help out."[8] Even the governor's finance director, Roy Bell, admitted that in many ways Proposition 13 coauthor Howard Jarvis's accusation that opponents were guilty of using scare tactics was accurate. "A lot of these scare tactics were on the basis that local government didn't trust the state to put any money in at all. Nobody promised them the state would put in $3 billion or $4 billion." In reply to a question whether the administration had soft-pedaled the amount of state financial aid that local governments could expect if Jarvis passed, Bell reportedly told the *Los Angeles Times*: "Yes. That's correct." "After all," Bell was quoted as saying, "we were supporting Proposition 8."[9]

Overall, with the exception of Alameda county, where supervisors initially made no move to rehire 1,300 employees laid off in June after the passage of 13, "most counties and cities either fired no one or only a handful . . . Most governments simply did not fill empty jobs or planned not to fill positions as they became vacant."[10]

In retrospect, the governor ought to have been politically crippled by his opposition to 13 since he had tried hard to mislead voters into believing that the proposition was a "ripoff" and a "can of worms." But such was not the case. The bailout legislation and the pay and hiring freezes for government employees helped convince the less cynical voters that Brown would implement the new amendment in good faith. The layoffs issue provided him yet another political weapon to allay voter concern. Brown adroitly exploited this issue to explain the need for the state pay freeze, insisting that despite labor union objections, "it was the only way to spread the work. The sacrifice must be shared and the number one priority is minimizing, to the maximum degree, the number of layoffs. I am very concerned that the mothers and fathers who have never been on an unemployment line may be there and with the money saved from the pay freeze and the cost of living freeze, I am hopeful to make the layoffs a very minute figure."[11]

Minute indeed. Not only did government statisticians have a remarkable inability to estimate the available surplus should Proposition 13 pass (they missed by $3 billion), they were also unable to estimate the number of layoffs accurately.

Before the election, legislative analyst William Hamm predicted that 270,000 persons would be fired. He based that number on the $7 billion drop in tax revenue from passage of Proposition 13. The governor, Finance Director Bell, and most other government officials who opposed 13 agreed that the amount available from the state surplus as bailout to local agencies would be no more than $3.5 billion. Voters who chose to believe the bureaucrats could expect 270,000 layoffs. Those with more faith in academics could expect 450,000. Post-13, both bureaucrats and academics hastened to adjust their calculations to reality.

On June 15, 1978, UCLA forecasters Kimbell and Williams released a new series of projections that assumed the state would use its huge budget surplus to bail out local governments. Instead of massive layoffs, they projected sustained economic growth for the next year, after which the effects of Proposition 13 would be felt. By the end of 1980, 401,000 jobs would be lost:

> The only essential positive change from our May numbers is in the timing of the distress and not in the magnitude. This stems from the fact that current plans are to use the full accumulated state of California surplus in the first year to prevent what Howard Jarvis claimed he wanted—reductions in local government spending on the order of $6 billion in the first year alone.[12]

The UCLA professors cautiously noted that once the state budget surplus was sharply reduced, higher taxes might have to be imposed to sustain government services.

This forecasting turnabout was highlighted on the editorial page of the *Wall Street Journal* on the same day.

> The new ideas that came to the econometricians resulted from the news that the state government, which has a $5 billion surplus, will be using that to ease the local revenue loss. It may have been that the voters of California knew of that $5 billion beforehand, and decided to plug it into their own electoral calculations.
>
> We must say the UCLA econometricians deserve a round of rousing applause. In a cursory search of our files, we find this may be the first time in this century where an economist admitted error.[13]

Professors Kimbell and Williams's reply appeared in the *Journal* on July 3, 1979. The May forecast was revised, they explained, because it assumed use of state surplus funds at the moderate annual rate of $1.5 billion. This was the sum of money estimated to be available on a continuing basis for the rival property tax relief measure (the Behr bill, or Proposition 8 on the June ballot). Proposition 13 had not stipulated the use of state surplus moneys for local assistance. "Accordingly, we could have reasonably assumed no use of state surplus to evaluate the impacts of Proposition 13." In contrast, the June simulation assumed that $5.5 billion would be used in the first year to assist local government. This sum would drop to $2.5 billion per year thereafter. "This greater use of the state surplus delays the effect we predicted in May but does not alter the essential prediction that California faces a difficult transition ahead," they explained.

The key in determining the reliability of the UCLA quarterly forecast, then, was the amount and use of state surplus funds. The pre-election forecast in May assumed minimal use; the post-election forecast assumed maximum use, at least for the first year. Evidently Professors Kimbell and Williams believed in June 1978 that the surplus would shrink dramatically by mid-1979.

Six months later, Professors Kimbell and Williams performed a complete turnabout. On December 7, 1978, they issued a revised forecast. With unbounded optimism they predicted the state could "bail out" local governments from the effects of Proposition 13 at an increased rate in the next four years and still maintain a budget surplus.[14] These projections contradicted the year-end forecasts of state officials and also reversed the professors' earlier predictions of massive layoffs.

The December 1978 model assumed that robust economic growth in the state would increase state government revenues by 12.5 percent a year through 1983. The forecast also assumed that state spending would rise 10 percent each year through 1983 and that local-assistance spending would rise 7 percent in 1980 and 1981 and 12.5 percent in 1982 and 1983. On that basis, state aid to local governments could increase for the next year by 7 percent above the $13.5 billion budgeted for fiscal 1979, rising to $19.5 billion by 1983. The bailout portion of total state aid could increase from $4.2 billion in 1979 to about $6.3 billion by 1983.

In reality, the distribution of the surplus to local governments for 1978–79 meant that the actual revenue drop was only $2 billion, not $7 billion as the government and legislative analyst Hamm had predicted. Using Hamm's formula, a $2 billion drop in revenue indicated only about 77,000 layoffs statewide—a far cry from the 270,000 he had predicted before the election. However, not only the legislative analyst but also the state's Employment Development Department (EDD) seemed to have difficulty with its estimates.

On June 23, 1978, the EDD issued the first in a series of special releases based on surveys made by EDD field officers that enumerated actual layoffs by public agencies. Between June 6, when 13 passed, and June 21, layoffs for cities, counties, and special districts totaled 2,145 and for school districts, 2,778. The EDD also announced the establishment of a special layoff information unit in Sacramento to collect field office surveys of public sector layoffs over the coming months. Prior to the bailout bill, the EDD had projected approximately 152,000 layoffs, but its June 23 pronouncement adjusted this estimate to 86,300 regular and CETA employees, due, it explained, to the bailout.

According to EDD announcements, their office intended to issue a weekly update of the ever increasing layoff figures. This intention was hastily abandoned in favor of monthly updates, as the expected large rise in layoffs embarrassingly failed to materialize. A survey released at the beginning of July reported that only 3,636 local government workers had been laid off by June 29. Missing from this survey were any data on 36 of the 58 counties, including San Francisco. Also, the cutoff date precluded listing layoffs as of July 1, the day Proposition 13 took effect. The news media were quick to note the glaring discrepancies in the EDD reports. Challenged by various reporters, the agency conceded that the two reports on post–Proposition 13 layoffs were incomplete and inaccurate. As EDD Communications Director Robert McCafferty told reporters, "I'm really distressed by the numbers we've put out so far. We are tightening up the way we get those numbers."[15]

Given the high number of "errors" in these first few reports and their exposure by the press, the governor's office became involved. "We were curious also about those constant changes," spokeswoman Elizabeth Coleman said in Sacramento. The governor's office had made inquiries to the employment department, but Coleman "could not confirm or deny whether the governor had personally initiated the 'inquiries.' " Officials at the EDD in Sacramento were less reticent. "It was more than an inquiry," one official said. "They told us to get it absolutely clear."[16]

The EDD's release of August 4 cited layoffs of 7,261 city,

county, and special district workers and 13,066 school district employees. However, the department explicitly acknowledged in this release that these numbers overstated the true impact of Proposition 13 on employment.

First, the reported figures were not solely layoffs, but included vacancies due to retirement and attrition that had been left unfilled because of the hiring freeze in effect in many public agencies. Second, the figures included layoffs of both part-time and full-time workers, without any breakdown. Moreover, the EDD showed education layoffs separately because several school districts surveyed had indicated they would recall many of the dismissed employees. In a final note, the EDD reported that some of the persons laid off had already found other employment.

The EDD's September 1 release estimated a total of 21,965 layoffs (13,970 school district employees and 7,995 local government employees). The following month's report, issued October 6, gave total layoffs at 19,004. Of these 11,708 were school district employees; in one month's time, school districts had rehired over 2,000 laid off employees. The report also noted that "California's seasonally-adjusted unemployment rate dropped sharply from 7.4 percent in August to 6.7 percent in September, the lowest in more than four years."[17] The last time California's rate had been lower than 6.7 percent was May 1974, when it stood at 6.6 percent. This was immediately before the beginning of the nationwide recession.

The final EDD report appeared on November 3, 1978, and showed that recalls and rehires had reduced school district layoffs to 10,600 and others to 7,221, a grand total of 17,821. Moreover, "California's unemployment rate dropped from 6.7 percent in September to 6.5 percent in October, the lowest point in five years . . . Total employment, at 9,950,000, set a new record and the number of unemployed at 692,000 was the lowest since August 1973."[18] In this report, an information officer stated that no further reports would be issued because the total number of layoffs had remained relatively constant from month to month since October 1978. By the end of the year, the EDD reported that "California's unemployment rate dropped sharply from 6.5 percent in October to 6.1 percent in November, the lowest rate since March, 1970. The number holding jobs was up by 46,000 over the month to establish a new employment record of 9,996,000. The number of unemployed dropped by 44,000."[19]

The November and December 1978 issues of *Tax Revolt Digest* succinctly summarized the overall total of the layoffs. In November it noted that "only about 19,000 public employees had lost their jobs so far as a result of Proposition 13." In December it could report that "about one-third of the local employees who lost their jobs in California following the enactment of Proposition 13 have been rehired."

Given the politics behind the No on 13 campaign and the predictions of massive unemployment, this extended examination of the actual number of layoffs helps to place the real effects of Proposition 13 in perspective. Moreover, if the passage of 13 was, as Neil H. Jacoby and some other notable economists believed, "simply a taxpayer protest against state mismanagement," then the government's response in the area of public employment provides an interesting example of its (non)attempt to implement the voter mandate to cut the fat and decrease a bloated bureaucracy. The "before" and "after" statistics speak for themselves.

Explanations for these surprising employment statistics are as varied as the figures themselves, depending at which point on the political spectrum the question is posed. Some, including the governor, believed that the hiring and pay freeze Brown ordered for state employees (which meant no cost-of-living increases for welfare recipients or for local government employees under terms of the state's surplus-sharing legislation) helped to prevent a fair number of layoffs. This action, the availability of the surplus, and the bailout legislation "saved the day" and ensured that the "doomsaying" did not come to pass.

Brown's Department of Finance, in justifying the pay freeze, prepared figures showing that a mere 1 percent cost-of-living raise for state employees would result in 3,000 to 6,000 layoffs in local government. Department Director Richard Silberman said in a July 1978 interview that current projections forecast 9,000–18,000 layoffs with a 2 percent increase, 18,000–36,000 with a 3 percent increase, and 42,000–84,000 with a 4 percent increase. "That's the summary of a hell of a lot of discussion and analysis," Silberman said. According to Brown's top aide, the governor "feels when you balance layoffs against salary raises for those already employed, there is no balance—notwithstanding a lot of people booing and shouting obscenities in the park."[20]

Given the figures produced by the Department of Finance, Brown's rationalizations for his decisions seemed sound. The only contradictions were provided by the reality of events once the "freezes" were overruled by the courts. Even with the retroactive court-ordered pay raises and rehirings, layoffs just never materialized in the expected numbers. Soon it was back to business as usual again in Sacramento. However, the overall effect of 13 from June 1978 to June 1979 was to reduce the number of local employees by 8 percent (although the majority of layoffs were in the schools, where layoffs might have been expected to occur regardless, due to declining enrollment).

Despite the lack of massive layoffs and the reinstatement of the pay raises, at the beginning of 1979 public employee unions were still perturbed by the message of 13 and its future effect on local government revenues. As Stephen P. Coony of Local 660 put it, "The era of those so-called responsible settlements [of 4 to 5 percent cost-of-living raises] is over. The era of public employee strife is coming to California in a big way . . . Whether or not that happens all at one time . . . or over a period of years, I think we've got tumultuous relations ahead of us. Everything is conspiring now—the entire climate just calls for a reaction by the public employees."[21]

However, in spite of this newfound feeling of discontent among California's public employees, the effect of Proposition 13 was to place "effective legal limits on government spending [which] also increase[d] the bargaining power of public officials." As neoconservative political thinker Professor Irving Kristol observed, "There is no way in which the politicians could be persuaded to stand up to [public employee] unions without something like Proposition 13 to provide the necessary backbone. It put their political futures on the line."[22] Proposition 13 placed limits on government spending to correct the overspending bias, but the outcome of this action pleased neither public officials nor their employees.

Forecasts about 13's impact extended even beyond the state's borders. It generated so much interest in Washington, D.C., that

Robert N. Giaimo, chairman of the House of Representatives Committee on the Budget, asked the Congressional Budget Office (CBO) to analyze the measure's impact on the nation's economy and the federal budget.[23] Among the report's key predictions were (1) marginally lower levels of real economic activity through the first half of 1979 and marginally higher levels of real activity by mid-1980; (2) a loss of about 60,000 jobs by the end of 1978, followed by a gradual improvement; and (3) a reduction in the Consumer Price Index of 0.2 percent by the end of 1978 and 0.4 percent by mid-1980. The CBO noted that the spending cutbacks implied by a property tax revenue loss of $7 billion would be attenuated by the state's $4.1 billion bailout, the availability of local surpluses, and a probable increase in user charges and nonproperty taxes. While small relative to the size of the national economy, a $6 billion–plus reduction in property taxes would have a stimulative effect. "The aftertax incomes of California's homeowners and owners of business property will rise, leading to increases in consumption expenditures and business investment spending."

Although the CBO forecast 60,000 layoffs in the short run and predicted recovery of employment by mid-1980 "as the stimulative effects create jobs in the private sector," the report pointed out that the number of available jobs "may be slightly lower than the level that could be expected in the absence of Proposition 13." Overall the net effect of Proposition 13 was seen to be harmful to employment.

THE REALITY

Predictions about widespread layoffs and sharp increases in the unemployment rate were part and parcel of the pre-13 election maneuvering. But the passage of time allows these forecasts to be compared with the real changes in public employment and the overall unemployment picture. Such comparison helps to account for the headlong rush to revise downward the predicted harmful effects of Proposition 13 so soon after its passage.

It is possible to compare unemployment figures for California with those for the nation as a whole beginning in 1973, the first year for which comparable sets of information were collected and published. Figure 4.1 plots changes in unemployment both in California and nationwide for all members of the civilian labor force aged sixteen and over. Between 1973 and 1978, California's unemployment rate routinely exceeded the national average by any-

FIGURE 4.1

UNEMPLOYMENT RATES
CALIFORNIA AND THE UNITED STATES

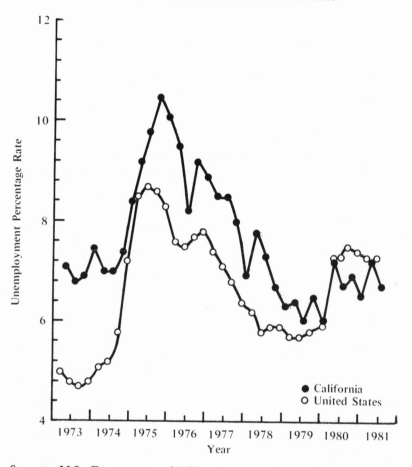

SOURCE: U.S., Department of Labor, Bureau of Labor Statistics, *Employment and Earnings.*

where between 0.5 and 2 percentage points. The gap stood at about 1.5 points at the time 13 passed. Since 13 became part of the state constitution, the unemployment rate in California has fallen sharply relative to the national average. By the first quarter of 1980, it had actually fallen below the national average for the first time in the decade. California clearly weathered the recession of 1980 better than did the rest of the country. In the first three months of 1980, the unemployment rate in the other states rose, but in California it actually fell. It continued to fall all through calendar year 1980, remaining below the national average through June 1981. In sum, the state's unemployment picture improved steadily over the first three years of Proposition 13.

Figure 4.2 plots the change in the state's unemployment rate relative to the national average. It shows even more dramatically the improvement in California state unemployment compared with the other 49 states.

These improvements in the state employment picture relative to the nation as a whole certainly cannot be ignored. In fact, we can draw some very definite conclusions about changes in the structure of the work force. As Figure 4.3 vividly demonstrates, Proposition 13 did halt what had been an inexorable yearly rise in government employment in the state. Indeed, stretching back for over thirty years, state and local government employment in California had risen in an uninterrupted fashion, with annual downward adjustments each summer due to schoolteacher vacations. It took three full years after 13 passed for the state's public sector to recover to its pre-13 level. Thus, virtually all of California's net new job growth in the first three years of 13 occurred within the private sector. It will be interesting to watch if government employment resumes its upward rise at the older pre-13 rates or remains stable at this lower level. In other words, was the effect of Proposition 13 a one-shot, three-year adjustment in the growth rate of government employment, or will it be more long-lasting?

As for job creation or destruction in the first three post-Jarvis years in California, just after Proposition 13 took effect, total civilian employment in the state at the end of July stood at 9.74 million. Three years later, in June 1981, that number had risen to 10.67 million, a gain of some 930,000 jobs. Since 5,000 government jobs were lost in the same period, a net gain of 935,000 jobs occurred in the private sector.

Between 1974 and 1978, California added more than 1.3 million jobs to its economy, roughly one in every six new jobs in the entire nation.[24] Between July 1978 and July 1980, California added nearly three in every ten new jobs, almost a doubling of its prior share. These gains constituted an increase of 7.4 percent in the state's civilian labor force, compared with an overall increase

FIGURE 4.2

UNEMPLOYMENT IN CALIFORNIA
ABOVE/BELOW NATIONAL AVERAGE

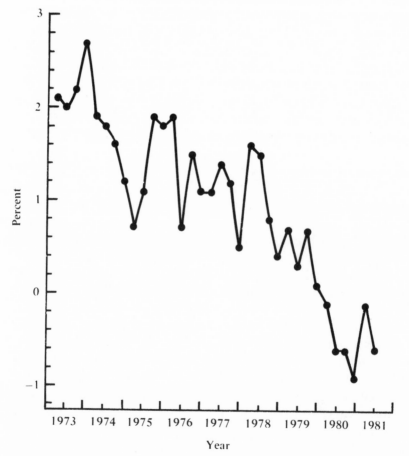

Year

in the nation's total civilian employment of only 2.7 percent in the same two-year interval. Moreover, all these new jobs in California emerged in the private sector. Those claiming that tax cuts stimulate the *private* economy can find comfort in the post-13 private employment record. However, critics of this view might

FIGURE 4.3

GOVERNMENT EMPLOYMENT IN CALIFORNIA

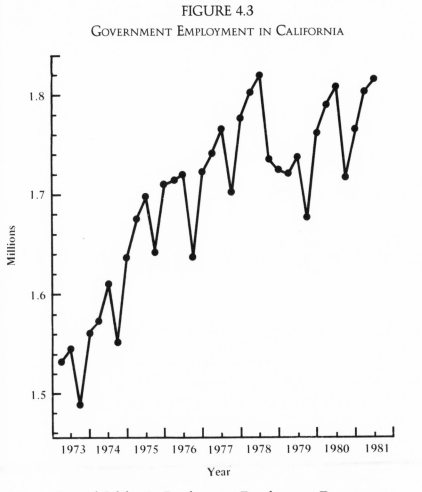

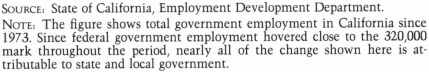

SOURCE: State of California, Employment Development Department.

NOTE: The figure shows total government employment in California since 1973. Since federal government employment hovered close to the 320,000 mark throughout the period, nearly all of the change shown here is attributable to state and local government.

contend that California has certain distinct advantages as a state, which helped to contribute to its post-13 economic growth.

California is a large and wealthy state. Its economy in 1980 was in the range of $250 billion. If it were a separate country, it would be one of the ten richest nations in the world. Diversity is the hallmark of the state's economic base. Construction, manufacturing (especially high-technology electronics and aviation), financial services, trade, transportation, and agriculture all make significant contributions to output and employment. California is not as vulnerable as most other regions of the country to a sharp economic downturn if adverse trends hit any one of the state's economic sectors. It weathered the recessions of 1974 and 1980 better than many one-industry states. But since the state's diversified, modern, high-technology economy was well in place before Proposition 13, the structure of its economy cannot be invoked to explain the historical reversal of unemployment trends that has arisen since 13.

We can credit the state's burgeoning economy in the past few years, in part, to the tax-cutting initiative. Proposition 13 injected several billion dollars into the state's economy, with no corresponding reduction in government spending. By tapping its multi-billion dollar surplus to bail out local governments, the total level of government spending in the state remained remarkably firm in real terms. But the property tax cuts injected into the economy billions of additional dollars in the form of individual spending and business investment. Five billion dollars represents about 2 percent of the value of California's annual output of goods and services, which means that the state's economy received an additional boost of private spending and investment, enabling it to create new jobs much more rapidly than could the rest of the nation.

The multibillion dollar stimulus to the state's economy was matched by a "supply-side" incentive effect on work, investment, savings, and productivity. The legislature's response to Howard Jarvis and his stunning victory included abolition of the business inventory tax and the indexing of the state's personal income tax rates to inflation, ending bracket creep–induced tax increases. In short, 13 improved the business climate in California, as the CBO study had accurately forecast.

An improved state economic climate was also the consensus of members of the business community.[25] On behalf of Governor Brown, the Advisory Council of the State Department of Economic and Business Development surveyed 4,500 of the largest employers in the state; 84 percent of the companies that responded said they felt 13 had improved the state's business climate. However, these business leaders were still wary of the state's future intentions, fearing that the legislature would seek ways to create new taxes.

Apart from private sector expansion in the form of new job creation, the initiative directly eased inflation because homeownership costs make up a significant component of the Consumer Price Index and property taxes, in turn, are an important element in homeownership costs. The $7 billion reduction in property taxes alone reduced the annual increase in the national Consumer Price Index by 0.2 percent in 1978. More dramatically, it reduced the state Consumer Price Index by a full percentage point.

CONSTRUCTION

A number of factors influence the price and quantity of new construction. On the cost side, key elements include the price of land and site improvements, the costs of material and labor, and the financing charges builders incur as they develop properties. In recent years, other costs have become more important—building permits, environmental regulations, greater limitations on density, and higher fees for water and sewer hookups. These costs rose steadily throughout the 1970s, especially in California.

On the demand side, the higher the cost of new housing, the fewer units potential owners buy. In the short run, as the costs of new housing rise, demand falls. Homeownership costs include mortgage interest (about 61 percent of the cost of homeownership), property taxes (about 18 percent), insurance charges, repair and maintenance expenditures, and fuel and utilities.[26] Since mortgage payments overwhelm property taxes as a cost of homeownership, even a sharp contraction in property taxes, say 50 percent, would reduce homeownership costs only about 10 percent.

Interest rates are by far the most important element affecting the demand for housing. Rising interest rates reduce the amounts buyers are willing and able to pay for new housing. A rise in interest rates means, therefore, that many potential buyers will buy only if house prices fall. The fall in house prices that results from a rise in interest rates makes house building less profitable, and the rate of new construction thus falls. Sharp cutbacks in the nation's monetary growth rate in 1966, 1969, 1973, 1978 (fourth quarter), and 1979 caused sharp rises in nominal interest rates and a falloff in new home building.[27]

It is difficult to calculate the effects of Proposition 13 on the price and supply of new construction. The reduction in property taxes, however massive, paled beside the other recent economic trends, especially the rapid rise in mortgage interest rates and the growing scarcity of land due to new environmental restrictions. But it is especially difficult to compare post-13 trends in California with national movements in construction activity due to a purely unique set of regulations that took force in California on July 1, 1978. On that date, more costly energy standards were imposed on all new construction, and so developers rushed to begin scheduled building plans before the June 30, 1978, deadline. These new standards explain a dramatic upsurge in the value of new construction permits from a seasonally adjusted annual rate of about $15 billion in the first quarter of 1978 to $21 billion in the second quarter. The number collapsed to $14 billion in July, the first month of life under 13. Fluctuations in nonresidential construction were even more dramatic: the dollar value of residential permit valuations rose about 20 percent in the second quarter of 1978 compared with about 70 percent for nonresidential construction and 100 percent for the industrial component of the latter. Due to these circumstances, pre- and post-13 comparisons are severely distorted. Had these new standards not been imposed, it might have been possible to compare state with national trends in order to isolate any effects solely attributable to 13.

In the eighteen months following implementation of Proposition 13 (through the end of 1979), the total increase in dollar valuations of new permits for nonresidential construction rose 53 percent in the nation as a whole and 60 percent in California. The dollar value of private housing, both single and multiple-family, fell by nearly 50 percent in both categories.[28]

In addition, 13 had little perceptible effect on the average purchase price of a home in California. Home prices have risen steadily since 1971 and continued to increase throughout 1978 and 1979. The first major break in this trend occurred in mid-1980 and was directly attributable to a sharp rise in the mortgage interest rate to 14 percent. Even higher interest levels in 1981 further depressed sales.

Economic theory implies that a reduction in property taxes should be reflected in higher values for houses. This sharp rise did not occur. The reason is the provision in 13 that requires reassessment of every home to full market value on resale. While existing homeowners enjoy more spendable income, new purchasers must face the higher property taxes that reassessment brings. These closely approximate pre-13 levels. Sellers of homes cannot convert property tax reductions into higher selling prices. New buyers benefit from 13 only in subsequent years because future property tax reassessments, and corresponding tax increases, can rise by a yearly maximum of 2 percent.

RENT CONTROL

Rent control is one of the more controversial issues arising from Proposition 13. The concept of rent control first came to California in 1972, when students in Berkeley qualified an initiative on the local ballot. Although it obtained voter approval, the state Supreme Court subsequently ruled that specific measure unconstitutional, but asserted the general principle that local jurisdictions have the legal ability to enact such controls.

Rent control remained dormant as a political issue until 1976, when Berkeley and Palo Alto voters defeated two proposed local measures. Two years later, in June 1978, voters in Santa Monica and Santa Barbara also rejected rent control propositions.

On June 6, 1978, the history of rent control took a different turn. Proposition 13 provided rent control activists and tenants with the best opportunity they ever had. After 13 passed, rents did not immediately and uniformly fall and in some instances they even rose, generating a tremendous uproar among renters. Many renters felt betrayed since Howard Jarvis had promised that they, too, would get a break if they voted for 13. Between June 1978 and October 1979, proponents of rent control qualified eighteen petitions around the state. Such measures passed only in Berkeley, Davis, Santa Monica, and Cotati during this period.

Proponents of rent control have been far more successful in front of city councils and county supervisors than with voters. By January 1980, more than fifty cities in California had considered rent control. City councils and county supervisors adopted controls in such populous communities as Los Angeles (by a vote of eleven to one), Los Angeles county, San Francisco, and San Jose. Altogether, some 30 percent of the 2.9 million rental units in the state were under rent control by late 1979.[29] Indeed, the California Poll taken the first two weeks of May 1979 showed that state residents supported rent control by a margin of 56 to 31 percent; among renters, the margin was 73 to 20 percent. Sixty percent of all Californians and 81 percent of renters said that landlords were charging excessive rates, considering the cost of operating rental property.

Fears that rent controls would stifle new apartment construction prompted the California Association of Realtors, in conjunction with the California Apartment Association, the California Housing Council, the California Building Industry Association, the California Mortgage Bankers, and the state Building and Construction Trades Council, to sponsor a constitutional amendment to limit the authority of state and local governments to impose rent control. The proposed amendment (known as Proposition 10 on the June 3, 1980, state ballot) prohibited statewide rent control but permitted local rent control through a majority vote of the people (not by act of city councils or county boards of supervisors). Any specific rent control measure would have to conform to guidelines in the amendment, which allowed landlords to raise rents each year by a percentage equal to the previous year's increase in the Consumer Price Index. Additionally, the amendment required any locally adopted rent control measure to be put to a vote of the people every four years for retirement or ratification. If adopted, Proposition 10 would also have repealed all existing rent control laws. After this, new controls could be adopted only by a vote of the citizens, beginning with the November 1980 elections.

The campaign for Proposition 10 was highlighted with lively radio and television advertisements. Proponents blamed rent controls for the shortage and high price of rental housing throughout the state and claimed that their measure was designed only to set fair rentals. Opponents claimed that 10 would eventually force higher rents because new facilities would be exempt from control. The complex language of the measure made it difficult to understand if a yes vote on 10 was for or against rent control. In the end, 10 lost by a resounding 65 to 35 percent margin. Mervin Field said that the massive defeat signaled a feeling by voters that backers of the proposition were trying to "bamboozle" the public.

With the defeat of Proposition 10, city councils and county boards of supervisors still retain the authority to adopt rent control ordinances without direct voter approval. Since overall economic trends largely determine activity in the construction sector, however, it will take many years to judge how fears of rent control affect new apartment construction.

N GOVERNMENT

Like the expected decline in employment, the widely predicted post-13 collapse of public services failed to materialize. After an initial drop, public employment returned to its pre-13 level. Surplus state funds poured into local government agencies to offset losses in property tax receipts. Local governments dipped into their own surpluses. Some fees rose. A few agencies were forced to tighten their belts. By and large, however, in the first three years of the tax revolt, government in California went about its business as usual.

Propelled by the upcoming elections, the state legislature fashioned a bailout program for local governments in literally a matter of days. Bailout I (SB 154) authorized $4.4 billion in relief to local governments to compensate, in part, for the loss of billions of dollars in property taxes. This was followed, in turn, by Bailout II (AB 8), which was adopted by the legislature in July 1979. Bailout II was a long-term plan for fiscal relief that gave back to local governments about $4.85 billion in 1979–80 and $5.5 billion in 1980–81.

Before looking at the structure of Bailout II and what happened to specific government services, it is useful to compare the state of public finances of California governments in the three years since Proposition 13 with those of the preceding decade. Figure 5.1 shows the steady rise in overall revenues and spending since 1968–69. Note that revenues actually fell in 1978–79, the first year of Proposition 13, but that surplus state funds enabled overall spending to continue its decade-long upward path. What is extraordinary about the increase in total government spending in California in fiscal 1978–79 through 1980–81 is that it took place

FIGURE 5.1

TOTAL REVENUES AND SPENDING
OF STATE AND LOCAL GOVERNMENT

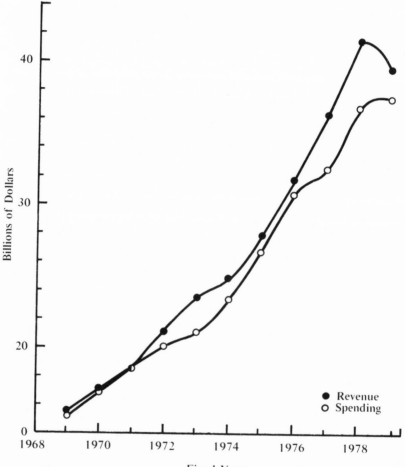

SOURCE: U.S., Department of Commerce, Bureau of the Census, *Governmental Finances*, 1968–69 to 1978–79.

after massive property tax cuts and several billion dollars of additional reductions in individual income and business taxes.

It is easy to trace in Figure 5.1 the emergence of the state's general fund surplus: revenues exceeded expenditures, often by substantial margins, in the several years immediately preceding Proposition 13. (Figure 5.2 plots the annual and accumulated state

FIGURE 5.2

GENERAL FUND UNRESTRICTED SURPLUS
AND ANNUAL SURPLUS/DEFICIT, 1973–74 TO 1980–81

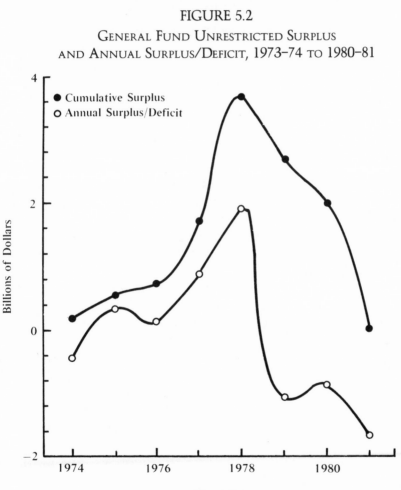

Fiscal Year

SOURCE: Analysis of the 1981–82 budget bill (report of the legislative analyst).

surplus.) Despite fears that the entire surplus might be exhausted in one massive payout to local governments, however, the state has been able to sustain its multibillion dollar bailout for three years, in ever increasing amounts, due largely to an upward turn in revenues. Figure 5.1 shows that state and local revenues fell from $41.6 billion in 1977–78 to $39.5 billion in 1978–79, a decline of 5 percent. Total revenue of state and local government for 1979–80 came to just over $46 billion. After a one-year contraction in state and local revenue, moneys flowing into government rose by more than 16 percent in the second fiscal year under the provisions of Proposition 13. Security Pacific National Bank estimated $50.8 billion for 1980–81.[1]

One source of the increase in local government revenues was the unexpectedly rapid rise in assessed valuations and property tax collections. Assessed valuation rose 9.6 percent in 1978–79 due to sales of existing homes (consequently reassessed to reflect market values) and substantial new commercial and industrial construction.[2] Assessed valuation rose about 14.4 percent in the following year, and the State Board of Equalization reported the growth in assessed value for 1980–81 at nearly 14 percent.[3] Thus, despite Jarvis-Gann's 2 percent annual limit on property tax increases, total property tax collections may well exceed Proposition 13 dollar levels as early as 1984 or 1985.

Actual spending by local governments is found in the state controller's reports on local governments, which are typically released the April following the conclusion of the prior fiscal year. For example, information on public school expenditures for 1980–81 is not available until April 1982 at the earliest. But the evidence through 1979–80 indicates a leveling of spending in the first year of Proposition 13 followed by renewed upward growth in the second year (see Table 5.1). Surplus funds combined with record revenues for 1980–81 doubtless fueled higher spending that year, too.

These facts and figures show that the moneys flowing into and out of state and local government treasuries have not been curtailed in any sense. Indeed, the available figures are somewhat misleading. In the case of education, for example, some programs were dropped, resulting in a significant rise in per-capita expenditures on students in basic academic programs. At this point, therefore, it is difficult to determine or measure what changes, if any, have taken place in either the quality or quantity of public services. The bailouts have sustained government spending at steadily rising levels, thus deferring until 1982 or later the promised impact of Proposition 13, the so-called day of reckoning that government officials have warned about since 1978. But those cuts, if they ever come, must remain the subjects of a future study. Here

TABLE 5.1

LOCAL GOVERNMENT SPENDING
1977–78 TO 1979–80 (millions of dollars)

	Actual 1977–78	Actual 1978–79	Actual 1979–80	Percentage Change 1977/78–79/80
Schools, K–12	$9,020	$8,999[a]	$9,807[b]	8.7
Community colleges	1,442	1,399[c]	1,576[d]	9.3
Cities[e]	7,306	7,699	8,660	18.5
Counties[f]	8,441	8,811	9,563	13.3
Enterprise special districts	2,814	3,085	3,749	33.2
Nonenterprise special districts	1,298	1,323	1,532	18.0

SOURCES: State Controller's Annual Reports Concerning the Financial Transactions of Cities, Counties, School Districts, and Special Districts.

NOTES: [a] ADA fell 8.3 percent.

[b] ADA fell 1.2 percent.

[c] ADA fell 10.6 percent.

[d] ADA increased 7.2 percent.

[e] Includes city and county of San Francisco; includes city-owned enterprises, such as water, electricity, gas, sewers, airports, transportation systems, harbors, cemeteries, hospitals, parking districts, and housing.

[f] Excludes city and county of San Francisco; includes county-owned enterprises, such as hospitals, airports, refuse, harbor, parking, golf courses, parks, and transportation systems.

we return to the immediate past and how government coped with 13's aftereffects.

BAILOUT II

Year-to-year financing of local government left much to be desired. For Sacramento it entailed an annual political struggle; for local governments, it meant uncertain annual budgets and a virtual inability to adopt long-term plans. Thus the governor and legislators sought a viable long-term solution that would enable local governments to maintain services at or near 1978 levels.

In all, it took the legislature from January to July 1979 to fashion a solution acceptable to both parties in both houses. After nearly six weeks of almost daily meetings, a six-member joint conference committee put together the specific bill. Known officially as AB 8, and popularly as Bailout II, the measure was largely the work of Democratic Assemblyman Leroy Greene of Carmichael. The bill's permanent solution to local government funding is to use general fund revenues to aid local governments. The sum of this aid can be increased by several hundred million dollars each year. However, if the state's economy and government revenues weaken, the law includes a "deflator" mechanism to apportion the reductions in state revenues between the state and local governments, thereby protecting both from precipitous losses of funds.

The deflator mechanism automatically reduces relief funds to local governments if the combined total of state revenues and surplus funds drops below a given point. For the 1980–81 fiscal year, the given point was $20.6 billion, a figure released by the new Commission on State Finance and based on the best estimates of 1980–81 state financial resources at the time the bailout plan was being developed in 1979. Under the terms of the law, if available state revenues fell $100 million or more below the $20.6 billion figure (which they did not), the entire shortfall would have been deducted on a 50–50 basis from the amounts (1) public schools and community colleges and (2) cities, counties, and special districts were due to receive in state bailout funds. Under AB 1019, a follow-up measure to AB 8, the corresponding figures for the 1981–82 fiscal year and subsequent years will be adjusted by the changes in the California Consumer Price Index and state population.

The Senate approved the bill 28 to 12 and the Assembly 67 to 11. On July 20, 1979, the legislature sent the bill to Governor Brown for review and signature. Calling it "the most massive program ever enacted by the legislature," Governor Brown signed the $4.85 billion bailout bill into law on July 24, 1979.[4] Brown chose to leave the bill intact rather than make any additional cuts, for, as he pointed out, there were "very few things that could be vetoed without forcing the poor to bear the brunt of the state's fiscal problems."[5] (In California, the governor may veto portions of bills.)

But, Brown continued, in the future "a recession will not spare California and we will have to apply a much more stringent approach."[6] Such stringency was represented by what Brown called the "fail-safe" mechanism, the deflator formula that would adjust the amount of state funding available to local governments in accordance with future economic tides. He also added that as long as the state of California had a surplus, legislators would not cut down on spending.

Opponents charged that the bill was too generous with state revenues and did not reflect the public's wishes. In fact, despite the tax-cutting message of Proposition 13, the new bailout terms amounted to "business as usual in Sacramento."[7] Proponents of the bill argued that it was designed to end the annual contest among cities, counties, special districts, and the schools for limited state dollars. Its purpose was to make local governments independent from the state by granting long-term relief without strings.

Bailout II shifted about 28 percent of the remaining school property taxes to cities, counties, and special districts, thereby eliminating these jurisdictions' dependence on state block grants. It also significantly increased state aid to schools. Between 1978 and 1980 this aid rose from 40 percent to 68 percent of all public education funds. The state takeover of county programs for the aged, blind and disabled, along with Medi-Cal, was made permanent. In addition, the bailout also established a new matching program to fund local health services. Finally, Greene's bill eliminated the majority of restrictions that the legislature had placed on the use of bailout funds during the previous year.[8]

One clear effect of Proposition 13 was greater centralization of local government finance in state hands.[9] The state absorbed much of the revenue loss incurred by local governments, but it also set specific conditions for new sources of revenues such as benefit assessments. School districts, in particular, became far more dependent on state funds and subject to state regulation. Greater centralization threatened a general decline in home rule. Increasingly, local discretion and responsibility gave way to burdensome state laws and guesswork on annual levels of state assistance, thereby complicating the tasks of budget makers and local government administrators. Recognizing these difficulties, the legislature loosened some of the strings tied to state aid in Bailout I.

ESSENTIAL SERVICES: POLICE

Bailout I (or SB 154) mandated that police and fire services were to be maintained at pre-13 levels. However, the measure did not totally preclude reductions in spending for these services. "Local governments were specifically authorized to effect cost savings if such steps did not impair the protection provided. The public protection programs most affected by budget reductions in 1978–79 were agricultural commissioners, the sealers of weights and measures, and local planning and flood control programs."[10] These were not crucial to the maintenance of public safety.

The public, the press, and even scholars have all too often erroneously equated or confused the amount of dollars spent on public services with the quality of service delivered by government agencies. The standard presumption is that an increase in public spending means more and better services. Conversely, a decrease in public spending is presumed to imply cuts in both the quality and quantity of those services. The deeper the spending reductions, the sharper the service cuts.

This view incorrectly links the dollars and staff used in providing services with the benefits taxpayers receive.[11] The concept of productivity relates the value of inputs used in any productive process to the value of goods and services produced. This concept can be quantified because producers must pay for the inputs they use in creating goods and services they subsequently sell in the marketplace.

It is more difficult to value output that is not sold in the market. Most public services are largely tax supported and distributed free of charge. National economic accounting typically values government services at their cost of provision, that is, wages paid and goods purchased. Input thus equals output. Improvements in business productivity are measured by changes in the ratio of the cost of inputs to the value of outputs. No corresponding measure exists for public services. In the absence of a widely accepted gauge to determine the value of public services, it is essential to examine each service separately and try to reach some tentative agreement about it.

In deciding to cut the fat out of local government, voters clearly excluded police and fire services, on the unverified assumption that these services operated efficiently in protecting both life and property. However, as Robert Poole, a specialist on local government services, points out, "Like other public agencies, police and fire departments are run as bureaucracies. They have little of the cost-consciousness typical of competitive, profit-making companies. Consequently, it should come as no surprise that they are often quite inefficient."[12]

A 1975 Rand Corporation study showed many inefficiencies in police departments. In particular, detectives spent much of their time shuffling papers and continuing useless examinations of cases that should have been closed long before for lack of any significant probability of getting further information. Similarly, officers wasted much time going through the motions of taking fingerprints and engaging in other pseudo-investigative activities at crime scenes where it was evident that little or nothing could be accomplished. On the basis of such findings, the study concluded both that too many officers were being assigned to detective units and that "far more criminals will be caught . . . by more alert patrol units and improved citizen cooperation than by refinement in investigative work."[13]

Studies completed in Kansas City have shown that routine patrols have limited deterrent value. They do not reduce crime or increase citizen security, and a few minutes difference in police response time makes little difference in whether a crime is solved or a suspect apprehended.[14] Palmer Stinson, a California police consultant and former Oakland police captain, blames the structure of police departments and the misuse of officers' time:

> Public safety agencies are not uniformly managed and efficient. Impartial law-enforcement surveys have consistently reported two unresolved problems . . . top-heavy staffing and badly deployed patrol forces. Many cities have experienced "grade creep" and have too many deputy chiefs, captains, lieutenants, and sergeants. In some agencies there is one management person for every two or three patrol officers . . . Also few police forces do a good job of matching officers' work hours and days off with the ebb and flow of citizens' call for service. In some jurisdictions, officers have one or more weekend days off, even though the weeks' peak of calls may fall on the weekend.[15]

Figure 5.3 shows the massive increase in public expenditures on police services since 1968–69. However, over this period it is clear that crime rates have continued to increase steadily (see Figure 5.4). These trends suggest the failure of either execution or resource allocation in police work—or even the possibility that a reduction in expenditures might have little direct effect on crime rates since these depend on other variables. Nevertheless, it is apparent that despite continuing increases in police budgets and personnel over the years crime has continued to increase in California. Perhaps the whole concept of law enforcement needs rethinking.

The public's mandate to maintain existing levels of police services was instrumental in bringing about a closer examination of the actual services delivered. Bailout I's failure to define "service level" soon made the lack of data on current service delivery apparent. As the California Taxpayers' Association pointed out, "Budget, service, work load, and patrol data did not enter the debate over how much aid the state should channel to local government in support of police . . . functions." The association helped to remedy this gap in research with a study of the change in sheriffs' work loads and performance between 1968 and 1978. A survey of 57 county sheriffs departments, to which 42 responded, disclosed that after adjusting for inflation, budgets for California sheriffs increased 78 percent over the ten-year interval. Budgets for detention facilities also doubled in real dollars.[16] The survey did

FIGURE 5.3

POLICE PROTECTION EXPENDITURES

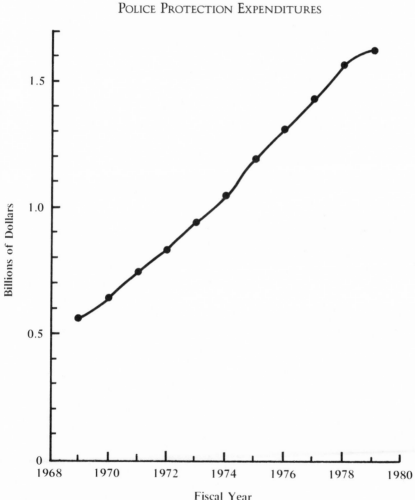

Fiscal Year

SOURCE: U.S., Department of Commerce, Bureau of the Census, *Governmental Finances,* 1968–69 to 1978–79.

not obtain precise information on equipment or facilities, but its authors speculated that increased mechanization and sophistication of sheriff operations, in addition to increases in staffing, had boosted costs.

FIGURE 5.4

CALIFORNIA CRIME RATE
(Per 100,000 People)

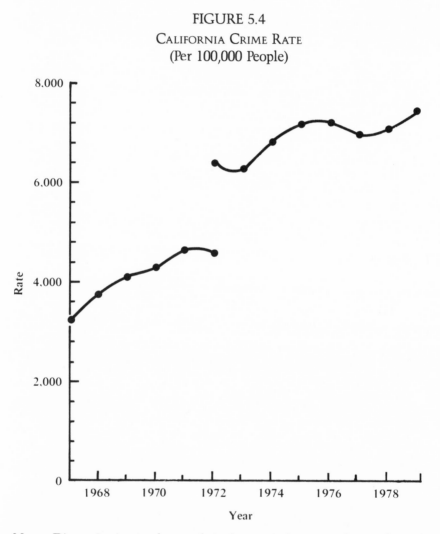

NOTE: Discontinuity in the graph is due to a change in the method of reporting crime rates in 1972.

The survey also found that a sworn officer served 47 percent fewer persons and 46 percent fewer square miles in 1978 than in 1968. Such reductions were taken to mean that there had been an improvement in service levels. However, arrest rates actually declined from 3.3 per month per officer in 1967–68 to 1.8 per month in 1977–78. On the subject of patrol, the survey noted that over the ten-year period this coverage had increased 65 percent. (Potential patrol capability was defined here as a measure of the frequency of patrol over any given road mile.) This phenomenon may be explained, according to the study, "by more patrols on the road, which in turn would explain the higher service levels and higher expenditures."[17]

Note that in this instance more spending does not equate with more public safety. Less spending might further accelerate the erosion in public safety or possibly reverse the trend. But this thought must remain speculative at present since such cuts have yet to occur in police budgets.

In the first two years of Proposition 13, county expenditures for all public safety and protection programs rose from $1.56 billion in 1977–78 to $1.62 billion in 1978–79 to $2 billion in 1979–80, rising from 18.8 percent of county spending to 24.5 percent in two years. Spending rose by nearly $500 million (32 percent), well beyond the rate of inflation.[18] Spending on police services in the state's 419 cities increased from $956 million in 1977–78 to $1,045 million in 1978–79 to $1,299 million in 1979–80, a gain of about 36 percent in two years.[19]

Given this rapid increase in expenditures, it is not surprising that a number of ballot measures to levy a special tax for police services have failed to win the two-thirds approval required under Proposition 13. On November 4, 1980, only one of nine police-funding measures met the requirement. Most obtained only a simple majority. On June 2, 1981, four cities, of which only Los Angeles was important in size, voted on a special tax for additional police protection. Voters said no in San Pablo, Pinole (by four to one), and Los Angeles (58 percent) and yes in San Ramon Valley. Although crime remained a major political issue in 1981, voters had seen public spending on police rise since passage of Proposition 13 and refused additional tax levies.

ESSENTIAL SERVICES: FIRE

The legislature mandated that California's fire services, like those of the police, remain unchanged for 1978–79 and allotted bailout moneys to ensure compliance. Bailout II removed those strings, allowing cities and counties discretion in setting budgets. To date, fire services have not been cramped for funds.

Prior to Proposition 13, three types of fire services existed in the state, each with its own funding structure and specialty. Special fire districts set the property tax rates for their services; city fire departments looked to the cities for their budgetary needs; and the California Department of Forestry, which provides fire protection for both California wildlands (which are the state's responsibility) and structures under contract to a county, was funded in part by the state and in part by the counties. County funding was of two types—one based solely on the property tax (Structural Fire Protection Fund) and the other based on county general funds.

With passage of 13, fire protection districts (as opposed to city fire departments funded from city budgets) lost their major funding source—the property tax. Fire protection districts are single-purpose units of government with no source of revenue other than the property tax or related revenues (such as interest on property taxes deposited with the county treasurer). Only the bailout funds enabled these districts to meet the fire maintenance mandate.

In its first-year assessment of 13's effect on fire protection, the legislative analyst's office examined data collected by the Department of Finance and the several state fire services agencies (State Fire Marshal, California Department of Forestry, and Office of Emergency Services, Fire/Rescue Division). In addition, it also interviewed officials in fire protection districts and county fire departments. The results of this survey showed that "statewide fire protection has generally been maintained at or close to 1977–78 program levels." Table 5.2 shows no significant cutbacks in expenditures by fire protection agencies in 1978–79; the few cuts were confined to such peripheral programs as public education, weed abatement, and safety inspections.

The final state controller's reports on cities for fiscal 1978–79 and 1979–80 showed that spending on fire services rose respectively by $38 million and $142 million over the $537 million spent during 1977–78, a two-year gain of 34 percent.[20] Since 34 percent exceeded inflation over this period, spending on municipal fire services rose in real terms.

Several fire protection agencies came up with innovative ideas to augment revenues. The city of Inglewood, for example, imposed a "fire-flow" fee on property. The fee for each structure was

TABLE 5.2

LOCAL EXPENDITURES FOR FIRE PROTECTION
1977–78 AND 1978–79 (thousands of dollars)

	Actual 1977–78	Budgeted 1978–79	Percentage Change
Counties[a]	84,000	92,741	10.4
Cities[b]			
(89 percent of all cities reporting)	467,631	467,344	0.0
City and County[b]	63,915	65,614	2.6
Special Districts[b]			
(75 percent of all districts reporting)			
Fire Protection Districts			
(350 reporting)	206,536	225,923	9.4
County Service Areas			
(53 reporting)	2,984	3,912	31.1
Community Service Districts			
(20 reporting)	574	617	7.5
Recreation and Park Districts			
(2 reporting)	202	136	−32.7
All Others			
(11 reporting)	1,414	1,627	15.1

[a] SOURCE: State Controller's Report of the Financial Transactions of the Counties of California and 1978–79 County Budgets.
[b] SOURCE: State Department of Finance survey.

based on size and building materials used, with credits for sprinkler systems and other fire prevention devices.[21] In 1979 the legislature authorized general law cities, counties, and special districts to levy standby and availability charges, or special taxes, for fire services if two-thirds of the voters approve. In the November 1980 election, 41 city or special fire districts in 23 counties had such measures on their ballots, and 13 passed.[22]

In a case study of fire services in San Mateo county, an independent research group at the Governmental Research Council made a number of recommendations for cost-savings. The group surveyed fire services in the county after passage of Proposition 13 in order to identify the most viable alternatives for reorganizing present service delivery to reduce costs. Among their recommendations were (1) an alternative approach to providing emergency medical services in San Mateo county; (2) different methods for delivering fire services to unincorporated urbanized areas; (3) consolidation of fire services.

The study found "placing a paramedic service within selected county fire departments using existing fire personnel" feasible because the departments themselves had the capacity to assume the additional service. "Using existing fire personnel, trained to the level of paramedic, would be less costly than the present service." According to the group's research, "the scheme envisioned would involve a sharing of costs and revenue between the county and participating fire agencies."[23] Such a scheme represented not only an all-around cost-savings but also allowed the county to maintain existing emergency medical service levels permanently.

In the case of fire service delivery to unincorporated areas currently served by the California Department of Forestry, the analysis found that it was feasible for city and district fire agencies surrounding or adjacent to unincorporated pockets to provide them with fire protection. The results of the analysis clearly indicated that "the calls generated by these unincorporated areas could be absorbed by city fire departments without increasing personnel or affecting their capabilities to provide timely response to city fire calls." Furthermore, "implementation of this alternative approach could significantly reduce the cost of servicing these unincorporated areas and generate revenue for the cities involved. . . . Overall, the county could realize a net saving of over $147,000 per year."[24]

On the subject of consolidation, the study indicated that "a county-wide fire service agency has the potential to increase fire service quality and significantly reduce county-wide costs." It estimated cost savings to be "in the order of $3.5 million annually compared to current expenditures." Even further savings were possible: "Regional fire service consolidation provides nearly comparable opportunities to improve fire service cost and organizational effectiveness." Overall, the study pointed out, "analysis of fire service consolidations, at whatever level, indicates that there is potential for major positive impact on the provision of fire services in San Mateo County."[25]

It is clear that in most instances fire departments and districts received priority funding and suffered very few cutbacks, despite isolated instances cited by some fire chiefs. Still, there are certain areas where cost-savings could be greatly increased, but implementation of these particular areas, such as consolidations and paramedic services, are fraught with political problems, and it is these political difficulties that will require greater efforts to overcome on behalf of both providers and consumers of fire services.

Taking stock, it appears that overall spending on the essential services of police and fire protection has not been curtailed and such services have not been adversely affected. In all, the first bailout in 1978–79 gave block grants of $250 million to the cities, $190 million to special districts, and $437 million to the counties, in addition to the state's buyout of health services. The Bailout II formula transferred a portion of the remaining school property taxes to other local agencies. For 1979–80, this transfer gave $207 million to the counties. In Proposition 13's first year, the state attached several conditions to the acceptance of bailout funds by local agencies: limits on salary increases, maintenance of police and fire service levels, prohibition of health-care program cuts, and so forth. The courts eventually overruled a number of these conditions, including salary freezes and police-service maintenance. Spending on police services grew even more rapidly under Bailout II, however. Despite Bailout II's reductions in the dollar amounts that went into city and county treasuries in the form of block grants, property tax revenues still rose more than $700 million in 1979–80 over the previous year, and again by $700 million in 1980–81, thereby more than offsetting the modest reductions in bailout revenues. County revenues grew 13.5 percent and city revenues 11 percent in 1980–81.[26] Overall, cities and counties have fared well under 13.

ESSENTIAL SERVICES: EDUCATION

Of all state and local government services, education is by far the most costly. Yet it is also the one essential service that has come under great criticism—for the bizarre reason that steadily rising expenditures on public education have been accompanied by a steady erosion in quality.

Between 1967 and 1976, public school expenditures rose 114 percent—outstripping the 98 percent rise in personal income of all Californians and the 60 percent rise in the Consumer Price Index. On the average, in 1978, California taxpayers spent $1,750 per pupil for public education. What they got back for that amount is uncertain.[27]

How did the public school system get into such dire straits? Many reasons have been offered to account for declining standards and soaring costs. Some causes may be "directly attributable to recent education trends: grade inflation, the reduction in basic course requirements and the proliferation of electives, social promotions, less homework and easier textbooks."[28]

A national blue-ribbon panel, formed to explain why College Board scores declined over the preceding fourteen years, cited both of these causes, together with other "pervasive" factors, to account for the decline; for example, the effects of TV, less reading, more broken homes, and low student motivation due to social causes, such as the unrest of the 1960s. This period was also cited as a cause of lower scholastic aptitude test (SAT) scores since educational opportunities increased for larger numbers of disadvantaged students who had not previously attended college and were now taking the tests.

Figure 5.5 displays the steady erosion in test scores in California since the 1971–72 school year. These declines have occurred despite a steady rise in total spending on public education and in per-pupil expenditures since enrollments are no longer rising (see Figure 5.6). It is tempting to suggest that some budget cuts might actually improve educational performance since growing budgets have been accompanied by a steady decline in levels of achievement. As yet no such cuts are contemplated.

Educators frequently cite lack of student motivation and greater numbers of minority students as causes for the present

FIGURE 5.5

SCHOLASTIC APTITUDE TEST SCORES

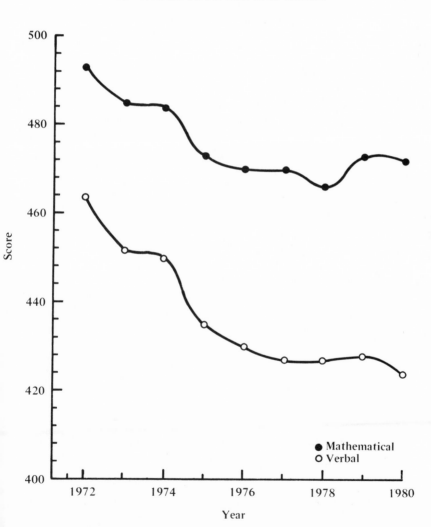

problems of public schools. Defenders of public schools, in contrast, argue that too much has been asked of the schools. "In the last ten years, schools have been asked to accomplish what no one else could do: to integrate society. In addition, they have been

FIGURE 5.6

SCHOOL EXPENDITURES

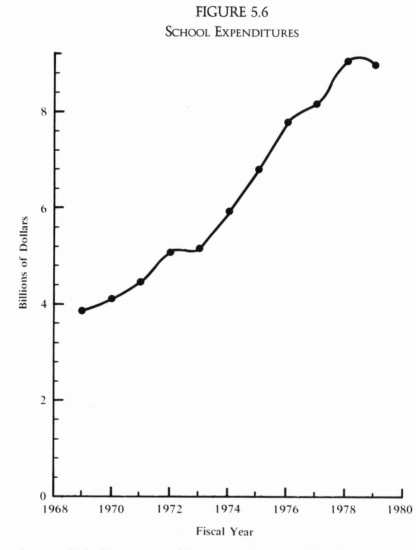

Fiscal Year

SOURCE: U.S., Department of Commerce, Bureau of the Census, *Governmental Finances*, 1968–69 to 1978–79.

asked to provide bilingual and adult education, to care for preschoolers and to teach youngsters to drive, sew and swim. Above all they were expected to teach kids to read and write. When it became apparent that the schools were doing none of these things very well, public disenchantment began growing in earnest."[29] One specific example well illustrates how such public disenchantment was fueled. "Since 1974, the student enrollment in San Diego city schools has dropped from 123,000 to 119,000 and the number of classroom teachers cut from 5,064 to 4,922. Yet, there are: 8 more principals, 5 extra vice principals, 100 new nonclassroom certificated people, 340 more clerical workers and 120 extra custodians and gardeners. The overall district employee rolls have grown from 9,230 to 9,813."[30] A comparison with statistics for 1970 is even more disturbing. Then the city had 130,000 students. In 1978, with 11,000 fewer students, the city had 507 fewer classroom teachers. But there were 16 more principals, 180 more counselors (for a total of 343), 586 more clerical and technical staff, 101 more gardeners and custodians. The total district staff had grown by 1,544 employees.

In August 1981, the California Taxpayers' Association released a research bulletin entitled "Measuring Education." It examined changes in funding, enrollment, and employment for the state's public school system between fiscal 1971–72 and 1979–80. The report's findings echoed the experience of San Diego. Overall, average daily attendance (ADA) fell 13 percent, enrollment 11 percent, and the teaching staff 4 percent. At the same time, State Department of Education staff increased 41 percent and other school personnel (nurses, psychologists, counselors, administrators) increased 29 percent. Total revenues for kindergarten through twelfth grade (K–12) increased 116 percent over this period, exactly keeping pace with the state's inflation rate. Declining enrollment thus meant real increases in per-pupil revenues over this period of 22 percent. The report also points out that declining public school enrollment of 11 percent during the last decade contrasted sharply with an increase of 21 percent in private school enrollment, suggesting growing disenchantment with the public schools.

Finally, while the report also cited a statewide decline in SAT scores since 1971, it noted improved performance since 1977 on the California Assessment Program tests given annually to third, sixth, and twelfth graders to determine skills in reading, spelling, written expression, and mathematics. The greater part of these improvements have occurred since passage of Proposition 13.

Proposition 13 was both a timely and convenient means by which the public could express its dissatisfaction with public education, especially since education consumed the greatest proportion of local property taxes. Indeed, Jarvis himself was prompted to say that "cuts to education would not be serious since schools aren't teaching anyway."[31]

Jarvis later elaborated his overall views on 13 and education:

Schools have fat that can be trimmed but essential services are not endangered.

Schools by law have first call on the state dollar.[32]

Serrano can best be implemented by passage of 13, with the state assuming the burden of educating students.[33]

In countering Jarvis's arguments, those running the No on 13 campaign felt that education did not provide them with a good issue because the subject evoked widespread negative feelings on (1) teacher militancy, unionism, and collective bargaining; (2) continual litigation and forced busing in cities; (3) large expenditures on basic educational programs (particularly important in the light of the growing popularity of the back-to-basics movement); and (4) steadily increasing costs in California, which rose 19 percent above the national average between 1970 and 1976.

Additionally, according to polls taken by Winner & Wagner, the public clearly preferred cuts in education over cuts in other essential local services since the latter were clearly felt to provide better "value-for-money." A 1978 Gallup poll confirmed the public's dissatisfaction with education; confidence in education experienced another annual decrease, "continuing a trend which has seen that portion of the public rating the schools 'A' or 'B' decline from 48% to 36% over the last four years."[34]

Amid the debate over the effects of Proposition 13, the legislative analyst published a study that attempted to outline its consequences for education. It pointed out that "over half of all property tax revenues (52.2 percent) is used to finance K-14 school expenditures." The property tax is "the major source of revenue for California's 7,000 elementary and secondary public schools and for the 105 community colleges." College financing is "based on a sharing of expense for average daily attendance (ADA) between the State and local community college districts. The State's share of funding is determined by the State support for ADA in the prior year. This support amount is then increased for inflation. The adjustment for inflation is equalized based on the property wealth of the community college district in order to provide low wealth districts proportionately greater amounts of state aid."[35]

The study estimated support for community colleges at $568.8 million in 1978-79 (4.2 percent of the proposed state budget) and the total local property tax revenue to community colleges at $880 million. Combined with state and federal aid, according to the legislative analyst's estimate, the total revenue for the colleges would be $1.7 billion. For K-12, the report estimated revenues of approximately $5.6 billion from local property taxes (1978-79) and $3.6 billion from the state.

To counteract the effects of 13 on education, the analyst's study noted several ways that reductions in school revenues could be alleviated, including (1) full state funding; (2) a statewide salary schedule; (3) a voucher system; and (4) state replacement of local property tax revenue losses.[36] After passage of Proposition 13, each of these alternatives received considerable attention from those concerned before the final funding solutions were adopted.

The legislative analyst's study also surveyed selected school districts in order to assess the plans districts might adopt if 13 passed. Proposed areas for cutbacks included transportation, maintenance, summer schools, preschools, libraries, adult education and counseling programs, nursing services, athletics, and supplies. However, even the total elimination of all these programs would result in only a 5-10 percent reduction in total K-12 expenditures. But overall, as the study pointed out, without replacement revenues from new taxes or other levels of government, Proposition 13 could result in a 30 percent reduction in total K-12 revenues.[37]

After Jarvis had characterized education as being in need of a fat cut, educators and their powerful lobbies tried to focus voter attention on the short- and long-term consequences of tampering with the education system. They confronted teachers with the possibility of huge staff layoffs, closed classrooms, and lack of supplies and parents with the collapse of a system that, despite its shortcomings, had undertaken to educate their children. As one Santa Barbara parent expressed it: "Proposition 13 is a sword hanging over everyone's political head. There is guerilla warfare being waged and we and our kids are the victims."[38] However, these threats lacked credibility. Numerous Education Code provisions severely limit a district's ability to reduce staff, in particular Section 44892, which specifically prohibits school districts from laying off permanent employees because of a reduction in revenues. This provision is especially important since school district personnel costs account for approximately 85 percent of expenditures.

Wilson Riles, state superintendent of schools, added to the scaremongering by quoting the dollar losses that schools could sustain under 13. He estimated that as much as $500 million in federal funds might be lost in addition to the estimated $3.7 billion cutback in property tax support. The cuts, Riles pointed out, "would come in programs that require some local funding. Loss of local funds to the programs would mean an end to federal matching dollars . . . An estimated $205.7 million would be cut out of the school lunch program . . . In addition, special programs for children from low income families would lose $194 million." Using figures compiled by surveying schools around the state he also noted that Proposition 13 "would jeopardize $17 million for experimental programs; $19 million for libraries; $7 million for study centers and reading programs; $35.7 million for handicapped children; $62.3 million for vocational and adult education; and $6 million for Indian education."[39]

Yet, California voters ignored the threats and dire predictions about the imminent demise of public education. After passage of 13, there was no doubt that without state aid the schools and community colleges would have faced serious financial straits. Consequently the legislature's division of initial bailout funds allotted 45 percent, or $2.27 billion, of the $5 billion aid package to schools and community colleges. These new state funds "enabled education to escape with but a 10.5 percent overall reduction from the anticipated 1978–79 figure."[40] Overall, for 1978–79, schools emerged with more than 95 percent of the 1977–78 statewide financing figure. Further, because boards in many districts responded to 13 by eliminating summer school services, the state bailout allowed them to exceed 1977–78 spending during the 1978–79 academic year.

The education bailout met with mixed reactions from school administrators, teachers, and parents. The conditions for receiving bailout funds tended to equalize low- and high-spending districts since low spenders were reimbursed up to 91 percent of what they would have received in 1978–79 had the initiative failed. High-spending districts had to absorb a greater reduction—up to 15 percent of sums anticipated for 1978–79. Overall, lost revenues ranged from 9 to 15 percent, depending on a particular district's position on a statewide ranking of per-pupil expenditures. State aid to finance special programs was distributed to local districts with a flat 10 percent reduction, with the exception of funding for handicapped students, which remained at previous levels.

As with other units of state and local government, the gubernatorial decree prohibited school districts from granting 1978–79 cost-of-living increases to their employees. School administrators' reactions to these new limitations varied, but some districts immediately eliminated summer school programs and services and introduced fees. For example, the San Mateo Union High School District reduced busing to and from nearby Foster City by 74 percent, and Mt. Diablo Unified School District cut $167,000 from its transportation budget. This meant that "youngsters in grades 7–12 living less than seven-and-a-half miles away will also have to find their own transport." Other districts began charging for such transportation. "In Orinda, the charge will be $105 per student per year, with a $200 family maximum. In the San Ramon district ... parents must begin paying 35 cents per ride or roughly $150 per year per student."[41]

The cancellation of summer school programs, one of the major fiscal reductions that most schools made immediately, saved about $107 million in state funds. Savings in this area aided the regular school program, but Wilson Riles decried the cutbacks: "Summer school will never be the same. The profit motive for districts will be removed ... and the state will pay only actual district costs in the future."[42]

In spite of the clamor surrounding the cutbacks in summer schools, Proposition 13 left districts *far better off* financially than they might have been since, under the terms of SB 154,

> districts did not have to maintain summer school and adult education enrollment in order to receive state support for these programs based on 1977–78 ADA (commonly referred to as a "phantom" ADA). Thus, even though summer school enrollment dropped from an estimated 202,500 to 7,400, and adult enrollment fell from an estimated 236,000 to 181,000, districts remained eligible to receive the funds *as if they were operating these programs at the 1977–78 level* [emphasis added]. On a statewide basis, approximately $270 million was built into the base for summer school and $202 million was built in for adult education while only $11 million was spent on summer school programs, and $166 million was spent for adult education. This left an excess of $295 million which was used to support the regular program.[43]

Because of cutbacks in adult and summer school programs, school districts' general aid income *per ADA* actually increased by 9.2 percent in 1978–79, since ADA itself fell 8.6 percent.[44]

After 13, the school boards also lost their ability to enact "permissive override taxes" without a vote of the electorate. "Previously, these taxes could be levied to provide meals for needy students, community services, child development funds and development centers for handicapped students."[45] After 13 the school districts had no way to raise additional revenues for the canceled programs and cutbacks.

However, despite these cutbacks the schools were not financially bereft since their funding with the bailout was equal to 98.8 percent of their 1977–78 funding (see Table 5.1). The key shift was in the proportion of funds from state and local sources. Before Proposition 13, over three-fifths of school budgets came from property taxes. After Proposition 13, the fraction fell to less than three-tenths.

Community colleges also cut back on a number of their programs and summer schools. According to a December 1978 survey of the 70 community college districts by the Chancellor's Office, nearly 6 percent of 61,000 courses and 13 percent of 125,000 sections were eliminated statewide. Sixty-two percent of these reductions were directly attributable to Proposition 13. Fifty-eight of the reporting districts (83 percent) also indicated that Proposition 13 had changed their ability to meet intended "mission and function," and 35 districts (out of 69 responses) indicated difficulty in meeting "mandated maintenance of effort."

To cope with the consequences of 13, community college administrators focused primarily on ways to replace lost revenues over the long run, without affecting the philosophy behind the formation of these institutions; namely, that they should represent "the dream of higher education for anyone who wants it . . . [since] they actively recruit those who mightn't otherwise go to college—the poor, the elderly, racial minorities, women whose children have grown up." However, with the passage of Proposition 13, tuition charges and fees became a possibility. While officials did not initially advocate the move, some observers worried about a more restrictive possibility. "A tuition would cut some people out," said Clark Kerr, former president of the University of California, "but that wouldn't be nearly as harmful as imposing admissions requirements to limit enrollment in the community colleges. That would be a fundamental change. It would break the universal access."[46]

Prior to Proposition 13, community colleges received total revenues of $1.5 billion, 56 percent of which came from local property taxes. After 13 passed, total revenues fell to $1.4 billion, of which 26 percent came from local sources.[47] Spending fell somewhat less, from $1.44 billion to $1.40 billion (see Table 5.1), but far less than had been feared, largely because property tax collections in 1978–79 exceeded everyone's predictions. Cost per pupil rose 8.5 percent from $2,008 to $2,179.

Professor Gregory Jackson of Stanford University conducted a survey of six community colleges on the immediate effects of Proposition 13 on their programs. He found only "modest impacts," compared with the rather dire predictions that both preceded and followed Proposition 13. Class size might increase somewhat and enrollments fall slightly, but only minor adjustments would occur, which would not change the exemplary role or fundamental nature of higher education.[48]

Proposition 13's passage made it apparent that despite the instant rescue provided K–12 schools by the first-year bailout, long-term solutions were needed to solve their fiscal problems. Governor Brown appointed the Post Commission to look into the most viable solutions to these problems and to determine the most acceptable means of implementing solutions. Wilson Riles appealed to the legislature to set up "a long-range adequate financial support system" for schools. He also pointed out that failure to plan for the future could make California "the first state in this nation that comes up without a public system of education . . . It is indeed a crisis situation." Moreover, Riles said, a September 1978 California Poll had found that 75 percent of those surveyed did not want to see cuts in education spending.[49]

By the end of 1979, the legislature had heard numerous suggestions for solving the schools' long-term problems not only from the Post Commission but also from various lobbies for education and educational administrators themselves. At the end of all this discussion on the financial future of education in California, the legislature finally approved a long-term mechanism for the transfer of some state revenues to schools. This measure, known as AB 8, not only solved the future funding problems of schools but also put about 50 percent of the state's students in compliance with the *Serrano* ruling, which took effect in 1980–81.

These formulas provided that high-spending districts (more than $2,000 per pupil) would receive an $85 per-pupil inflation increase, while low-spending districts (under $1,500) would receive $150 per pupil. Districts spending $1,500 to $2,000 would receive between $85 and $150, on a sliding scale. According to the court's ruling, by 1983–84 per-pupil support for 87 percent of the students in the state may not vary more than $100.

For the community colleges, the long-term bailout legislation was good only for two years, and as with schools, the new legislation did not eliminate disparities among college districts. Despite this state aid, community colleges still wanted to preserve local control of programs, even though property taxes made up only 20 percent of the funding. However, the bailout legislation did not totally clarify this problem. "The bailout law included strong legislative intent language regarding strengthening of local control of education . . . Yet the Legislature also adopted budget language that leans towards greater state decision-making."[50]

Furthermore, the legislature directed the California Post-Secondary Education Commission to evaluate the community colleges and to submit proposals on (1) improvement of interdistrict coordination of academic programs and the sharing of physical facilities; (2) the utilization of underused high school facilities; and (3) the development of comparable program and support-service costs for the three segments of public higher education and to include community colleges in the annual survey of faculty salaries and benefits.

Under Bailout II, total state and local funding for K–12 for 1979–80, including special categorical programs, was $9.9 billion, an increase of 10.5 percent over the first year's funding. Allotments for ADA remained virtually unchanged. Thus per pupil expenditures rose by more than 10 percent. Overall, funding for education in the second year approached an 80–20 split between state and local sources. The legislation clearly reflected the view, however, that local control of education should be strengthened, not weakened.

Bailout II equalized per-pupil expenditures, maintained adult programs as well as summer school programs for graduating high school seniors, and imposed proficiency standards on high school students. It also supplied funds for maintenance, teachers' pensions, and capital outlay for new school construction. Only activation of the deflator mechanism in the event of an economic downturn would jeopardize full funding of public education.

Revenues flowing into the 70 community college districts rose from $1.4 billion in 1978–79 to $1.6 billion under Bailout II, an increase of 13.2 percent. As Table 5.1 shows, spending shot up 12.7 percent. Community colleges, having tightened their belts under Bailout I, were able to breathe more freely under Bailout II.[51]

The 1981–82 state budget increased general education aid by 8 percent. Thus the continued erosion in test scores and other measures of educational performance cannot be blamed on spending cuts, which, to all intents and purposes, have yet to take place in public education.

LIBRARIES: THE BELEAGUERED SERVICE

Proposition 13 forced greater proportional spending cuts on California libraries than perhaps on any other major government service. The California Taxpayers' Association carried out a survey of major library systems in Los Angeles, Orange, Sacramento, Santa Clara, and San Diego counties to determine where cutbacks were occurring. According to its findings (see Table 5.3), even after receiving bailout funds "county library systems remain among the institutions hardest hit by Proposition 13's property tax cuts." Library hours were reduced 10 to 25 percent, and new book purchases dropped sharply. However, in none of the five county library systems had book circulation dropped by more than 12 percent. The study concluded that "library clientele have adjusted well to reduced library hours. At the same time, a dramatically reduced library work force has had to handle more clientele per hour than ever before in recent times."[52]

According to a survey conducted by the California State Library and the California Library Association, California libraries suffered (1) a 17 percent decrease in operating income from $207 million in 1977–78 to $171.8 in 1978–79; (2) a 22 percent cut in total hours of all branches from 48,457 in 1977–78 to 37,580 in 1978–79; (3) a 20 percent decrease in funds for purchasing books and magazines from the 1977–78 level of $27.2 million; and (4) a 21 percent reduction in total full-time equivalent staff from 9,060 to 7,154. According to the survey, the "actual numbers of persons affected are even higher, since libraries traditionally employ many part-time persons. However, the comparison includes positions eliminated and positions vacant but not filled, so layoff totals are difficult to estimate." A total of 1,228 persons (part-time and full-time) had been laid off.[53]

However, the reductions were uneven statewide. The survey showed that "libraries serving 4.6 million people received funding equal to 70 percent or less of their previous year's budgets; libraries serving 7.6 million people are funded at 86 to 100 percent of their 1977–78 budgets; libraries serving 2.9 million are funded at 100 percent or above of their 1977–78 budgets."[54]

The survey also looked at how libraries coped in general with the budgetary cutbacks. In addition to reductions in staff and library hours, some libraries in outlying areas closed permanently, and others made cuts in acquisitions budgets, bookmobile programs, interlibrary loan programs, reference services, film services, and summer programs for children. Other communities mounted

TABLE 5.3

IMPACT OF PROPOSITION 13 ON FIVE MAJOR COUNTY LIBRARY SYSTEMS
1978–79 FISCAL YEAR ESTIMATES (percentage changes)

County	Budget	Personnel	Library Hours	Book Circulation	Book Acquisition
Los Angeles	−30	−36	−25	−9	—[a]
Orange	−15	−15	−11	−10	−10
Sacramento[b]	−23	−30	−18	−10 to −12	−20
Santa Clara	−7	−5[c]	−12	−10	−30
San Diego	−17	−15	−10 to −15	−1	−20

SOURCE: Cal-Tax phone survey, May 1979.
NOTES: [a]No new books purchased since April 1978.
[b]Consolidated city-county system.
[c]Excludes 28 percent reduction in temporary work force.

fund-raising drives and examined fee charges for library cards. Where fees already existed, these were raised; however, "library officials were virtually unanimous in their opposition to charging for basic library services."[55]

The study concluded that "in general, services that are part of cities' and counties' budgets fared better than libraries that are special districts."[56] Cities and counties had other revenue sources in addition to property taxes, whereas few special districts did. Pre-13 municipal expenditures for libraries fell from $116 million to $111 million under Bailout I, but reached $120 million under Bailout II.[57] In comparison with the other areas of local government, library officials felt that libraries suffered heavy losses because data used by the legislature to calculate the bailout for special districts were incorrect and fire and police agencies received the bulk of special district allocations. Libraries received only $7 million out of the $162 million allocation.

Furthermore, library services had a low priority rating with both city and county officials. Figures from the Library Association survey "show that library layoffs of full- and part-time persons totaled 1,200. Statewide layoff figures show that about 27,000 persons were laid off due to Proposition 13, out of a total statewide local work force of 1.1 million." The study concluded that "clearly library reductions have been disproportionate to the number of other layoffs." Other explanations for the cutbacks of libraries ranged from vengeful local officials to the libraries' lack of political clout because they usually do not have vocal, organized constituencies.[58]

HEALTH AND WELFARE

The first bailout package set aside $1.1 billion for the state to assume, that is, to buy out, county expenditures on Medi-Cal and major welfare programs. Additionally, the bailout mandated that counties maintain essential health services. This requirement was effected by a complex "disproportionate-cut" formula (section 20 of SB 154), which limited the amount each county could trim from the health section of its budget. These limitations applied only to public health outpatient and inpatient services, not to county mental health, drug, and alcohol programs.

Before passage of 13, the state and counties between them had split the net cost of mental health, drug, and alcohol programs on a 9 to 1 basis (after federal funds and fee collections were taken into account). Under the emergency bailout legislation, the counties' 10 percent share was made optional for the year. Among California's 58 counties, some 26 responded by contributing to the mental health program, 20 to the drug program, and 38 to the alcohol program. Overall, county health expenditures fell from $1.12 billion in 1977–78 to $958 million in 1978–79 to $912 million in 1979–80, reflecting the end of the 10 percent matching payment.[59]

Prior to the passage of Proposition 13, opinion polls had shown conclusively that voters most wanted to halt the high cost of Medi-Cal and welfare programs. Over the preceding few years, total health expenditures had risen from 6.2 percent to 8.8 percent of the U.S. Gross National Product. This growth rate outpaced inflation and population increases in both California and the nation as a whole and had become an increasing burden to taxpayers. Proposition 13's mandate clearly expressed voter sentiment that the time had arrived to re-examine these health expenditures in light of the need to curb government spending at all levels. Yet, despite this mandate, the dollar level of public assistance spending remained steady, falling from $3.23 billion in 1977–78 to $3.17 billion in 1978–79 and rising back to $3.23 billion in 1979–80.[60]

The welfare budget comes not only from state and county funds but also from federal funds. Because of these diverse funding sources, it is difficult for one level of government to control overall expenditures. In general counties are responsible for administering welfare programs, but they have no control over eligibility criteria or levels of cash grants. In addition, state and federal regulations severely limit the extent to which counties can reduce spending or benefits.

Proposition 13's effect on the counties was to make them even more dependent on state and federal decisions and funds. Before 13, "more than one third of county property tax dollars went to welfare related programs, including the counties' share of the

Medi-Cal program. In 1977–78 this was about 36 percent, or an estimated $1.15 billion out of $3.15 billion in county property tax revenues."[61] Since adoption of 13, the property tax no longer supports county welfare programs to any significant degree.

Since 13, the size of the annual appropriations increase for welfare recipients has become a political football. Legislators and the governor were fully aware that voters most wanted budget cuts in this area, yet welfare recipients have been traditional clients of the Democratic party. Bailout I did not award a state-paid cost-of-living increase to Aid to Families with Dependent Children or Supplemental Security Income/Supplemental Security Payment recipients (the latter received only the federal cost-of-living adjustment). Year two gave a full cost-of-living increase. Year three held the state increase to 13 percent, about 2 percent below the 15 percent statutory increase. For year four, the legislature authorized a 9.2 percent increase for the state's 2.1 million welfare recipients and reduced Medi-Cal abortions by 90 percent, unless the state Supreme Court ruled new abortion restrictions unconstitutional.

PARKS AND RECREATION

Parks and recreation services also received state assistance. As "special districts," they shared in the $162 million in additional state assistance funds awarded these jurisdictions. In November 1978, the California Parks and Recreation Service surveyed public agencies that provide park and recreation services to determine the impact of Proposition 13 on their 1978–79 budgets and programs.[62] These findings were summarized by the Pacific Southwest Regional Office of the Heritage Conservation and Recreation Service. Of the 383 agencies asked to complete the questionnaire, 166 responded, including 42 special districts, 10 counties, 74 small cities (population under 50,000), 25 medium cities (population 50,000 to 100,000), and 15 large cities (population over 100,000). The responding agencies provided information on budget and staff cuts, other post–Proposition 13 impacts, and agency survival strategies and assistance needs.

The survey concluded that the "typical" agency made the

greatest cuts in the area of new acquisitions, which some voters had seen as undue expropriation of land for potential development, but planned to complete projects under way. To make up for budget cuts in operations and maintenance and recreational programs, the typical leisure service agency increased some of its user fees. Agencies also relied more on volunteers to supplement reduced staff. Increasingly, agencies turned to private sector groups to sponsor recreation programs, donate funds, or assume maintenance functions. Despite these measures, most agencies had to cut some services, particularly park-school cooperative programs. Adequate funds to operate and maintain facilities were the typical primary concern.

Table 5.4 shows that 85 percent of leisure service agencies increased user fees. Those agencies that had not increased fees either had increases pending or had suffered no cutbacks or were already self-supporting. Eighteen jurisdictions mentioned self-supporting recreation as either a reality or a goal. A number of agencies reported across-the-board increases in existing fee schedules, but the majority were more selective. Many agencies identified new fees on services or privileges, such as dog entrance fees, court-lighting fees, field preparation and class cancellation fees. Other increases targeted specific user groups, such as nonresidents, adults, or those who could afford to pay. Agencies expected to rely increasingly on fee-generated revenues. Indeed, a number of agencies reported that they were building revenue-producing facilities, planning revenue-generating events, and directing public relations efforts at their revenue producers.

Table 5.4 also shows that 69 percent of the agencies instituted either partial or full-scale volunteer programs. However, this figure is misleading since it includes agencies with volunteer programs prior to Proposition 13. Of the nineteen agencies with parks foundations, several noted that the foundations had been formed *prior* to the passage of Proposition 13.

Overall, the most evident finding from the survey was the increased cooperation with private sector groups. Forty-eight separate agencies reported that as a result of Proposition 13 they were soliciting funds, equipment, or sponsorship from various private sources. Few of these agencies were using foundations or gift cat-

TABLE 5.4

SURVEY OF PARKS AND RECREATION SERVICES

Type of Jurisdiction	Increased user fees	Instituted a volunteer program	Established a parks foundation	Carried out acquisition or development in 1978–79
Counties (10)	7	5	3	8
Special Districts (42)	39	34	5	30
Cities, up to 50,000 population (74)	62	47	7	66
Cities, 50,000 to 100,000 population (25)	21	20	2	22
Cities, over 100,000 population (15)	13	10	2	15
Total (166)	142	116	19	141
Percentage of total	85	69	11	85

SOURCE: "Results of the C.P.R.S. Post–Prop. 13 Park and Recreation Survey," mimeo. (November–December 1978).

alogs to approach the private sector. Most frequently, agencies reported working with parents, user groups, service clubs, neighborhoods, or businesses for a specific purpose.

Very few agencies were examining their own internal operations in a comprehensive way in order to lower operation and maintenance costs. Similarly, few agencies planned any large-scale reorganizations, such as consolidations with other agencies. More frequently cited was streamlining in-house procedures, realigning staff responsibilities, or converting all recreational programs to a contractual basis. In an attempt to enhance their image in response to 13, a few agencies reported that they were increasing public relations efforts and would drop any program that could not demonstrate support.

Newspapers, radio, and television have told hundreds of valid human interest stories about the distressing effects of Proposition 13 on the lives of Californians. There is no doubt that people living within the jurisdictions of the state's 6,000 units of local government have experienced closures of neighborhood fire stations, reductions in course electives and extracurricular school programs, cuts in library hours, and higher entrance fees for parks, and other changes. But most of these cuts were modest; few were significant.

An in-depth study of fiscal trends in the city of Los Angeles for the period 1973–78 provides an interesting example of the bureaucratic bloat that could be reduced without painful cuts in service.[63] A team of researchers at the Rand Corporation found that despite a 50 percent increase in city property taxes, total employment remained constant, but the number of front-line people actually giving services to the public fell. Inflation accounted for about three-quarters of the spending increases, but a phenomenon dubbed "upward grade float" consumed 11 percent. By 1978 a larger fraction of the city's work force consisted of administrative and support personnel rather than of front-line policemen, firemen, and sanitation workers. In addition, the staffs of the mayor, city council, city attorney, and the controller grew absolutely and relatively. These are examples of the fat that voters believed could and would be cut from local governments without harming services.

Given the media presentation of 13's effects and the demonstration that there was fat to cut in city and county governments, a look at some actual figures is informative. Data on state and local spending present an entirely different picture. In every major service area, spending steadily increased. For public safety, it has outpaced inflation. Spending on education has kept even with inflation in per pupil terms. State bailout funds have sustained pre-13 levels of local services well into the fourth year of Proposition 13. The state controller's annual reports on local spending sharply contrast with the media's human interest stories of hardship and deprivation.

Proposition 13 may one day bite into state and local government budgets. Future budget cuts may shrink services. But it is equally plausible, given the bizarre history of rising spending and deteriorating services, that spending reductions may improve local services. Given government's propensity to grow, however, the latter is likely to remain a matter for speculation.

THE AFTERMATH OF 13

It is not necessary to rehearse how most California politicians, bureaucrats, public employees, and newspapers adamantly opposed Proposition 13 all through the spring of 1978. Nor is it necessary to reiterate their defeat at the hands of Howard Jarvis, his United Organization of Taxpayers, and the state's electorate. But even after 13's landslide passage, many of the state's establishment continued to warn of future perils, if not in 1978–79, then surely in the second or third year of life under Jarvis, when the state had exhausted its much vaunted surplus.

Not all analysts of 13 carped about the voters' hedonism and selfishness in approving the measure. Gradually, as the months and years wore on and none of the disastrous consequences materialized, even major city newspapers came around to the views of their audience, who had overwhelmingly supported 13 at the ballot in defiance of editorial advice.

Six months after implementation of 13, on December 31, 1978, the *Los Angeles Times* issued a *mea culpa*.

> Those of us who opposed Proposition 13 have a problem: Now that the measure has been in effect almost six months, how do we account for the fact that civilization as we know it has not come to a sudden halt? In contrast to earlier predictions of doom the problems brought by its passage have turned out to be manageable and public services continue largely unaffected. Many public administrators have a ready answer. Doomsday still awaits California government, they say, but it has been delayed

a bit. These officials grudgingly admit that we may scrape through this fiscal year, but next year will be a disaster. Others push the timetable on back a little further, to 1980–81. Having helped deal with Proposition 13 as it affects Los Angeles, the state's largest city, I offer an explanation: We who thought that Proposition 13 could not, would not (perhaps even must not) work were simply wrong. We public administrators, officials, those whose interests are closely tied to public spending—in short, we in the governing class—made a fundamental if all too human error in confusing our own convenience and welfare with the people's interest.

To wit, the *Times* confessed not only that its doomsaying was totally wrong, but also that opponents of 13 were guilty of confusing their own self-interest with the public interest. The view that government must be able to levy all the revenue it needs in order to carry out all the programs society apparently demands, the editorial insisted, must in future contend with the electorate's opposition to unconscionable increases in taxation.

Just after the first anniversary of Proposition 13's passage, the *San Jose Mercury* (June 11, 1979) followed suit.

Just a little over a year ago, most California politicians, bureaucrats and newspapers—including this one—were opposing Proposition 13.

We said it would cripple local government. When it didn't happen last year, the doomsday chorus said just wait, the ax will fall next year.

Well, now it's next year. We've been watching San Jose's City Council put the finishing touches on a budget for fiscal 1979–80. And we have to admit, Armageddon is not exactly upon us. Looking at what Howard Jarvis's brainchild has wrought at San Jose City Hall, we see some things we don't like. *But we also see some things we do like* [emphasis added].

The editorial went on to note that San Jose's $128 million operating budget and the $117 million capital improvement budget trimmed the size and scope of city government *without impairing basic necessities.*

Writers for the *San Diego Union*, in California's third largest metropolitan area, were more cautious. Associate Editor Edward Nichols wrote (June 3, 1979) that "the sky hasn't fallen, but all is not serene." Staff writer Otto Kreisher was more specific. Based on interviews with state and local officials, Kreisher reported that Proposition 13 cutbacks implied possible time bombs in the form of deteriorating streets and public buildings, inability to provide new facilities or services to sustain growth, and decreased performance by public employees. He repeated a prediction from the president of the Special Districts Association that 1,000 cases of mosquito-caused encephalitis were possible in 1980, compared with just one in 1978, due to a reduction in mosquito abatement activity. These did not occur. (In fact, according to the National Center for Disease Control in Atlanta, in 1979 of the 134 recorded cases of viral encephalitis in California, only one was attributable to mosquitoes. For 1980, the total was 128 cases, and again only one was attributable to mosquitoes. Clearly the threat of increasing encephalitis due to a cutback in mosquito abatement activities was unwarranted.) The president of the Special Districts Association also predicted greater risk of crime, floods, and fire as spending cutbacks affected lighting, flood control, and fire protection districts.

Overall, the consensus on the first anniversary of Proposition 13 was that California had survived, with its public services virtually intact. A new debate then began on when (and if) cutbacks might adversely affect the quality of life. For the time being, the critics postponed the day of reckoning until the 1980–81 fiscal year or even later.

Most editorial writers have come to moderate their hostility to Proposition 13 in the light of its real effects, namely, a boon to private economic activity with minimal disruptions in public services. No longer do they denounce taxpayers for their selfishness over property taxes.

How have the state's registered voters reacted to Proposition 13 since its implementation? The answer is that support for 13 has wavered only slightly throughout 1978, 1979, 1980, and 1981. In its polls, the *Los Angeles Times* has periodically asked a sample of registered voters to give their impression of Proposition 13. Responses encompassing August 1978 through November 1981 demonstrate the measure's sustained popularity (see Table 6.1). More than three years after its adoption, Proposition 13 remained as popular as it was on the day of its landslide victory.

TABLE 6.1

LOS ANGELES TIMES POLLS: IMPRESSION OF PROPOSITION 13
(percentage)

	August 21–25 1978	September 25–28, 1978	October 15–21, 1979	May 4–7, 1980	July 12–22, 1981	November 1–5, 1981
Favorable	65	64	62	60	58	70
Unfavorable	30	32	31	34	36	27
Unsure	5	4	7	6	6	3

However, such uninterrupted support for the measure did not carry over to those officials responsible for its implementation. Several weeks after passage of 13, the *Los Angeles Times* Poll asked voters if "public officials were making an honest effort to carry out the will of the people on Proposition 13." Sixty-two percent said no. Two months later, in August, 71 percent said no. Within a few weeks, the electorate had grown more cynical about the responsiveness of its government.

It is also possible to trace a streak of cynicism in the public's perception of 13's impact on the behavior of public officials. In late June 1978 and again in early May 1980 the *Los Angeles Times* Poll (see Table 6.2) asked voters what they thought the "final lasting result of Proposition 13 would be [1978] or has been [1980]?" In 1978, 29 percent replied that Proposition 13 would cut waste. In 1980 only 10 percent of the electorate thought so. An October 1979 *Los Angeles Times* Poll asked voters if 13 had been effective in cutting waste: only 20 percent said they knew of any wasteful program eliminated due to 13. The share of the electorate that believed 13 would prompt public officials to cut waste fell from 29 percent in June 1978 to 20 percent in October 1979 to 10 percent in May 1980. We cannot overstate the significance of this trend. Public officials may have tried to eliminate waste and inefficiency in government following passage of 13, but the voters thought otherwise. In fact, voters had come to believe, two years after 13's passage, that services were more likely to be cut back than be made more efficient, due to what some observers have termed the "spite syndrome."

TABLE 6.2

Los Angeles Times POLLS: FINAL LASTING RESULT OF 13
(percentage)

	June 1978	May 1980
Services cut back	8	21
Other taxes raised	36	15
Cut out waste	29	10
Find other money	18	42
Not sure	6	11

Chapter 8 analyzes this overall shift in voter sentiment in detail. Here, it is interesting that voters in May 1980 still had faith in the state's remarkably resilient surplus: 42 percent said that the state would continue to find other money to make up for lost property taxes *without* having to raise other taxes.

AN INTERLUDE WITH JERRY BROWN

Despite Governor Jerry Brown's vehement opposition to 13 before its passage, he displayed remarkable political agility by seizing the tax revolt issue away from Republican challenger Evelle Younger, who, initially at least, had warmly endorsed the measure. Although the public was growing increasingly cynical about the words and deeds of public officials in implementing Proposition 13, they continued to accord Brown higher and higher marks throughout the fall 1978 campaign. In addition, the initial postelection poll showed that more people thought Brown rather than Younger had favored the measure.

The *Los Angeles Times* conducted pre-election polls in late August, late September, and late October. In the first of these polls, respondents were asked "which candidate for governor is more likely to cut waste in government and make it run more efficiently?" Forty-six percent thought Brown would, compared with 36 percent for Younger. The *Los Angeles Times* correspondent felt that Younger, by failing to endorse 13 more forcefully during the primary election, had missed an opportunity.

By late September, Brown's lead over Younger had begun to widen. In the second of three polls, voters were asked which candidate they felt would be more likely (1) "to cut waste in government and make it run more efficiently," (2) "keep taxes down," and (3) "try hard to make Proposition 13 work." Brown won by margins of 26, 23, and 25 percent, respectively. On the specific question of Proposition 13, 51 percent said that Brown would try harder to make the measure work, compared with just 26 percent for Younger. In just one month, Brown's lead on this issue had widened from 10 percentage points to more than 20. Indeed, during September Brown even gained support from Republicans.

The final pre-election *Los Angeles Times* Poll (October 22–25) showed Brown an overwhelming winner over Younger. Younger took strong stances on crime and nuclear power, which, to Younger's detriment, were among the least important issues in the voter's calculus at that time. The two major issues were cutting waste in government and making Proposition 13 work, and these turned out to be Brown's two strongest points. So what had been predicted in early June to be a close contest turned into a rout.

However, despite this victory, Brown viewed Sacramento as only a temporary way station in an eastward journey. His obvious ambition was four or eight years in the White House. His strategy consisted, in large measure, of riding the white horse of the tax revolt across the Sierras to all parts of the nation. Although more than twenty state legislatures had passed resolutions calling on Congress to invoke Article V of the Constitution and convene a constitutional convention to write a balanced budget amendment, Brown was the first nationally known political figure to join the movement. In an interview with the *National Journal* (February 24, 1979), Brown said that a constitutional amendment to balance the budget would help solve a number of our national ills— among them the declining value of the dollar, lagging investment in the economy, and shrinking gains in productivity—by ensuring greater fiscal discipline. Such discipline could be enforced only by an amendment since political will was sorely lacking.

Brown's statements brought the movement additional publicity, but his motives were nevertheless transparent. As Milton Friedman noted in his *Newsweek* column of March 26, 1979, Brown's endorsement "has been widely interpreted as using the budget-balancing issue as a launching pad for Presidential ambitions." Friedman's prediction that Brown would fail was borne out. Brown's national candidacy never did get under way, despite his move into a position of leadership on the 13–tax revolt bandwagon. Moreover, in 1980, in the second round of Howard Jarvis's tax-cutting efforts, Brown was back on the other side of the fence, this time opposing further tax cuts. So strong was his commitment to this issue that he chose to present his case to Californians in a statewide television broadcast.

seven
THE REVOLT

CONTINUES

Overnight Proposition 13 thrust Howard Jarvis into the national limelight and made him an international celebrity. In an effort to translate the California mandate into a national movement to cut federal taxes and reduce spending, Jarvis proposed to cut federal taxes by $50 billion over a four-year period, index income tax brackets to inflation, and reduce the capital gains tax rate to 15 percent. This proposal became known as the American Tax Reduction Movement. By slashing federal spending $100 billion over the same four-year period, Jarvis sought to reduce the national debt by 2 percent each year. Offices were opened in Washington, D.C., and Los Angeles, and two congressmen, Robert Dornan, a Republican from Santa Monica, and Tom Luken, a Democrat from Ohio, introduced the essentials of Jarvis's plan in Congress as H.R. 100.

Jarvis was not content to limit his foray into national politics to tax and spending cuts. His American Tax Reduction Movement contained a political action committee to support candidates for Congress who supported his viewpoint and to oppose those against it. Here Jarvis overplayed his hand. His promises of help in national campaigns were rejected and his threats of opposition ignored. In the end he was wholly unable to turn his West Coast success into a national political force. In partial defeat, he returned home and initiated another tax-cutting drive, this time to slash state income taxes in half (see Chapter 8).

Meanwhile, in California, Proposition 13's less flamboyant

cosponsor, Paul Gann, remained hard at work on a spending lim-itation. Shortly after passage of 13, he began gathering signatures for a new initiative that would restrict future increases in spend-ing for all governmental units in California. The "Spirit of 13" initiative, or Proposition 4 as it was known on the November 1979 ballot, proposed that spending by state and local governments in California rise no more rapidly than increases in inflation or personal income (whichever was lower), adjusted for changes in population. (For complete text, see Appendix B.)

This was not a new idea. In 1973 Governor Ronald Reagan had put forth a similar measure known as Proposition 1 limiting the size of government spending and reducing its share of state income (see Chapter 2). Unfortunately for Governor Reagan, the measure failed by a 54 to 46 percent margin. Still, Proposition 1 became the model for subsequent spending limits that were pre-pared and sponsored by the National Tax Limitation Committee. Its chairman, Lewis Uhler, had helped draft the original measure.

In 1976, Michigan became the second testing ground for spending limits. The Michigan measure, Proposition C, excluded the scheduled shrinkage in government spending that Proposition 1 had included, but otherwise paralleled the objectives of its Cal-ifornia precursor. However, this measure also had little success, gaining only 43 percent of the vote.

But in Tennessee the idea of a spending limitation was more popular. State Senator David Copeland's proposal of a spending limit was ratified in March 1978 by a constitutional convention. Copeland later joined the National Tax Limitation Committee to help promote tax and spending limits in other states.

Gann's Spirit of 13 measure evolved from the trials and errors of earlier measures both in California and other states. Its team of authors included experienced scholars and activists in the tax-cut-ting business: Professor William Craig Stubblebine of Claremont Men's College (later chairman of the National Tax Limitation Committee's group to draft a federal spending limit amendment), Lewis Uhler, Kirk West of the California Taxpayers' Association, together with representatives from the California Association of Realtors and the California Chamber of Commerce. Other organi-zations that actively supported the measure in its petition drive and advertising campaign included the National Federation of Independent Business, the California Farm Bureau Association, and the California Apartment Owners Association.[1]

THE MEASURE

The Spirit of 13 initiative (Proposition 4) differed from 13 in both method and appearance. While 13 exemplified the cutback approach to controlling government, 4 represented the growth-limit approach. Thirteen cut property taxes by more than half and limited future annual increases to 2 percent—how the reduced funds were apportioned among the different units of government was of no concern to Jarvis. In contrast, the spending limit provision of 4 applied to several thousand governmental units—cities, counties, school districts, some special districts, and the state. Proposition 4 was also more democratic: 13 required a two-thirds vote of the legislature or the electors in any given jurisdiction in order to raise tax rates or impose new taxes; 4 allowed a simple majority vote of the electorate at the state or local level to revise spending limits upward or downward. Furthermore, 13 was a briefly written, narrowly focused tax cut; 4 had a much lengthier and complex set of provisions (although nowhere near the 5,700 words of its 1973 precursor, Proposition 1).

In the light of 13's massive tax cuts, why did the advocates of 4 think their measure was an essential element in the fight to control government? Between 1969 and 1978 state expenditures grew 161 percent. During the same period, the Consumer Price Index rose only 92 percent. Had Proposition 4 been in effect throughout this period, aggregate state spending would have been billions of dollars lower. Moreover, the tax refund provisions of 4 would presumably have forced massive refunds to taxpayers, thereby preventing buildup of the surplus. Despite the cuts made by 13 in property taxes, sales, income, and other tax receipts continued to rise, permitting a corresponding expansion in the size of state and local government. Proposition 4 put a cap on allowable expenditures, regardless of the rise in tax revenues.

What were the main features of Proposition 4?[2]

Spending Limit. Section 1, the appropriations limit, said that each jurisdiction of government in California could increase its spending from tax sources over the preceding year by no more than the increases in the cost of living and population. In establishing these limits, each entity of government had to first determine its "proceeds of taxes" for fiscal 1978–79, the base year. These included all tax revenues, proceeds from the investment of tax revenues, excesses over all reasonable costs of regulatory fees, licenses, and user charges, and subventions received by local governments. Proposition 4 used allowable annual spending, instead of actual annual spending, of the base year to determine permitted levels of spending in subsequent years.

Tax Refunds. To prevent the accumulation of government surpluses, excess revenues over the spending limit in any year had to be returned to the taxpayer by a revision of tax rates or fee schedules within the two following fiscal years.

Adjustments to the Limit. In the event that financial responsibility for providing services was transferred from one entity of government to another, the limits of the participating entities had to be decreased and increased accordingly. Similarly, the limit had to be reduced if financial responsibility for providing services was transferred from an entity of government to a private entity or if the means of financing a government service shifted from taxes to licenses, user charges, or fees. Finally, the spending limit could be exceeded in an emergency, but the limit in the subsequent three years had to be reduced to prevent any overall increase.

Direct Vote on Spending Levels. A key feature of Proposition 4 was its democratic flavor. A simple majority vote of the electorate could adjust the spending limit of any entity of government up or down for a period of four years.

Special Funds. Jurisdictions could establish contingency, emergency, unemployment, reserve, retirement, and other funds. Contributions from taxes into these funds in any given year fell within the appropriations limit, but withdrawals did not. That is, when receipts from taxes were deposited into these special funds, the dollar amounts were to be counted against that year's limit. But when the funds were withdrawn and spent in future years, they were not.

Mandated Programs. The state government had to reimburse local jurisdictions for new programs or higher levels of service in existing programs that it mandated upon them, with the following exceptions: mandates requested by the local governments, mandates provided for in legislation defining a new crime or changing the definition of a crime, or mandates enacted prior to January 1975 (that is, a regulation implementing legislation enacted prior to January 1, 1975).

Bonded Indebtedness. The amendment was not intended to impair bonded indebtedness obligations of state or local government. (Legally incurred debt service was excluded from the limit.)

Some Definitions. To clarify the foregoing provisions, the amendment spelled out several definitions. Subventions to local governments counted against the limits of local government, not that of the state. User fees and charges were exempt from the definition of "proceeds of taxes" unless such charges exceeded the cost of providing the service; any excess of fees over costs was within the limit. Funds received by government from gifts, sales of property, royalties, rents, and admission charges were not "proceeds of taxes." This meant, in practice, that expenditures from reasonable fees and charges for revenue bonds and sewer hookups, for example, were exempt from the lid and could be used to finance necessary structures associated with new development.

Exemptions. All debt service "legally authorized" as of January 1, 1979, was exempt from the limit, as was debt service on bonds approved by the voters in the future. Exemptions to the limit also included appropriations required to comply with court or federal government mandates that required additional services and imposed greater costs and expenditures of all special districts that had less than a 12.5¢ tax rate as of January 1, 1978. The purpose of the latter provision was to free literally thousands of extremely small single-purpose districts, such as mosquito abatement, cemetery, street lighting, and so forth, from the requirement of voter approval to raise small sums that nonetheless exceeded the limitation formula of population and consumer prices. (In the aggregate, such expenditures comprised less than 1 percent of all state and local expenditures in California.)

The Campaign. On September 22, 1978, Paul Gann filed his spending limit initiative with the state attorney general.[3] He hoped to make history by collecting the requisite half-million signatures in a single day. Volunteers from the California Association of Realtors set up tables 100 feet away from polling places around the state on election day, November 7, 1978. Although Gann fell somewhat short of his goal, supporters accumulated about 378,000 signatures within one week of the election.

The petition drive continued throughout the winter. On March 17, 1979, Gann announced that his Spirit of 13 spending limit measure had qualified for the ballot, having obtained some 900,000 signatures—third highest total in the state's history. Although originally scheduled for the June 1980 ballot, the Gann measure was eventually included with a bill before the state legislature to put a proposed measure on school busing before the electorate on the November 6, 1979, ballot.

Opponents of Proposition 4 were few and far between and, for the most part, quiet. Although Governor Brown officially maintained a discreet silence on this issue, Assembly Speaker Leo T. McCarthy, an outspoken opponent of 13, was listed on the ballot as one of the proposition's principal sponsors. The opposition included the state AFL-CIO, led by public employee unions, major education groups, many local officials, and the liberal-minded California Tax Reform Association, but their campaign was virtually invisible.

Local politicians were most critical of the "straitjacket" implications of 4.[4] San Francisco Mayor Dianne Feinstein called the measure "overkill," labeling it unfair to a city like San Francisco that was actually losing population. Even though commuter traffic imposed an enormous burden on city resources, the Gann formula compelled a reduction in spending as the population base declined. Mayor Ilene Weinreb of Hayward, an industrial enclave on San Francisco Bay, argued that 4 would retard the town's fast-growing industrial sector. Despite a declining population, Hayward had been adding industrial space that required additional police, fire, and traffic-related services; a declining population would force spending cuts, despite the urgent need to expand essential services. Janet Gray Hayes, mayor of San Jose, feared that 4 meant a possible chill on development and a trend toward government by referendum. Los Angeles Mayor Tom Bradley stood aside from the fray, leaving the evaluation of the overall implications of the measure to his staff.

Not all local officials cried wolf. The mayor of San Diego, Pete Wilson, noted that San Diego voters had adopted a spending limit in 1978. He claimed that "what Mr. Gann is proposing isn't all that stringent."

Some neutral observers alleged that Gann's spending limits might succumb to a number of possible loopholes: exemption of user fees, exemption of programs ordered by the courts or federal government, and base-year loading.

Financial supporters of 4 included former donors to the No on 13 campaign. Gann's $1 million in contributions included funds from Southern Pacific Company and BankAmerica Corporation.

PUBLIC OPINION

From the moment of its inception, the fate of Proposition 4 was never in doubt. Unlike 13, which enjoyed only a modest lead in the polls until landslide momentum developed in the final weeks of the campaign, Proposition 4 burst out the starting gate with an overwhelming lead. Mervin Field's California Poll testified to its broadbased support.[5] In the first poll on Proposition 4 conducted in May, about 53 percent of those interviewed said they had heard about the proposed amendment; these respondents favored the measure by three to one. Those not aware were read a summary of the measure. Among this latter group, supporters outnumbered opponents by about two-and-a-half to one. The most cited reason for favoring the measure was "controlling government spending." The second California Poll on Proposition 4, conducted in late August, also demonstrated a better than two-to-one lead.

The *Los Angeles Times* completed the final pre-election poll between October 15 and 21. Among the 70 percent of the respondents who had made up their minds, 68 percent said they would vote for Proposition 4.[6] The *Los Angeles Times* Poll surveyed 1,128 adults, of whom just over two-thirds were registered voters. Interviewers asked a variety of questions that included voter intentions on Proposition 4, impressions of 13, awareness and inclinations on Jarvis's new proposal to cut state income tax rates in half, along with background data on each respondent's income, education, other personal factors, and attitudes toward government.

Support for Proposition 13 cut across conventional divisions of class, race, income, geographical region, and education. Support for 4 was even more broadly based. A thorough statistical analysis of the prospective vote on Proposition 4 revealed the most important determinant to be each voter's impression of 13. Of those with a "very favorable" impression of Proposition 13 (267 respondents), fully 85 percent either had decided to or were leaning toward a yes vote on Proposition 4, compared with 74 percent of those with a "somewhat favorable," 50 percent of those with a "somewhat unfavorable," and 32 percent of those with a "very unfavorable" impression.

Two important results were apparent from these numbers. First, the overwhelming majority (68 percent) of the 737 respondents were favorably impressed with 13. Second, among every category of voter save those who were very unfavorably impressed with 13, a majority of registered voters favored Proposition 4. Here, the link between 13 and 4 was forcefully direct.

So broad was the measure's support that it included even 59 percent of registered Democrats. Except for the 10 percent of the sample with over four years of college, of whom only 49 percent supported Proposition 4, overwhelming majorities of persons, with levels of education ranging from elementary through high school up to a college or university degree, supported 4.

In addition, voters' political views were closely associated with support for 4. About three-quarters of those respondents who identified themselves as middle-of-the-road, somewhat conservative, or very conservative supported 4. Even 57 percent of those who described themselves as somewhat liberal also planned to vote yes.

Only those who identified themselves as very liberal—about 10 percent of the sample—rejected Proposition 4, and by the modest margin of 57 to 43 percent at that. Thus 90 percent of the voters across the entire political spectrum fully endorsed Gann's spending limit. (Our statistical analysis showed that neither income nor the respondent's race or ethnic background affected support for Proposition 4.)[7]

A final set of questions in the *Los Angeles Times* Poll asked respondents to assess whether public services had changed for the better or the worse in the wake of Proposition 13. The list of services included schools, police, fire, parks, libraries, public transportation, road maintenance, and garbage collection. In every instance but education, between 70 to 80 percent said they either had not used the service in question or, if they had used it, had experienced no change. Only about one-fifth to one-fourth praised or condemned the changes in public services. Although worsening evaluations of public services correlated with negative impressions of Proposition 13, the percentages of people affected were too small to weaken, in any significant way, the overall favorable view of Proposition 4. Those people formed a small minority of the 26 percent who opposed 4.

On election day Gann won by 74 to 26 percent, a three-to-one avalanche that surpassed 13's two-to-one margin.[8] The measure won in every one of the state's 58 counties, with support ranging from a high of 87 percent in Glenn county to a low of 54 percent in San Francisco county. Just over 3.4 million voters went to the polls for the first special statewide election since 1973, a modest 40 percent of all registered voters, the lowest for any statewide election since 1935.

IS THE LIMIT EFFECTIVE?

The bitter experience that befell the vocal critics of 13 partially stifled public opposition to 4. In addition to the futility of resisting Proposition 4's seemingly inevitable victory, some analysts and critics were not sure that Gann's limits would constrain future government spending and consequently were reluctant to stick out their necks to oppose it. A combination of overall economic trends, conflicting interpretations of certain terms and provisions in the initiative, and the ease with which its loopholes could be exploited by the legislature and local entities effectively served to vitiate the measure, almost to the point of insignificance.[9]

Inflation. According to the spending limit formula of 4, appropriations from proceeds of taxes could increase as much from year to year as the cost of living (or per capita personal income, whichever was lower) adjusted by population changes. With inflation running at double-digit levels in 1979, 1980, and possibly at or near those levels throughout the early 1980s, state and local governments had ample opportunity to expand their budgets without overrunning these limits. Until revenues surpassed the allowable spending limit, refunds of taxes were not necessary. Only school districts faced potential problems due to declining enrollments (in computing spending limits for public schools, ADA was the measure of population change). As we see below, the legislature attempted to grapple with this problem.

Fees and User Charges. Proposition 4 authorized the imposition of user fees and charges by state and local government up to the full reasonable cost of services. However, any collections in excess of costs were to be counted as general revenue and were thus subject to the limitation. If any given service was shifted from tax revenue financing to user fees, the limit had to be proportionately reduced. However, nothing in the amendment prevented the introduction of new or expanded services so long as the fees did not exceed the reasonable cost of that specific new service. While the Gann amendment eliminated the use of fees for general government support, it did not preclude the imposition of new fees and charges for new services. Thus some government expansion could be financed on a pay-as-you-go basis, outside the limit. (Of course, this remained true only so long as fees and user charges were not a "tax" since Proposition 13 allowed new taxes only if two-thirds of the local electorate approved.)

Base-Year Loading. No issue was more important to the true impact of Proposition 4 than the question of "base-year loading." Since future levels of government spending were tied to the 1978–

79 base year, accurate specification of that allowable dollar limit constrained growth in spending for all future years. Section 5 of the Gann amendment allowed reserve or contingency funds so long as appropriations to these reserves were included within the limit. Actual spending from these funds on some future date was not subject to the limit. Therefore, so long as general surplus funds of state and local governments were appropriated into a reserve or contingency fund during the 1978–79 base year, the appropriations limit would presumably include those moneys.

However, there remained the question of the state's massive General Fund surplus, together with surpluses of local governments that were carried over from prior years and not explicitly appropriated into any given reserve or contingency fund. Were these sums also to be added into the 1978–79 base year? This would have increased the state's base-year limit by more than $3 billion and vitiated the limit for years to come. This additional sum of money would have increased the state's base year by more than 15 percent and, when added to cost-of-living and population changes, created a limit so high that revenues would not have exceeded the limit for years to come. Indeed, spending could have increased dramatically and no tax refunds would have been required.

Professor Stubblebine believed the inclusion of the general surplus into the base-year formula improper for two reasons.[10] First, it would have created a limit that was unrelated to any given year's revenue since it included excess revenue collections carried over from prior years. Second, it would have permitted a one-time action that could not be duplicated in future years and thus should not be allowed to determine allowable limits for future years. At present it is likely that a court ruling will be required to clarify this dispute, should state or local governments collect sufficient revenues and spend as if the 1978–79 base year included general fund surpluses from prior years.

Lame Duck Adjustments. Although Proposition 4 passed in November 1979, it was not scheduled to take effect until July 1, 1980. The purpose of this grace period was to enable both the state legislature and local governments to make whatever adjustments they deemed necessary for life under the new limits for the beginning of the next fiscal year. One example of such adjustments was SB 1426, a bill signed by the governor five minutes before the Gann limit took effect. SB 1426 placed $208 million in reserve-status money in the State School Building Lease-Purchase Fund and $126 million in the State School Fund. This appropriation of $334 million from state revenues fell within the appropriations limit for 1979–80, but the spending of this money at any future date would be outside the limit for that year.

Mandates. The amendment stated that government spending mandated by the courts or the federal government would be excluded from the limits. Some thought that, over time, many governmental activities would come to fall under this heading, for example, education.

Prior to the enactment of 13, the state was under a court order to alter the system of school financing, which provided much more money for some schools than others. By freezing spending totals for each school district, the Gann measure may have made compliance with the spirit of this court mandate—the *Serrano* case—more difficult by preventing low-spending districts from expanding per-pupil expenditures more rapidly than inflation to bring them closer to those prevailing in higher-spending districts. The courts could subsequently issue another order exempting all school expenditures from the Gann limits, although they could also rule that the limits in the constitution constrain the speed with which lower-spending districts are allowed to accelerate spending plans. The former ruling would free more than a thousand school districts from the Proposition 4 limits. Since half of local government spending is for public education, the single largest chunk of government spending would no longer fall under the amendment.

Legislative Definition. It took the state legislature two full months after the July 1 date of implementation to approve a bill defining the terms of the initiative. This amendment, SB 1352, was in turn scheduled to take effect on January 1, 1981. Apart from required definitions of "cost of living," "per capita personal income," "agencies covered under the limit," "state subventions," and other technical details of implementation, several items in the language of Proposition 4 were accorded greater legal clarity.

First, regulatory and license fees (for example, a beautician's license) were defined *not* to be "proceeds of taxes" and thus did not come under the limits. This specific provision avoided separate accounting to justify that such fees were reasonable and did not exceed costs borne in provision of a service or regulation.

More important, the implementing legislation explicitly recognized the state's primary responsibility in funding local schools under the permanent bailout legislation (AB 8). SB 1352 allowed the state to equalize spending in the public schools (as mandated by the court), to provide categorical aid programs targeted to specific education needs, and to underwrite costs in schools with declining enrollments by charging any excess spending of any given school district against the state's overall limit. This provision essentially freed school districts from the limit. The rationale was that since the state provided most of the funds for local public education, excess spending in the districts could be charged to the state. (This also allowed unimpeded implementation of the *Serrano* ruling.)

Another unique modification of Proposition 4 helped to ease San Francisco's plight. Because the Gann limit used population as a key element in its limitation formula, San Francisco faced a potential decline in its allowable spending, even though commuters to the city might increase in the future. The new amendment authorized San Francisco to use population changes for the entire Bay Area, affording the city and county more room for budgetary expansion.

In light of these modifications, one might be inclined to suggest that the legislature's overall approach to Proposition 4 was to take any and every step it could to ease the constraints on state or local governments in order to avoid even the smallest of rebates to the taxpayer. In fact, the appropriations limit contained in Proposition 4 may not come into play for years to come if carryover surplus funds are permitted to count in the 1978–79 base year. Even if the authors of 4 win court approval to exclude this surplus from the base-year figure, it is still unlikely that 4 will compel tax rebates anytime in the near future. The reason is that state and

local government revenues show little prospect of surpassing inflationary increases to any significant degree. Thus the spending
"lid" will remain inoperative. What is likely to emerge in coming
years is a far greater reliance on fees and charges as a means of
financing local government.

'Yes, it looks like more rain and I'm not opposed to that—even with water still rising from the last storm—but I don't necessarily favor it, either, though there are perfectly good arguments for it as well as against it, so I'd rather not commit myself at this point in time.'

IZZLES

Howard Jarvis and Paul Gann parted company soon after passage of Proposition 13. Jarvis shifted his American Tax Reduction Movement to the nation's capital, without much success. Gann stayed home and won an overwhelming victory with his Spirit of 13 spending limit initiative in November 1979.

Temporarily defeated but not dismayed, Jarvis brought his tax-cutting efforts back to his home state of California. On Monday, April 16, 1979, the day on which state and personal income tax returns were due, he announced plans for his newest initiative. The measure, known formally as Proposition 9 on the June 1980 ballot, informally as "Jarvis II" or "Jaws II" by critics, proposed (1) to cut state income tax rates in half, from the current progressive range of 1 to 11 percent to a new range of 0.5 to 5.5 percent, (2) to index the rates permanently to inflation to prevent bracket creep, and (3) to abolish the state's business inventory tax. As with 13, this measure was both short and concise, with none of the added technicalities found in Gann's spending limit initiative. (For text, see Appendix C.)

Jarvis easily qualified this new tax-cutting initiative; his 820,-000 signatures surpassed the state requirement by more than a quarter of a million. However, the cost of accumulating these signatures exceeded the $28,500 spent on Proposition 13 almost a hundredfold. Proposition 9 was the first initiative ever to be qualified entirely by mail. The Irvine-based consulting firm of

Butcher-Forde used computer mailing lists from Proposition 13 contributors in order to solicit signatures and campaign contributions, raising more than $2 million in contributions by direct mail, but spending $2,075,000 just to qualify the initiative.[1]

While the Proposition 13 tax revolt was brewing, the state legislature bumbled away the 1977 session. When it finally enacted the Behr bill in 1978 as an alternative, the public deemed this response too little, too late. But the legislature learned from this mistake and did not idle away the remaining months of the 1978 and the upcoming 1979 session. Even before Jarvis circulated his petitions, Governor Brown and the legislature were fashioning their own brand of tax relief. In late 1978, they enacted a one-shot increase in state income tax credits for 1978—from $25 to $100 for single persons and from $50 to $200 for joint returns—and partially indexed the tax brackets for 1979 (after the first 3 percent of inflation, to prevent excessive bracket creep). In 1979, they fully indexed the income tax brackets for the next two years and also abolished the state's business inventory tax. These latter measures were not embedded in the constitution, as proposed in Proposition 9, and could be overturned by a simple majority vote in the legislature. Nevertheless, the two measures symbolized to the public a responsible and responsive state government. In this round of the tax-cutting wars, both the governor and the legislature decided not to play Nero and fiddle while the taxpayer burned.

Behind Proposition 9 lay a sizable increase in the state income tax burden. Between 1971 and 1980, total personal income in California rose from just under $100 billion to over $250 billion (see Table 8.1). During the same period, personal income tax collections increased from $1.79 billion to $6.8 billion. Whereas personal income increased 166 percent, state income tax collections rose 280 percent. Every 1 percent rise in personal income generated a 1.7 percent rise in state income tax revenues. California's progressive taxation system thus managed to transfer more and more personal income from private to government hands. Howard Jarvis's new proposal was as plausible a response to this trend as 13 had been to the spiral of property tax increases.

THE CHANGING CLIMATE OF OPINION

At the outset, the "experts" considered Proposition 9 a certain winner come June 3, 1980. In a January 30, 1980, story entitled "California Voters Appear Sure to Approve Proposition to Slash Personal Income Tax," the *Wall Street Journal* called Jarvis II an "almost certain-to-pass referendum." Citing a survey by Mervin Field (the California Poll) that found Californians favoring by two-to-one some kind of personal income tax cut, the article said that most experts expected the measure to pass with ease.

The trend of public opinion on 9 was a reverse image of the shift in opinion on 13. Proposition 13 started with weak support and finished strong; 9 started strong, but finished weak. Resistance to Proposition 9 increased throughout the spring. By May both the

TABLE 8.1

CALIFORNIA PERSONAL INCOME AND
STATE PERSONAL INCOME TAX COLLECTIONS
1971–1980

Year[a]	Personal Income (millions)	Percentage Change	Fiscal Year[b]	Personal Income Tax (thousands)	Percentage Change
1971	$94,206	—	1971–72	$1,785,618	—
1972	102,539	8.84	1972–73	1,884,058	5.51
1973	112,641	9.85	1973–74	1,831,964	−2.76
1974	125,579	11.48	1974–75	2,581,584	40.92
1975	139,472	11.06	1975–76	3,089,963	19.69
1976	155,626	11.58	1976–77	3,761,356	21.73
1977	175,155	12.54	1977–78	4,667,887	24.10
1978	199,010	13.62	1978–79	4,761,571	2.00
1979	226,510	13.82	1979–80	6,275,000	31.78
1980	251,237	10.92	1980–81	6,800,000	8.37

SOURCE: *Cal-Tax News,* February 15–March 14, 1980.
[a]Calendar-year basis.
[b]Fiscal year ending June 30.

California and *Los Angeles Times* polls uncovered the makings of a disastrous defeat for 9 on election day, when an overwhelming 61 percent of the electorate voted against it.

Field's February poll found that only 40 percent of the public had any specific knowledge about Proposition 9 (see Table 8.2). Those without such information were told about the initiative by the interviewer. In all, the measure was favored by an impressive 54 to 34 percent margin. The major reasons given by voters favoring Proposition 9 were that it would cut taxes, cut unnecessary government spending, and reduce bureaucracy. Opponents feared that additional tax cuts would jeopardize routine government operations and force cuts in needed services and major programs.

By mid-April a dramatic shift in public attitudes had taken place. Even before the protagonists actively crossed swords, and with the bulk of advertising and campaigning still to come in May, increasing numbers of voters worried that further major cutbacks in revenues would threaten needed government services and important programs. In his review of the April poll, Field identified a possible key to the outcome: the surplus available to offset the reduction in state income tax receipts and maintain government services at current levels.[2]

The sole *Los Angeles Times* Poll (mid-May 1980) highlighted the public's growing rejection of Jarvis II. By this time, just a few weeks before the election, a full 80 percent of voters had heard about the initiative. Such increased awareness went hand in hand with greater opposition to the measure. By a margin of 49 to 44 percent, voters felt the state income tax to be "fair." Nearly two-

TABLE 8.2

TRENDS IN PUBLIC OPINION
(percentage)

On Proposition 9 would vote:	February 28 (Field)	April 13 (Field)	May 11 (*Los Angeles Times*)	May 20 (Field)
No	34	48	52	57
Yes	54	43	38	31
Undecided	12	9	10	12

thirds were satisfied or neutral about the amount of state income taxes they had paid in the past year. In sharp contrast with their expectations of the consequences of 13, voters worried that 9 would endanger public education and grant an undue windfall tax break to the rich. Californians now professed that the "final, lasting result" of 9 would be to "reduce government services," not "eliminate government waste." Since 13, greater efficiency in government and the elimination of fat and waste were becoming a will-o'-the-wisp.

The final Field Poll accurately approximated the final election results. Between February and May of 1980, a 20-point plurality in favor of Proposition 9 changed to a 26-point plurality against the measure. Not only had the tide turned against Howard Jarvis, but the lopsided defeat of his income tax–cutting initiative presaged defeat in November of a host of tax-cutting measures in a dozen states. Was this to be the beginning of the end of the tax revolt? In the short span of just three months, public opinion had backed away from tax reduction. Why did this occur?

THE ISSUES

Three major issues and several interesting related stories dominated the 9 campaign. The major issues revolved around who would benefit most from the tax cuts, how state revenues and spending would be affected, and what would happen to public services if 9 passed. Minor issues were the personality of Howard Jarvis himself, the opposition of Nobel laureate Milton Friedman from the ranks of the tax cutters, Governor Jerry Brown's reconversion to bigger government, and the surprising outspending of Jarvis by the No on 9 forces in the final month of the campaign.

Who Benefited? Any personal income tax cut leaves some people better off than others, but the big question is always *who*. The opponents of 9 repeatedly charged that 9 would "soak the poor" of needed services in order to provide windfall tax breaks "for the wealthy few." In dollars and cents, half the savings realized by the measure would have gone to about 10 percent of the taxpayers. Supporters of 9 countered this charge by pointing out that lower-income households would receive a larger percentage reduction. Thus dollars were set against percentages and percentages against dollars.

Income tax payers in the lower brackets would have received a greater percentage tax cut than higher-income households because the initiative did not change personal credits. After the income tax is halved, the taxpayer subtracts his unchanged allowable credits, which are proportionately greater as a share of smaller incomes than of larger incomes. Thus the percentage reduction in state income taxes for lower-income taxpayers is higher. Table 8.3 shows that for a hypothetical family of four filing a joint return, the percentage savings in state income taxes falls from 100 percent at a taxable income level of $10,000, to 70 percent at $15,000, to the low 50s at a taxable income level above $30,000. Thus lower-income households would clearly have received substantially higher percentage savings under 9.

A look at Table 8.4, which gives both the percentage of returns filed and percentage of total taxes paid by different income groups in 1976 and 1977, reveals where the bulk of the dollar savings would have gone. Just over 45 percent of the state's taxpayers reported adjusted gross incomes below $10,000 and paid about 3.1 percent of total state income taxes. At the other end of the income distribution scale, the 2.2 percent of Californians filing returns with adjusted gross incomes over $50,000 paid 31.5 percent of all state income taxes. Combining the two highest income categories together, the 15.2 percent of taxpayers with incomes over $25,000 paid 66 percent of all state income taxes. So, an across-the-board rate reduction of 50 percent would have granted the major share of dollar savings to higher-income taxpayers.

Approximately half of the state's taxpayers itemize deductions. For these households, lower state taxes mean less to deduct on federal returns. The savings realized under Proposition 9 would have been counteracted by increased federal tax liabilities (see the right-hand column in Table 8.3 for amounts). The higher the rate of federal taxation, the greater the leakage of state tax savings into the federal treasury. Opponents of 9 reminded the voters that the federal government would be the real winner if 9 passed since it would collect an additional $1.1 billion from Californians in 1981. Was this a benefit Californians wanted to convey to the federal

TABLE 8.3

IMPACT OF PROPOSITION 9 ON 1981 STATE AND FEDERAL INCOME TAXES*

State Taxable Income	Current Law			Proposition 9			State Tax Savings		Federal Tax Increase	
	Computed Tax	Credits	Net Tax	Computed Tax	Credits	Net Tax	Amount	Percentage	Marginal Rate	Amount
$ 5,000	$ 50.00	$88	$ 0	$ 25.00	$88	$ 0	0		.14	$ 0
10,000	150.20	88	62.20	75.10	88	0	62.20	100.0	.18	11.20
15,000	313.80	88	225.80	156.90	88	68.90	156.90	69.5	.21	32.95
20,000	536.20	88	448.20	268.10	88	180.10	268.10	59.8	.24	64.34
25,000	817.60	88	729.60	408.80	88	320.80	408.80	56.0	.28	114.46
30,000	1,158.00	88	1,070.00	579.00	88	491.00	579.00	54.1	.32	185.28
40,000	2,034.20	88	1,946.20	1,017.10	88	929.10	1,017.10	52.3	.43	437.35
50,000	3,111.00	88	3,023.00	1,555.50	88	1,467.50	1,555.20	51.5	.49	762.20
100,000	8,611.00	88	8,523.00	4,305.50	88	4,217.50	4,305.50	50.5	.59	2,540.24
1,000,000	107,611.00	88	107,523.00	53,805.50	88	53,717.50	53,805.50	50.0	.70	37,663.85

SOURCE: "Analysis of Proposition 9, June 1980 Ballot," *Cal-Tax News*, February 15–March 14, 1980, p. 4.

*Married couple, with two dependents, filing joint return, no renters' credit.

government to the detriment of those individuals most dependent on services funded from state revenues?

Apart from any impact that such state tax cuts might have had on state and local services, the No on 9 forces insisted that even if voters deserved an additional break in personal income taxes, Proposition 9 was the wrong measure to accomplish this. It provided vast benefits only for the truly wealthy, with little for the overwhelming majority of the state's residents. As shown later, it was the effectiveness of this argument that helped to defeat the measure.

Impact on State Revenues.   In the process of putting money back into the taxpayers' pockets, Proposition 9 would have reduced government revenues. Estimates of the potential revenue losses varied by several billion dollars. Similarly, there was much disagreement over the potential loss of billions of dollars in federal revenue-sharing grants. The size of the state's surplus became a heated political issue, so much so that a private Eastern consulting firm was retained to generate a nonpartisan estimate. Predictably the UCLA economic forecasting team became embroiled in the dispute, but this time in support of Howard Jarvis.

How was it possible that estimates of the impact of Proposition 9 on state revenues varied by several billion dollars? Explanations are not hard to come by. Economic and budgetary forecasting is

TABLE 8.4

ADJUSTED GROSS INCOME AND PERSONAL INCOME TAXES
1976 and 1977

Income	Percentage of Returns	Percentage of Total Taxes
Under $10,000	45.7	3.1
$10,000–25,000	39.0	30.9
$25,000–50,000	13.0	34.5
Over $50,000	2.2	31.5

SOURCE: Special Report on Proposition 9, *San Jose Mercury News,* May 25, 1980, p. 5.

difficult in the best of economic climates. In the case of Proposition 13, the State Department of Finance grossly underestimated revenue for five consecutive years, resulting in an "obscene" surplus. The cumulative total of underestimates amounted to $3.55 billion.[3] Proposition 9 was contested during a period of growing economic uncertainty, and any of the following developments could have significantly affected state tax collections.[4]

1. State tax receipts from windfall oil-related revenues in 1980–81 could have ranged from a low of $200 million to a high of $400 million.

2. If the Department of Finance's highest estimate of revenue had materialized, the state would have collected $950 million in unanticipated 1979–80 and 1980–81 general fund revenues beyond the original January 1979 projections.

3. If legislative proposals to make June 4, 1980 (election day) the effective date for Proposition 9, rather than January 1, 1980, had succeeded, some $1.4 billion in first-year tax savings would have been eliminated and added to government revenues.

4. About $600 million in first-year tax savings would have been eliminated by halving 1978 income tax brackets, rather than those of 1980, which had been considerably widened due to indexing.

5. Proponents of Proposition 9 claimed that $600 million in additional revenue would be generated by the increased economic activity associated with a major tax cut—a feedback effect associated with the supply-side economic theory of tax cuts and revenue growth put forth by Professor Arthur Laffer of the University of Southern California.

The most optimistic scenario calculated first-year tax losses at about $2.9 billion. Given an estimated state surplus of $2.6 billion on June 30, 1981, the state's balanced budget requirement would have compelled only a modest reduction in spending. In the most pessimistic scenario, revenue losses ran to $4.9 billion and the surplus to only $874 million, mandating a $4.03 billion cut from proposed spending during the 1980–81 fiscal year. Three years after Proposition 13, such a large cut in state spending would have brought about substantive cuts in services.

Had Proposition 13 failed, the state of California would have enjoyed a surplus of $6.8 billion during the 1978–79 fiscal year, rising to $10 billion the following year unless, of course, new or expanded spending plans or other tax cuts were quickly implemented. But a $7 billion property tax cut in the face of a $6.8 billion state surplus guaranteed that money to bail out local government was available if the political will to implement it could be found. In this regard, Proposition 9 was no different; it assumed the state surplus remained large enough to offset a halving in state income tax receipts. So the likely size of the surplus on June 30, 1980, was every bit as important as it had been two years earlier, and the guessing game continued as to its total.

In 1979, legislative analyst William Hamm made the first prediction on the size of the uncommitted surplus available for the 1980–81 fiscal year as of June 30, 1980, during deliberations on AB 8, the second-year bailout program. He forecast a $611 million surplus based on the general national economic slowdown that was widely expected to occur during 1980. Hamm hedged his forecast somewhat by saying that a mild economic slowdown in California could depress the surplus to $532 million. But if the previous two years' economic growth rates were maintained through the 1979–80 budget year, the surplus could reach $1.2 billion. However, Hamm added that the latter case was highly unlikely.[5]

In the face of a continuing high level of economic activity in California, such a slowdown failed to materialize. In January 1980, when the *1980–81 Governor's Budget* was introduced, the Brown administration estimated a General Fund surplus of $1.835 billion as of June 30, 1980, which did not include $290 million from the Federal Revenue Sharing Trust Fund.

In late April 1980, in response to a series of questions by John Vasconcellos, chairman of the Assembly Ways and Means Committee, Hamm reassessed the projected level of the General Fund surplus. He noted that cash-flow patterns of revenue collections indicated that General Fund revenues would be between $250 million to $500 million *more* than estimated in January and that expenditures would be $100 million less. Prior-year adjustments would add another $50 million to the surplus. Overall, the June 30, 1980, surplus would range from $2.25 billion to $2.5 billion, exceeding the January budget estimate by $400 million to $650 million.[6]

State Finance Director Mary Ann Graves added to the scare mongering for fiscal 1981–82. In January 1980, when the 1980–81 budget was introduced, Graves said that the June 30, 1981, surplus would collapse to only $112.7 million, although she had set aside another $400 million to ward off economic uncertainties. By these accounts, even without passage of Proposition 9 forcing new taxes or spending cuts, the state faced a deficit in the 1981–82 budget year.[7]

In order to avoid another round of political embarrassment such as had afflicted many state lawmakers over the huge surplus surrounding Proposition 13, on January 1, 1980, the legislature established the independent, bipartisan Commission on State Finance to make revenue and expenditure predictions. Membership of the commission included the Senate president pro tem, the speaker of the Assembly, the minority floor leaders of both houses, the director of finance, the state controller, and the state treasurer. The commission invited private accounting and consulting firms to offer their services to estimate the surplus. However, since no forecasts would be ready until just about election time, this commission was unable to neutralize the "surplus" issue. Finally, on May 27, Ed Moskovits of Data Resources, an independent consulting firm in Massachusetts retained to estimate the surplus, told the new state commission that the surplus would be $2.5 billion, a figure in clear contrast with the government's pessimistic scenario.[8]

To help ease fears about the possibly severe impact of Proposition 9, Senate Republican leader William Campbell introduced a bill, SB 1464, to implement the new tax cuts starting July 1, 1980, instead of retroactively from January 1, 1980. This bill would have eased a potential loss of $4.8 billion in state revenues for the eighteen-month period from January 1, 1980, to June 30, 1981, and converted it to only a $3.4 billion loss. The nonpartisan legislative counsel, Christopher J. Wei, confirmed that Campbell's bill was constitutional. Howard Jarvis himself stated that he had never meant the measure to be retroactive (the text of the proposition did not mention any date) but had wanted it to take effect for its first full year on June 4, the day after the election.[9]

However, in early May the Senate rejected Campbell's bill, by an 18–13 vote, 3 short of the 21-vote majority needed in the 40-seat upper house. Jarvis's critics contended that his support of Campbell's bill demonstrated that Proposition 9 took too large a revenue bite out of state and local programs and might be defeated because of this. Senate Democratic leader David Roberti said the people did not want the legislature to alter Proposition 9 before the election, but he no doubt quietly believed that defeat of Campbell's bill would work against Jarvis.[10]

In early May, California's congressional delegation entered the fray, warning that Proposition 9 could trigger major cutbacks in federal funds to the state. In all, more than fifty grant-in-aid programs sent $8 billion in federal funds into California, but Proposition 9 revenue losses might leave state and local agencies bereft of sufficient funds to maintain eligibility for federal matching programs. Several members of the delegation thought that Proposition 9 revenue losses might be of such magnitude that Californians would lose funds for school lunches, flood control, drug abuse programs, vocational training, school libraries, and other general welfare assistance.[11] None of the California congressmen of this persuasion supported Proposition 9.

The forecasting team of UCLA economists also joined the dispute. On Thursday, March 27, 1980, it announced that its "best guess" was that the Jarvis II income tax cut would translate into a reduction in state and local spending of no more than 7 percent through 1983. Indeed, the 7 percent spending reduction probably would be experienced toward the end of 1981, and the reduction would be lower in the following two years. Moreover, it could find no plausible rationale for expecting cuts as severe as the 30 percent budget cutbacks Brown had ordered if 9 passed.[12]

In the course of the extensive, and often heated, debate over the potential revenue loss to the state from Proposition 9, almost everyone overlooked one fact—a budget consists of both revenue estimates and *spending proposals*. One way to offset a portion of potential Proposition 9 revenue losses was through reductions in proposed spending. To that end, legislative analyst William

Hamm issued a 1,732-page report recommending cuts of $600 million from Governor Brown's proposed $24 billion spending budget.[13] But during the months of March, April, and May, Hamm's recommendations somehow got lost in the feud over the size of the revenue loss. It was as if the proposed level of spending remained an immutable given.

IMPACT ON PUBLIC SERVICES

A third important element in the campaign for 9 was its impact on state and local government services. The critics insisted that a multibillion dollar revenue loss would wreak havoc on essential public services and devastate the poorer sectors of California society. No government service received more attention than education.

Among leaders of the state's educational establishment, David Saxon, president of the University of California, acquired the most notoriety. Stating his explicit opposition to Jarvis II, Saxon warned in mid-January that if the measure passed, student fees would be pushed to $3,000 a year. By mid-February he had resolved to send letters to University of California students informing them that Proposition 9 could mean an annual tuition rate of $2,000. In March he wrote to all 130,000 students in the system to inform them that passage of Proposition 9 would necessitate, for the first time in the university's 112-year history, tuition charges. He denied the charge that this letter was his personal effort to campaign against 9, even though the letter's opening paragraph admitted that "I am doing all I personally can to see that it is defeated." Saxon insisted that he wrote the letter because he felt a moral obligation to prepare students for tuition fees should 9 pass.[14]

Others took a different view of Saxon's moral obligation. State Senator Paul Carpenter filed a lawsuit against Saxon, alleging illegal use of public funds for the mailing. In response to a request from Assemblyman Eugene Chappie, legislative counsel Bion Gregory concluded that Saxon had indeed acted improperly in spending $30,000 in university funds to oppose Proposition 9.

Many in the state's educational establishment echoed Saxon's fears for the well-being of higher education in California. William McElroy, chancellor of the University of California, San Diego campus, predicted an enrollment decline of 10 percent in the event of an annual tuition charge.[15] The *Chronicle of Higher Education*, in its February 19, 1980, issue, carried the tuition charge message nationwide. It reported that college and university officials in California believed that Proposition 9 would have "drastic," "calamitous," and "extraordinarily damaging" effect on their institutions. Besides the University of California system, according to Chancellor Glenn S. Dumke, the California state university and college system, with an overall budget of $852 million, faced the elimination of thousands of faculty and staff positions, curtailed enrollments due to higher fees and tuition, and even closure of several of its campuses. A similar warning was echoed by Gerald C. Hayward, chancellor of the California system of community colleges. In all, the 134 public colleges and universities in the state faced hard times. For the public schools, State Superintendent of Education Wilson Riles said in mid-February that passage of Proposition 9 would "dismantle" the California public school system.[16] And, in early March, Senate Finance Committee Chairman Albert Rodda told his committee that Jarvis II would "cut our throats," but that "we're not going to bleed to death until next year."[17]

In late May, the fire chiefs of San Francisco, San Jose, and Oakland convened a press conference to warn that passage of Proposition 9 would endanger Bay Area residents. They estimated dozens of layoffs, closure of many neighborhood fire stations, and delay of equipment purchases. Furthermore, they alluded to an "increase in lives lost" if voters approved Proposition 9 since response time to a fire would "almost double."[18]

In addition to the protagonists for education and fire, two of the "essential" services of government, A. Alan Post, the former legislative analyst and chairman of the blue-ribbon Post Commission, described Proposition 9 as an elitist measure that would inevitably take its toll on schools, Medi-Cal, welfare, and property tax relief. In mid-March, civil rights activist James Farmer also warned that the affirmative action gains of recent years would be threatened. In his view, Proposition 9 would be disastrous to minorities. It would not only "kill" an affirmative action program that had taken years to build but also drastically reduce public services that benefited poor people and minorities.[19]

Since Howard Jarvis and his supporters claimed that Proposition 9 entailed only modest spending cuts that could be accommodated by trimming fat and waste and promoting greater government efficiency, most of the opposition's claims were easily refuted. The Jarvis style on 9 was to compare his opponents of 1980 with those of 1978 and to ask the voters to question the truth of this new set of prophecies. It was, in fact, just another case of *déjà vu.*

MINOR EPISODES

Governor Jerry Brown's reconversion to bigger government showed his infinite flexibility. It was but one year ago, in 1978, as an aspirant for the presidency of the United States, that he had launched his campaign as chief champion of a constitutional amendment to require a balanced federal budget, and but eighteen months since he had adopted Proposition 13 as his own and earned the nickname "Jerry Jarvis." During 1979, as the momentum developed in favor of Proposition 9, Brown kept a very low profile.

On March 20, 1980, Brown made a live appearance on television to tell California voters that he, personally, was opposed to Proposition 9. First, 55 percent of the tax savings would accrue to the richest 10 percent of the taxpayers, and it was "unfair to give so much money to so few." Second, the spending cuts that would follow would most hurt "the aged, the disabled, and the mentally ill, and also savage one of the finest university systems in the world." Couched in terms reminiscent of a biblical injunction to help the poor, ill, and elderly, Brown's strong public rejection of 9 was interpreted in some quarters as a last-ditch effort to save his shaky presidential campaign before the Democratic primary in liberal Wisconsin.[20]

In late May, just as publication of the final Field Poll showed widespread opposition to 9, Brown spoke before the Commonwealth Club in San Francisco and warned that if 9 passed, the state's economy would suffer a major cutback.[21] It is a remarkable testimony to Brown's political agility that in the short span of two years he had opposed Proposition 13, became its champion, fought for a balanced budget amendment, opposed Proposition 9, and managed to end up on the winning side of things when all was said and done.

Less predictable was opposition from another quarter. The February 20 edition of the *Sacramento Bee* reported that Milton Friedman, the Nobel Prize–winning economist who had supported California's previous tax-cutting measures, Propositions 13 and 4, said he was opposed to Proposition 9. His reasons, as reported, were that if 9 passed, the state legislature would respond by raising business taxes (despite the two-thirds requirement of Proposition 13). He also felt that the Gann spending limit should be given time to operate. Furthermore, he was opposed to using the constitution to legislate any specific form of taxation that would lead to an inefficient administrative structure.

On March 11, 1980, the *Santa Ana Register* expressed editorial shock at Friedman's opposition to 9. The editors wrote that "just because the state government loses revenue it does not necessarily follow that business taxes will be raised to make up the loss. Another big victory for a tax-cutting initiative might, in fact, create a political momentum that would prevent passage of new tax proposals in the legislature." Indeed, the editorial suggested that defeat of 9 might encourage the legislature to raise new taxes on everyone.

On May 19, the *Wall Street Journal* indirectly expressed its chagrin with Milton Friedman in a full-page editorial supporting Proposition 9. Noting that class-baiting rhetoric had become the keynote of the No on 9 Committee, which was supported by public employee unions, the editors suggested that "the reputable economists who've tacitly lent it their names ought to rethink their situation."

Finally, on May 23, the *Santa Ana Register* entitled its lead editorial "Dr. Friedman, Won't You Please Come Home?" The editorial cited his 1978 book *Tax Limitation, Inflation and the Role of Government*, in which he wrote:

> Every step we take to strengthen the tax system, whether by getting people to accept payroll taxes they otherwise would not

accept, or by cooperating in enacting higher income taxes and excise taxes or whatnot, fosters a higher level of government spending. That's why I am in favor of cutting taxes under any circumstances, for whatever excuse, for whatever reasons.[22]

The third major human-interest episode in the 9 campaign had to be Howard Jarvis himself, who became his own worst enemy. Pontificating on every issue, Jarvis minced no words with any audience. At an appearance at the Sacramento campus of California State University, he called one student "stupid," another a "dumbhead," and told a third, "You've got a big mouth and no brains." He advised one lady in the audience, "Why don't you go to Nevada in a [bawdy] house they have there!"

During another campus appearance, at Cal-Poly in San Luis Obispo, Jarvis told a campus newspaper "God, if you want to see a lousy county, it is San Luis Obispo. That's the dumbest, crookedest bunch of goddamned crap in the whole country." Assembly Republican leader Carol Hallett, whose district takes in San Luis Obispo, and who was a supporter of Proposition 9, called Jarvis's performance vulgar and insulting and demanded an apology to her home county. Jarvis refused to apologize.

Finally, during a speech before the Commonwealth Club of California, Jarvis waved a piece of paper claiming the state had a $9 billion surplus. The document was the state's pooled-investment accounting that included just over $2 billion in unrestricted General Fund surpluses, but otherwise represented committed funds, trust funds, or funds pending expenditure. The newspapers had a field day with this error.[23]

Given his outrageous behavior during the campaign, did Howard Jarvis out of control cost Proposition 9 some votes? The answer to this question was undoubtedly *yes.* The No on 9 forces quickly capitalized on the arrogance of Howard Jarvis and made it a campaign issue. They successfully portrayed the man as a demagogue pursuing his own gratification and fame to the detriment of responsible state and local governments. A Jarvis in control might not have been able to turn the election around, but it would, in all likelihood, have meant a closer outcome.

Another unexpected by-product of Proposition 9's shifting political fortunes was the ability of the No on 9 forces to raise money. In late February, Citizens for California, a broadly based coalition, was formed to fight Howard Jarvis. Members of the organizing committee included Mickey Kantor, a prominent Democrat and Los Angeles attorney who had managed Governor Brown's 1976 presidential campaign, University of Southern California Chancellor Norman Topping, John Henning of the California Labor Federation, and John Mack, president of the Los Angeles Urban League. Chief supporters of the organization included the California Teachers Association, the California State Employees Association, the state Fire Chiefs Association, the California Labor Federation, the League of Women Voters, the state division of the American Association of University Women, and the Sierra Club. As of April 1979, Citizens for California had raised only $636,027, compared with more than $3 million for the Jarvis forces. But in the crucial month of May, Jarvis's opponents outspent him by two to one. Opponents of 9 raised $687,000 in May and could afford to finance a massive statewide radio, television, and newspaper advertisement effort. In contrast, Jarvis received $317,000 in May, spent only $277,000, and faced $370,000 in debts from prior campaign spending in excess of funds received.[24] When the more than $2 million Jarvis spent qualifying his measure was subtracted from his total contributions, spending on the actual election was nearly even. But in the crucial final weeks Jarvis could raise little money. Founders of Citizens for California had taken a long shot with their tactics and parlayed it into a marvelous victory.

Once again, the state's political, labor, and educational establishments led the opposition to this tax-cutting initiative, but this time they emerged victorious. With the exception of one national newspaper, the *Wall Street Journal*, and the local *Santa Ana Register*, most other newspapers urged rejection of Proposition 9. As shown in Chapter 6, several major papers had admitted overzealous opposition to Proposition 13 and later underwent some public soul-searching in their editorial columns. But remembrance of words past did not prevent a crescendo of editorials against 9, warning of "devastation to community colleges and other public educational institutions" (*San Francisco Examiner*, February 19, 1980), of "inequities in the tax benefits" (*Los Angeles*

Herald Examiner, May 1, 1980), of "a major dismantling of government programs and services" (*Sacramento Bee*, February 13, 1980), of effects that "would hurt people who depend on government—the poor . . . the children . . . the mentally ill" (*Los Angeles Times*, February 17, 1980), and so on. One irate reader was prompted to reply to such threats in the *Los Angeles Times* with "you trot out the same aged, sick, students and poor to defend profligate government spending as you did against Proposition 13," (Henry A. Morse, Montebello, February 24, 1980), but this letter was not typical of most published by the newspapers during the campaign.

EXPLAINING THE VOTE

The *Los Angeles Times* Poll of mid-May elicited basic background information on California voters and their expectations about the impact of Proposition 9 on the state's economy and local government services. The *Times* Poll assembled facts about each respondent's age, sex, income, employment status, housing situation, political party identification, race or ethnic origin, county of residence, and if he or she worked for the government. Since the *Los Angeles Times* Poll of June 1978 had demonstrated that expectations about tax cuts on government services and the economy largely determined voting on Proposition 13, the same questions were repeated. Answers to these questions afford a detailed look at the reasons for Proposition 9's defeat.[25]

In all, *Times* interviewers contacted 1,686 residents, of whom 1,125 (67 percent) were registered to vote. Among registered voters, 421 (38 percent) supported Proposition 9, 589 (52 percent) were opposed, and 105 (10 percent) were undecided. Among decided voters, 58 percent opposed and 42 percent favored Proposition 9, closely reflecting the actual election results of 61 to 39 percent. The following discussion focuses on this latter group of registered voters.

Support for Proposition 13 had cut across traditional partisan, ideological, and social class levels. Neither differences of race, income, party identification, area of residence, homeownership, or other social divisions had separated supporters from opponents. Instead, voters based their decision on whether they believed that 13 would stimulate the state's economy or endanger local services.

Did the vote on Proposition 9 signal a return to traditional politics of partisan, ideological, and social groups in opposition to one another? Or, did expectations of the effect on government services and the economy of halving the state income tax rates determine the election? A careful analysis of the survey sample disclosed that like 13, neither demography, politics, nor social class played a statistically significant part in the election results.[26]

Given this result, what dramatic shift in expectations occurred in the two-year interlude that converted a 65 to 35 percent landslide victory for 13 into a 61 to 39 percent stunning defeat of 9? One approach is to compare voters' expectations of the likely effects of 9 with those of 13. Table 8.5 shows the four main reasons voters gave for opposing the two Jarvis measures.

The figures are very instructive. In June 1978, only 25 percent of those polled feared a decline in public safety and 37 percent a deterioration in education, the two services the public generally views as essential. A majority of voters believed that a tax cut would not jeopardize vital public services. By May 1980, two years later, these percentages had risen to 44 and 59, a robust 20 percent swing in the electorate. By this stage, a majority of voters had come to equate further tax relief with deterioration in public education.

In addition, the campaign strategy against 9 was extremely effective. The No on 9 forces continuously stressed that a 50 per-

TABLE 8.5

REASONS FOR OPPOSING TAX REDUCTION
(percentage)

	Proposition 13	Proposition 9
Public safety will be endangered	25	44
Education will deteriorate	37	59
Rich will benefit most	57	66
Minorities will suffer most	43	45

cent across-the-board cut in rates was unfair because it would grant a majority of tax savings to the wealthy few. Two-thirds of those opposed to 9 offered that same reason for rejecting the measure.

Unlike Proposition 13, voters were not so certain about the beneficial economic effects of 9. While 40 percent of Proposition 13's supporters thought that it would stimulate the economy, only 35 percent of Proposition 9's thought the same. Similarly, the percentage of those who thought that the tax reduction initiatives would reduce inflation dropped from 41 to 35. In sum, growing fears that passage of 9 would harm essential public services, that the benefits of tax cuts would be unfairly awarded, together with a diminished belief in the magical powers of tax cuts led the public to send a message to Jarvis, not to Sacramento.

Two other issues influenced voters. First was Howard Jarvis himself. Although 53 percent gave him a favorable rating, only 68 percent of this group supported 9. In contrast, among the 47 percent rating the man unfavorably, 88 percent rejected the measure. Liking Howard Jarvis was less important to a yes vote than disliking him, which almost guaranteed a no vote. It is intriguing that Proposition 13 still enjoyed broad support (60 percent) but that its author, Howard Jarvis, was gradually slipping in esteem (53 percent).

The second issue was the state's income tax system. Although those voters who characterized themselves as "very angry" over the amount of state income taxes they paid supported 9 two to one, this segment comprised a modest 11 percent of the electorate. In the next category of voters, the "fairly angry" (some 26 percent), just over half supported 9. But of the remaining 64 percent of the sample who either had "no feelings" on the issue or were "satisfied" with their state income taxes, more than two-thirds opposed 9. The widespread public rage over state income taxes that would fuel an income tax revolt simply did not exist.

The *Los Angeles Times* Poll also asked each respondent to recall his or her vote on 13. Of those who voted against 13, 94 percent planned to vote against 9. Only 6 percent of Jarvis's detractors in 1978 had been converted to the benefits of cutting taxes. But fully 41 percent of Jarvis's 1978 supporters planned to abandon him in 1980. Two in five! To simplify somewhat, prior opponents

of tax reduction had not changed their mind, but massive deser-
tions occurred in the ranks of the tax-cutters. These defectors now
believed that tax cuts would endanger public services. What
caused this change of heart? One answer can be found in the link
between taxing, spending, and public services. What would have
been the fiscal impact of 9 on government, its ability to cope with
revenue losses, and the likely reactions of elected officials to this
new measure?

Table 8.6 shows how voters perceived the likely and actual
effects of 13 and the probable effects of 9. Overall, it suggests a
growing cynicism. Columns 1 and 2, from the 1978 poll on Proposition 13, show that voters, especially those voting yes, expected
significant cuts in waste and inefficiency in government. By May
1980, after two years of waiting, voters had not witnessed the expected cutback of waste and inefficiency in government. Indeed,
nearly half of all those who had made up their mind on Proposition 9 felt that other money had been found—no doubt the surplus—to sustain public services at 1978 levels (column 3).
Taxpayers' overall reaction was one of disappointment or shock or
stark realization that governments simply will not or cannot cut
waste and inefficiency, regardless of the electorate's wishes.

The importance of this shift in public opinion cannot be overstated. It was politically more expedient to use the state's multibillion dollar surplus to sustain virtually full funding of most
local services than to force major cuts in local budgets or grant
additional tax relief, with the result that state and local government agencies were not under the gun to order priorities or eliminate marginal programs. Many analysts and voters had also come
to believe that bureaucrats had no desire to make government
more efficient and, if necessary, would cut the most visible or
highly desired services first (the spite syndrome) or would quickly
rush to impose a variety of fees and user charges just to show the
voter who was in charge. Only 9 percent originally feared 13
would force cuts in services. In May 1980, 24 percent said the
effect of 13 had been a cut in services.

What about the potential effects of Proposition 9? Among all
decided voters (column 4), only 15 percent ventured that waste
and inefficiency in government would be cut. Almost three times
as many, 42 percent, said that other taxes would be raised to offset

TABLE 8.6
The Effects of Propositions 13 and 9
(percentage)

	Column 1 *June 1978* Effect of 13 will be (all voters)	Column 2 *June 1978* Effect of 13 will be (yes on 13 voters)	Column 3 *May 1980* Effect of 13 has been (all voters decided on 9)	Column 4 *May 1980* Effect of 9 will be (all voters decided on 9)	Column 5 *May 1980* Effect of 9 will be (no on 9 voters)	Column 6 *May 1980* Effect of 9 will be (yes on 13/ no on 9 voters)	Column 7 *May 1980* Effect of 9 will be (yes on 13/ yes on 9 voters)
Government services cut back	9[a]	5	24	15	20	15	5
Cut out waste and inefficiency	31	47	12	15	7	11	29
Other taxes raised	39	28	17	42	51	54	28
Other money found	20	19	48	27	22	20	38
	(n = 988)[b]	(n = 429)	(n = 904)	(n = 952)	(n = 553)	(n = 214)	(n = 307)

SOURCES: *Los Angeles Times* Polls, June 1978 and May 1980.

NOTES: [a]All percentages have been calculated to exclude those respondents who told interviewers "not sure" or failed to answer. In each case, this was a small fraction of the sample, 10 percent or less. Every effort has been made to ensure comparability in the seven columns.

[b]The number in parentheses indicates the numerical base, the number of respondents, on which the percentages listed in the table were calculated.

income tax revenue losses to the state. Only 27 percent said that other money could be found, a reflection of the public's belief that the surplus might not be large enough to sustain the bailout at current levels. Among no on 9 voters (column 5), only 7 percent said that 9 would cut waste. Twenty percent said that government services would be reduced, but just over *half* said that new taxes would be imposed. In sum, passage of 9 would not make for more efficient, leaner, or smaller government. Instead, it would lead to new or higher taxation. What, in the eyes of many voters, was the point of cutting income taxes (to benefit the wealthy few) if new taxes would result?

The final two columns, 6 and 7, show the expectations of those who had voted for 13, but were split on 9. Once again the key differences were the conflicting beliefs on attacking waste in government and fears of new taxation. The tax revolt "deserters" (column 6) believed that tax reduction would not eliminate waste in government. Nearly 70 percent saw in 9 new taxation or service reductions, neither of which was desirable. The tax revolt "sustainers" (column 7) still relied on the surplus and the belief that government agencies could deliver services more efficiently.[27] For Howard Jarvis, unfortunately, the sustainers had been transformed into a politically powerless minority.

BUSINESS AS USUAL

Among Proposition 9's less controversial features were its provisions for indexing income tax brackets to inflation and abolishing the business inventory tax. The reason these issues were not inflammatory was that a politically responsive legislature and governor had already passed the two measures into law in 1979. Critics of Jarvis saw little need to give these two measures constitutional stature.

Nevertheless, despite the defeat of 9, members of the legislature tried to express their continuing concern for the taxpayer's well-being. Assemblywoman Marina Bergeson introduced a measure to make full indexing of personal income tax brackets permanent (AB 2001). Earlier in 1979 Brown had signed AB 276, a bill also introduced by Bergeson, which established full indexing through the end of 1981. After January 1, 1982, income tax bracket adjustments would revert to the partial indexing formula adopted in 1978, which requires annual adjustments of brackets at a rate equal to the change in the Consumer Price Index, less three percent. Bergeson introduced AB 2001 to forestall this scheduled increase in state income tax rates.

AB 2001 was extremely popular in the Assembly and the Senate, securing a unanimous vote on the floor of each house. Governor Brown, however, vetoed the measure on July 15, 1980, fearing that its adoption would force cuts in existing programs or require new taxes during 1982, his last year in office. Despite the unanimous vote of both houses on the bill's initial adoption, Bergeson could not rally the two-thirds majority needed in each house to override Brown's veto. By a vote of 51 to 24, three short of the 54 necessary, the Assembly sustained his veto.

Brown's veto of full indexing gave new life to Howard Jarvis. During the first half of 1981, Jarvis gathered signatures for an initiative to prevent bracket creep. His proposed amendment would adjust state income tax brackets each year by the full percentage change in the California Consumer Price Index. As a statutory initiative, Jarvis needed 345,119 valid signatures to qualify his petition for the June 1982 statewide ballot. By June 12, 1981, Jarvis filed some 500,000 signatures, obtained in 58 counties.

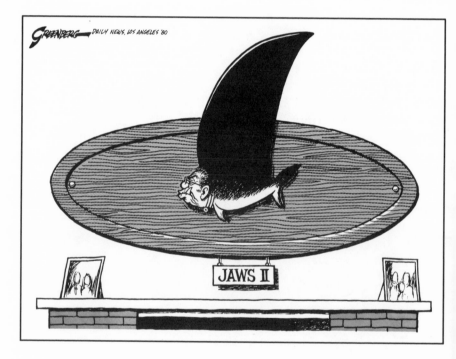

>F THE TAX REVOLT

During the bicentennial year, referenda to limit taxes and spending appeared on five state ballots, and all failed, but the tax revolt
was just beginning to smolder. It was Howard Jarvis who succeeded in igniting the fire. Given California's modest initiative
qualification requirements and its lively political culture, it was
perhaps not too surprising that the tax revolt should surface there.
Proposition 13 lit a bonfire whose flames eventually spread across
the nation. Throughout 1978, 1979, and 1980 voters in many
states evaluated ballot measures, and almost every state legislature
slashed one tax or another during its 1978 or 1979 sessions. Indeed, by spring 1979, 30 states had passed resolutions asking Congress to call a constitutional convention to write a balanced budget
amendment.
      On June 3, 1980, the flames were finally damped down by
California's overwhelming rejection of Proposition 9. With few
exceptions, tax-cutting ballot measures in other states were also
defeated. In two short years, the conflagration had died to a few
embers. State legislators spoke of austerity, tight budgets, vanish-
ing surpluses, and even the need for new or higher taxes to save
essential services. The movement to write a balanced budget
amendment into the Constitution also stalled, four short of the 34
state resolutions necessary to force Congress to convene a constitutional convention. As of late 1981, the tax revolt movement may
well be dormant. However, it was not Californians who caused
the tax revolt. They were just the first to give it focus and to force

their politicians and those in other states to heed voter complaints of runaway taxation and spending. Although conditions in California differed from those elsewhere, unhappiness with government finances became equally widespread in other states. For better or for worse, Jerry Brown became the first nationally prominent politician to champion the movement for a balanced budget.

ACROSS THE 50 STATES

Forty-seven American states, Puerto Rico, and the District of Columbia have either a constitutional or statutory prohibition or restraint on state deficit financing, some of which date to the nineteenth century.[1] Some provisions limit a state's ability to incur debt; others require balanced budgets; still others provide for the management of an impending or an incurred deficit. These rules of public finance, however, have not prevented excessive growth in taxation and spending at both state and local levels. Nationwide, state and local taxes rose from 6.4 percent of personal income in 1947 to 12.1 percent in 1977[2] as progressive tax rate schedules and inflation, which also drove up property assessments and sales tax receipts, yielded an ever increasing flood of dollars for state and local treasuries.

Precursors to Proposition 13

Before June 1978, three states had acted to limit taxes or government spending. New Jersey deserves credit as the first state to limit state and local government spending. In 1976 the state legislature approved a bill to tie increases in state spending to the annual increase in per capita income, which had averaged about 10 percent. Even more stringent were the limits set on local government spending; it could rise by no more than 5 percent per year. This measure was enacted during a period of debate on the controversial subjects of rising property taxes and the imposition of an unpopular new income tax. In order to show that it was serious about holding down spending, the New Jersey legislature adopted the spending limits even as it approved the new income tax. The statute had an initial termination date of June 30, 1980, and stated that the local limitations, which were initially scheduled to expire on December 30, 1979, had been imposed only as an experiment. The measure also incorporated two safety-valve clauses. Local residents could approve spending above the 5 percent limit by referendum, and the state legislature could approve emergency spending beyond the statutory limit with a two-thirds vote.

The second state to limit government spending was Colorado. In 1977 the Colorado legislature voted to restrict spending increases to no more than 7 percent per year. However, this measure is scheduled to expire in 1983.

On March 7, 1978, Tennessee voters approved an amendment to their state's constitution that limited the growth of appropriations from state tax revenues to the estimated rate of growth of the state's economy. Known as the Copeland amendment, after state representative David Copeland, the measure was approved by a 64 to 36 percent margin, although the size of this victory was marred somewhat by a very low turnout of 17 percent. Since its passage, the limit has not come into play because state revenues have lagged behind the growth in the state's economy. "Personal income," established as the pace-setting economic indicator by the 1978 legislative session, rose nearly 11 percent in fiscal 1978–79, but state spending grew only 9.5 percent.[3]

Fall 1978: The Revolt Spreads

In November 1978, voters in twenty states faced a tax or spending limit measure on their ballots.[4] In six states the issue was not so much one of limiting government spending or cutting taxes as it was of shifting the burden of taxation or changing the rules for assessments. In Illinois, the property tax ceiling was purely advisory. In Massachusetts, voters authorized cities and towns to tax residential property at rates lower than those for commercial property. Missouri voters, in anticipation of higher property assessments, authorized their legislature to require local governments to reduce property tax rates. Montana voters rejected a plan to transfer the assessing of property taxes from the state to local governments. In South Carolina, voters agreed to establish a "rainy day" reserve fund, equal to 5 percent of the general budget, to be used only for emergencies after approval by a two-thirds vote of the legislature. Lastly, in Colorado, voters rejected a constitutional amendment to tie spending to inflation, which could have liberalized the 7 percent statutory spending limit.

General tax or spending limits were approved in six states: Arizona, Hawaii, Idaho, Michigan, Nevada, and Texas (see Table 9.1). In other states, voters called for more specific tax reductions. Alabamans, in order to blunt the effect of a court order calling for reassessments, voted to restrict increases of any type of property taxes in any county to 20 percent. Residents of North Dakota approved a measure to reduce personal income taxes. Both North and South Dakota adopted amendments requiring a two-thirds vote of the legislature in order to raise selected taxes. West Virginia rejected a proposal to reduce the 60 percent majority vote required to raise school taxes and bonds, thus keeping levies more difficult to secure.

In contrast, Oregonians rejected two property tax relief measures. Voters in Michigan rejected a 2.5 percent maximum annual

TABLE 9.1

TAX AND SPENDING LIMITS ADOPTED IN 1978

State	Measure	Percentage Voting Yes
Arizona	Amendment to limit state spending to 7 percent of personal income	60.4
Hawaii	Amendment to limit spending increases to economic growth	66.8
Idaho	Amendment to limit property taxes to 1 percent of market value	58.4
Michigan	Amendment to limit state taxes to current percentage (9.5 percent) of state personal income	52.5
Nevada	Amendment to limit property taxes to 1 percent of market value (required a second vote of approval in 1980)	77.8
Texas	Amendment to limit spending increases to growth in the state's economy	84.1

property tax increase limit despite approving an overall state tax limit. In Arkansas, a state where per capita state and local government spending in 1976–77, other than capital outlay, ranked lowest in the nation, voters refused to repeal a 3 percent sales tax on food and prescription drugs. Finally Nebraskans rejected, by a modest majority, a measure to restrict future spending increases to 5 percent per year.

In most instances, however, approval of spending limits was overwhelming, running to as high as 84 percent in Texas. In only two instances did it fall below 55 percent. Even so, some defeated measures were almost approved. For example, the tax-relief measures in Oregon and Arkansas lost by small margins.

Overall, the voters' message was clear: runaway government spending and taxing had to stop. Specific limitation measures varied from state to state, reflecting differences in each state's level and composition of taxes, the perceived efficiency of public services, the size of state surpluses, and the political skills of interest groups who sponsored or opposed these limits. In the absence of available public opinion polls in these states, it is difficult to explain why some measures failed, but interesting to note their very small margin of defeat. States that had hitherto not been known for discontent over taxation suddenly became caught up in the contagion of Howard Jarvis's revolt.

1978–1979: The Responsive Legislatures

"So primal was the tax cutting urge among politicians that a stampede of tax relief measures thundered through 47 state legislatures in 1978 and 1979."[5] During these two sessions, 37 states reduced property taxes (to head off Proposition 13–type movements in their states), 28 states cut income taxes, 13 states restricted sales tax collections, and 12 states cut or repealed other taxes. Six states adopted at least partial indexing of income taxes, and five adopted statutory tax or spending limits (see Table 9.2). In all, taxpayers received more than $4 billion in tax relief. State and local taxes as a share of personal income fell from 12.1 percent in 1977 to 10.9 percent in 1979.

In some states, the cuts were massive—$710 million in Minnesota, $250 million in Nevada, $705 million in Oregon, $400 million in Utah, and $942 million in Wisconsin. Delaware lowered its maximum income tax rate from 19.8 to 13.5 percent. Even New York got caught up in the spirit of things and dropped its maximum rate from 12 to 10 percent. In 1978, unused state surpluses exceeded 8 percent of total state government spending. But many legislatures, fearing that these surpluses might fuel the fires of tax rebellion in their states, took pre-emptive moves to dissipate the surpluses in the form of tax relief.

By the end of 1979, fifteen states had adopted either a constitutional or statutory limit on taxes or spending. This number did

TABLE 9.2

TAX AND SPENDING LIMITS ADOPTED IN 1979

State	Measure	Percentage Voting Yes (if applicable)
California	Amendment to limit appropriations to increase in Consumer Price Index and population growth	74
Louisiana	Legislative statute limiting state tax revenue increases to growth in personal income	
Nevada	Legislative statute limiting spending increase to inflation plus population growth	
Oregon	Legislative statute, requiring voter approval in April 1980, limiting appropriations increases to personal income growth (extended by voter approval in 1981)	
Utah	Legislative statute limiting appropriations increases to 85 percent of increase in personal income	
Washington	Statute limiting tax revenue growth to average growth in personal income over previous three years (required voter approval)	62

not include a 1977 Rhode Island statute that limited increases in the governor's state budget request to 8 percent over the current year's general fund.

Throughout 1979, legislatures clearly had the tax revolt uppermost in their mind. In a transparent effort to squash more extreme proposals, some granted modest tax relief. The behavior of the Nevada legislature, in particular, demonstrated how responsible and responsive politicians became in the wake of the tax revolt.

Nevada's Question 6, a Proposition 13–type property tax limitation, was approved by a three-to-one margin in November 1978. Under Nevada law, an initiative can be adopted only if voters approve it in two separate elections. Within six months, the legislature enacted a comprehensive, $244 million tax reduction package for 1979, the largest reduction in the state's history. This package was made possible, in part, by an astonishing surplus of $168 million, in a total budget of $1 billion, due to rapid growth in both the gambling and tourist industries. Property taxes were cut 27 percent, renters were granted relief, and spending lids were placed on state and local budget requests. In addition, in a June 5, 1979, referendum, voters were given the option of eliminating the sales tax on most food items; they approved by a four-to-one margin. Overall, the Nevada plan cut taxes for a typical family of four with an income of $19,000 and home valued at $50,000 by $365. However, the state legislature stipulated that if voters approved Question 6 a second time, the entire plan would self-destruct. The legislature's rush to responsibility in April may have been impelled by an early March 1979 poll of 750 voters showing that 70 percent intended to vote yes a second time on Question 6. Another example of a responsive legislature was in Utah, where in order to encourage defeat of a Proposition 13–type initiative expected on the 1980 ballot, the 1979 legislature swiftly adopted an overall tax limit measure.

One of the primary causes of the growth in state revenues has been inflation-induced bracket creep. One increasingly popular solution to this problem has been indexing. In 1978, Arizona and Colorado, as well as California (see Chapter 8), adopted some form of indexing. The Arizona statute was on a year-to-year basis. In 1979, Wisconsin, Minnesota, and Iowa also adopted indexing.

Iowa provided for partial indexing of personal income tax brackets in the 1979 and 1980 tax years. In Minnesota, indexing was more comprehensive and included not only the income tax brackets but also the personal credit allowance, the maximum standard deduction, and the maximum exclusion level for the low-income allowance. Income brackets were adjusted by only 85 percent of the change in the Consumer Price Index, while the other three factors were adjusted by the annual change in the Minneapolis–St. Paul Consumer Price Index. Montana's legislature also passed an indexing bill, but the governor vetoed it.

In 1979 tax cuts were both politically attractive and affordable, given the existence of general fund surpluses in many states. Overall, in 1978, state surpluses amounted to 8.6 percent of general expenditures. Wyoming finished its 1978 fiscal year with a surplus of $45 million, equal to 30 percent of its total budget. The 1978 Wisconsin surplus exceeded $500 million, which led the state to cut taxes by $900 million over a two-year period. In 1979 this also included a suspension of the collection of state income taxes during May and June. On July 1, 1979, the Texas state surplus stood at $700 million and was expected to exceed $1 billion in 1981 in the absence of additional tax reduction. Governor William Perry Clements, Jr., the first Republican governor in over a hundred years, cut more than $2 billion from a $22 billion budget. This amounted to a tax cut of $1 billion in 1979, in addition to the $1 billion cut previously approved for 1978. Finally, in Oregon, which has voted down two tax and spending limitation measures, an estimated 1979 surplus of $550 million was used to grant tax relief.[6]

1980: The Revolt Slows

During 1980, three more states passed laws to limit taxes or spending. In April, the Delaware legislature passed a constitutional amendment limiting appropriations for any fiscal year to 98 percent of estimated general revenue funds and setting up a separate account for surplus funds of up to 5 percent of the estimated general fund. In June, the South Carolina legislature voted to limit state spending increases to the previous year's total multiplied by the average percentage increase in state personal income for the three previous years. Idaho adopted a statutory limit on general fund expenditures; henceforth they could not exceed 5.33 percent of total state personal income for the ensuing fiscal year.

If Proposition 13 catalyzed the tax revolt, Proposition 9 signaled its demise. The momentum that had been building since 1978 saw voters in eighteen states qualify a variety of tax proposals for the November 3 ballot. In its first postelection issue, the *State Tax Review* titled its lead article "Voters Reject Most Major Tax Measures."[7]

Initiative proposals similar to California's Proposition 13 were rejected, often by substantial margins, in all five states in which they appeared: Arizona, Nevada, Oregon, South Dakota, and Utah. In addition, Michigan voters defeated two property tax relief initiatives, the most controversial being the Tisch amendment to limit property tax assessments. Utah voters also rejected proposals to eliminate the sales tax on food and the ceilings on the homestead and personal property tax exemptions for individuals.

Elsewhere, relatively modest proposals to enact new property tax homestead exemptions or increase existing ones were approved in Arkansas, Louisiana, New Jersey, Virginia, and West Virginia. Very modest property tax reductions were also approved in Louisiana and Ohio.

Only three important proposals won out. Montana voters approved indexing personal income tax brackets, personal exemptions, standard deductions, and minimum filing requirements to the annual change in the Consumer Price Index, beginning in 1981. Missouri voted a spending limit. The one truly dramatic victory was Massachusetts's Proposition 2½: Voters passed, by a three-to-two margin, a bill to limit property taxes to 2.5 percent of real property value. This translated to a $1.3 billion reduction in funds for local governments. (Since the proposition was a law rather than a constitutional amendment, the state legislature can revise it at any time by a simple majority vote.)

As the tax revolt wound down, it was ironic that only in Massachusetts did public officials face the problem of a sudden shutoff in revenues. In the Bay State, older, poorer communities that had the highest property tax rates and the greatest demand for services were the hardest hit by the new measures. For example, property tax revenues in Chelsea fell from $24 million to $3.5 million. Boston lost 71 percent of its property tax receipts and had to cut

$97 million from a budget of $862 million.[8] *Forbes* magazine speculated that "eventually, common sense suggests, the state legislature will have to do something about 2½. Sooner or later the
populace will be more disturbed by the lack of services than they
are by the legislature's voting new taxes."[9] The article pondered
an increase in the sales tax and the replacement of Massachusetts's flat 5.3 percent state income tax with a graduated income tax. But Massachusetts was an anomaly in the fading tax
revolt.[10]

On January 17, 1981, voters in Dallas rejected a 30 percent
slash in property taxes, one of the nation's most sweeping tax cut
plans since Proposition 13.[11] Turnout was limited to a meager
100,000 voters, or 10 percent of Dallas' population, and the vote
was almost exactly two to one against. Apathy and opposition prevailed. The city charter amendment would have reduced the
city's property tax rate from 56.6 cents to 40 cents per $100 of
assessed valuation and would have limited increases in an individual's taxes to 5 percent a year. Dallas city officials claimed that
a rollback would have reduced municipal tax revenues by nearly
$40 million and forced major reductions in services. Indeed, this
measure would not have surfaced at all, save for a major re-evalua-
tion program in the summer of 1980 that had raised some homeowners' taxes by up to 300 percent.

Finally, on June 23, 1981, in Detroit, Mayor Coleman Young
submitted a tax increase referendum to his city's voters in order to
prevent municipal bankruptcy. He sought to raise $94 million in
additional revenues by increasing the city's personal income tax
rate from 2 to 3 percent for residents and from 0.5 to 1.5 percent
for nonresidents. Proponents spent some $450,000 and were re-
warded for their efforts with victory.[12] Voters in Detroit, at least,
were receptive to higher taxes.[13]

FROM THE STATES TO THE NATION'S CAPITAL

The frustration and anger over rising state and local taxes, which
Howard Jarvis had so successfully harnessed, was matched by a
growing chorus of agreement that the federal government, too,
needed restraining. Rising taxes, runaway spending, and mush-

rooming deficits all added to a growing public disenchantment with the nation's lawmakers. By 1978, some four-fifths of the population told pollsters that inflation had become the nation's most pressing domestic problem and, in turn, that federal budget deficits were a "chief" source of inflation.

Before 1900, the federal government was rarely troubled by budget deficits.[14] Rapid economic growth throughout the nineteenth century generated sufficient revenues, primarily from customs duties, to finance a modest level of federal spending, on the order of 3 percent of the Gross National Product. Although deficits sometimes occurred, due to economic decline or war, budgetary surpluses in good years quickly restored the overall balance. These infrequent deficits were clearly viewed as exceptions to the principle of fiscal balance, and corrective measures were invariably promised and soon taken to restore normal conditions. As a result, the real value of government debt per capita in 1891 was about the same as in 1791.

The philosophy that government should be self-supporting implied a practice of balanced budgets. Even in times of deficit, frequent surpluses made federal borrowing a rare event. Revenues and expenditures were not incorporated into an overall official federal budget until 1921, but the existence of a budgetary surplus each year during the 1920s suppressed debate on a statutory or constitutional requirement for a balanced budget.

Between 1932 and 1981, the federal budget was in balance nine times, but only once after 1962. The consequence of this was a trillion dollar national debt by 1981, up $450 billion since 1973. By 1977, real debt per capita was 23 times greater than at the start of the century.

Although President Roosevelt campaigned on a balanced budget platform in 1932 and in 1936 several bills were introduced in Congress to require balancing the budget, national interest in this issue lay dormant until 1975. In that year the Senate Judiciary Committee held hearings on the issue, but shelved the proposal. Despairing of congressional action, the National Taxpayers Union formed a movement to mobilize state legislatures to call on Congress to invoke a constitutional convention to write a balanced budget amendment.

In 1975, the first resolution was introduced into the Maryland legislature, and it attracted virtually no national notice.[15] Subsequently many state legislatures willingly approved a balanced budget resolution without hearings, debate, or opposition. By March 1978 Colorado had become the twenty-second state to give such approval.

By the end of January 1979, Arkansas, North Carolina, South Dakota, and Utah brought the total number of approvals to 26 states. In the same month, California's Jerry Brown endorsed the drive. His action served to sharpen political opposition for the first time. In his home state, the Assembly killed the resolution, due in part to Brown's personal conflict with Speaker Leo T. McCarthy. Then a new national committee, led by Massachusetts Lieutenant Governor Tommy O'Neill, was formed to oppose the balanced budget drive. In April 1979, New Hampshire became the thirtieth state to ratify, when the movement stalled. However, before it waned, dozens of individuals and organizations had joined forces to limit taxes and spending or to prohibit deficits.

By early spring 1979, some 238 lawmakers had sponsored either constitutional amendments or laws requiring the government to balance its budget except in times of war or other national emergency. Another 108 senators and representatives, led by Congressman Jack Kemp and Senator William Roth, proposed a 30 percent reduction in tax rates over three years. Yet another 131 lawmakers advocated indexing in order to adjust tax brackets each year to account for inflation. Regrettably, for those seeking to limit the federal government, in 1979 or 1980 not one single dollar of taxes was cut nor any expenditure prevented. Instead, during fiscal years 1979–80 and 1980–81, total federal tax revenues rose by nearly $140 billion and the accumulated deficit for the two years approached $115 billion.

Federal Tax Cuts in 1981

Tax-cutting discussions pervaded the 1980 presidential campaign. President Ronald Reagan's first year was filled with tax-cutting plans both for individuals and businesses. The centerpiece of the Reagan program was a modified version of the Kemp-Roth proposal, an across-the-board reduction in personal income tax rates by 25 percent over 33 months, beginning October 1, 1981. Starting in 1985, after the rate reductions are in place, income tax brackets are to be fully indexed. While indexing will not lower taxes, it effectively ends tax increases due solely to inflation. In order to stimulate investment, the Reagan proposals also called for accelerated business depreciation, together with a bevy of other proposals that, in all, constituted a significant package of tax relief. However, this cut did not represent an extension of the tax revolt from state and local levels to the federal level. Rather, it was the eighth in a series of congressional tax bills, dating from 1954, enacted largely to offset a series of cumulative de facto tax increases due to bracket creep and social security tax increases.

Of course, Congress could have corrected inflation-generated bracket creep well before 1985 by indexing, but politicians can get more mileage out of periodic tax cuts than from automatic adjustments of tax rates. Permanent indexing would give politicians only a one-time credit. Meanwhile, federal income tax yields have grown about 75 percent faster than Gross National Product—and income tax receipts make up about 45 percent of all federal receipts—allowing Congress to collect a growing stream of revenues, while avoiding explicit votes for tax increases and every so often granting a tax cut. Furthermore, Congress can target tax relief to selected constituencies, whereas indexing benefits all taxpayers. This process will end in 1985 unless indexing is repealed.

Figure 9.1 shows that since 1949 federal tax receipts as a share of Gross National Product have ranged from a low of 15 percent in 1950 (reflecting postwar tax cuts) to a high of 21 percent in 1969. Beginning with the recodification of the tax code in 1954, Congress passed tax-reform measures in 1964, 1969, 1971, 1976, 1977, and 1978—once in the 1950s, twice in the 1960s, and four times in the 1970s. The accelerating frequency of congressional action directly reflected the higher rates of inflation in the 1970s. In each instance of tax reform, a rising trend of taxation was interrupted, and a lower burden restored.

The years of major tax cuts—1954, 1964, 1971, and 1976—show sharp reductions in tax receipts as a share of Gross National Product. This series of tax measures did not benefit all taxpayers equally since the bulk of relief in dollar terms went to lower and lower-middle income households in the form of greatly increased personal exemptions and standard deductions.[16] In postwar tax reform, rate reductions, either across-the-board or for upper-income households, have been more the exception than the rule, and increasing numbers of taxpayers now face higher and higher rates.

Even if the entire Reagan package of tax proposals became law, federal tax receipts as a share of Gross National Product might still rise to a postwar high. Some forecasters have projected federal tax

FIGURE 9.1

FEDERAL TAX RECEIPTS AS PERCENTAGE
OF GROSS NATIONAL PRODUCT

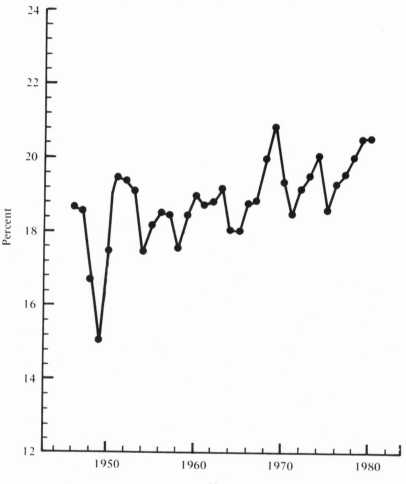

receipts for 1981, 1982, and 1983 at 21.4, 21.4, and 21.5 percent of Gross National Product.[17] A series of increases is already built into the tax system, of which the most significant are increases in the social security and the windfall (excise) oil profits tax. In addition, bracket creep continues to generate enormous revenues, offsetting much of the promised individual rate reductions. The Joint Congressional Committee on Taxation calculated that if the Kemp-Roth tax reductions had been adopted, in 1981 bracket creep–induced tax increases due to inflation would offset 86 percent of the total dollar value of tax relief. In 1982, this figure would reach 72 percent and in 1983, 68 percent. Given this background, the Reagan tax cut proposals should be viewed as the eighth in this series of postwar congressional corrections rather than as a national culmination of the tax revolt. Such proposals may halt the trend of rising tax burdens; they will not lower them significantly.[18]

CONCLUSION

In 1978, most Americans were highly enthusiastic about cutting taxes and telling government that it had to reform its spending habits. By 1981 public opinion had changed. In fact, the wheel had come full circle. Once again government had resumed its old habits, warning the electorate of empty treasuries and the disruption of public services if the tax-cutting vogue continued. After the defeat of Proposition 9, taxpayers did not fare well with either Congress or state legislatures, and two years of tax cuts and spending limitations soon gave way to proposals for new or increased taxation in various forms.[1] Voters, it seemed, had lost their enthusiasm for another round of cuts and proceeded to reject most of the tax-cutting proposals. The new interest was not tax cuts but austerity and saving essential public programs. Almost overnight, it seemed, the tax revolt had died. Yet its demise was not totally unpredictable.

WHY ARE TAX REVOLTS SO BRIEF?

Throughout history tax revolts have always been easier to initiate than to sustain. One reason is that the individual taxpayer is ill-equipped to fend off the coalition of taxing and spending interests that links together politicians, bureaucrats, public employees, and recipients of government benefits.

Taxpayers, as individuals, have interests that cover a broad spectrum of issues. They focus their attention on taxation only when it becomes of paramount importance to them. When run-away taxation becomes a pressing issue, as, for example, in the California case where a doubling or tripling of property taxes had taken place within a few years, taxpayers will unite to cut taxes. But, as soon as this common goal has been reached, each individual usually returns to private concerns, and the solidarity of the group is dissolved. It is almost impossible for any organization representing an ad hoc group of taxpayers, with only one common goal, to sustain interest, loyalty, and participation in longer-term goals once the short-term goal has been accomplished. With the tax cut successfully achieved, Proposition 13 voters had little else to bind them together.

However, in contrast with individual taxpayers, the proponents of taxing and spending—a coalition of elected and appointed officials, public employees, and direct beneficiaries of government spending—are a far more unified and enduring group whose view of the future is usually tied to the next annual budget or election. This group enjoys access to an army of tax-supported statisticians and researchers, who can be marshaled to back up announcements of impending cuts in services if tax cuts are enacted. The very existence of this group depends on the government's continued power to tax and spend. But, if expediency demands acquiescence to a tax cut, the coalition may temporarily accommodate; however, once the crisis is over, it quickly resumes its natural inclination to tax and spend. The California case well illustrates this point.

After a year and a half of tax cuts, from 1978 to 1980, the establishment succeeded in defeating Jarvis's second cutback assault. Since then, Governor Brown has vetoed a measure to index income taxes fully, and the legislature has succeeded in easing the constraints imposed by Proposition 4 and lessening its overall effect. Such action was made possible by the language of the measure, which lent itself to wide interpretation. In addition, the California Supreme Court, having read the June 1980 election returns, ruled that Proposition 13 did not apply to 1978–79 unsecured property taxes.

Throughout 1981, Governor Brown, big-city mayors, county supervisors, and other public officials also warned of impending cuts in budgets that would cripple the ability of local governments to provide even a minimum of service. These were the very same threats that had been uttered three years earlier. But with the wisdom of hindsight, this time public officials correctly interpreted the change in voter sentiment.

SOME LESSONS FROM THE TAX REVOLT

During the 1980s, the long-term effects of the tax revolt will remain the object of continued observation. However, experiences in the first three years of the movement permit some tentative conclusions.

Economic Effects

Employment: Up.   One noticeable aftereffect of Proposition 13 was the explosive growth of jobs in California. Between 1974 and 1978, the state's robust economy created one out of every six new jobs in the entire country. In the two years following 13, it created nearly one out of every three jobs, all in the private sector. This boom in employment was partly attributable to the transfer of billions of dollars of additional spending power into private hands; partly to an improvement in business expectations (since future property taxes could rise no more than 2 percent a year); and partly to a cut in income taxes and the abolition of the business inventory tax.

Government Revenues: Stable.   Post-13 government revenues did not visibly weaken. In fact, thousands of new workers paid income, sales, and property taxes. By 1981, public employment recovered to its pre-13 level. The total tax take since 1978 was large enough to cut income and business taxes, bail out local governments at ever increasing levels, *and* finance most state and local public services at their pre-13 levels. In sum, between 1978 and 1981, taxpayers got $30 billion in tax cuts—without a decline in public services.[2]

Public Services: Intact. Proposition 13 devastated neither the state's economy nor its public services, yet many school officials, fire chiefs, mayors, state legislators, and others still maintain their opposition. Sooner or later, they claim, and present evidence to the contrary, dire consequences will materialize from the cutbacks. However, given the current state of California's economy, any future curtailment of state services will be due to the failure of state and local governments to reduce unnecessary expenditures. Rising tax yields and the surplus have been used to postpone such action. State and local governments continue to act as if underspending, not overtaxing, were the cause of voter discontent. This spendthrift approach to public finance is reflected in the state government's haste to exhaust the surplus. After 1982, with the surplus gone, government officials can portray further talk of tax cuts as both reckless and irresponsible and an immediate threat to "vital" services.

Property Taxes: Up. In 1977 property taxes amounted to just over $10 billion. In 1979, they fell to about $5 billion. Rising assessments and taxes since 1978 will result in total property taxes surpassing the pre–Proposition 13 dollar levels by the mid-1980s. The reason for such increases is that turnover of existing homes has continued at a high level, in part because buyers can count on future assessment increases of no more than 2 percent per year.[3] In addition, since 1978, nonresidential construction has sharply increased. However, only time will tell if these upward trends will serve to foster another property tax revolt in the 1980s.

Political Lessons

Politicians' Stances: Evanescent. State and local government officials have consistently tried to loosen or circumvent the restraints of Propositions 13 and 4. To raise additional revenues, local governments have imposed new and higher user fees and charges and a growing variety of benefit assessments. The legislature has interpreted and amended Proposition 4 in ways that effectively weaken its restraints on future government spending at state and local levels. Governmental recalcitrance has prevailed over voter aspirations.

For a short period, Governor Brown became the champion of 13 and the politician most responsive to tax-cutting, earning the nickname "Jerry Jarvis." At the outset, Brown and his political ilk misjudged the direction of voter sentiments. But, as the saying goes, they had the good sense not to stand in front of the bus. They moved quickly to run alongside it, until they were able to board it, work their way to the driver's seat, and finally change its course for a new route. Even liberal Assembly Speaker Leo T. McCarthy became an official spokesman for Paul Gann and cosigned the arguments for Proposition 4 printed in the state's official ballot guide.

Despite government warnings, a total collapse of public services never materialized. Three years later, politicians and bureaucrats still continued to warn of this impending event. In October 1981 Jerry Brown talked of severe cuts in the state budget to avoid the constitutionally prohibited deficit. Yet, few public officials in California, apart from Mayor Pete Wilson of San Diego, championed greater efficiency and cutting of waste as a solution to the problem of decreased revenues.

Public Opinion: Equivocal. From an examination of various public opinion polls, it is clear that while critical of excessive public spending and taxation in general, most Americans strongly value, and often want to expand, a number of *specific* state and local government services.

During the 1970s, increasing numbers of Americans said that governments spent too much and that taxes were too high. At the same time, the majority of Americans continued to say the country spent too little on a number of important services. A 1978 National Opinion Research Survey disclosed that 67 percent said too little was spent on crime control, 57 percent said too little on health, and 54 percent too little on public education. This apparent contradiction in public demands was responsible for the immense change that took place in voter behavior between Proposition 13 and Proposition 9. Overall, public support for Proposition 13 and the measures it spawned in other states was both widespread and lasting. However, by the time Proposition 9 and subsequent measures appeared, public support for tax cuts and spending limits had virtually disappeared.

An examination of the vote analyses for California's three tax-cutting propositions disclosed that divisions of class, race, income, geographical region, level of education, religion, homeownership, political party affiliation, ideology, and other social and economic categories did not separate yes from no voters. This finding held true for both the lopsided yes on 13 and the almost equally lopsided no on 9. Traditional political alignments simply did not explain the causes of the vote on either measure.

Proposition 13 was not a vote to fire all the bureaucrats, sharply cut public services, close down the public schools, or totally abolish welfare and other programs for the needy. Rather, it was a vote to moderate what had become an overly rapid growth in taxation. Nevertheless, between 1978 and 1980, California voters awoke to a number of political realities, and their cynicism steadily increased. First, it was not easy to remove fat, waste, and inefficiency from government spending. In place of the cuts that most voters had requested, bureaucrats cut other areas. State and local governments continued to maintain pre-13 levels of spending. Such action succeeded only in exhausting the state's surplus in a short period of three to four years. Voters realized that with the surplus nearly gone, any further tax cuts (such as those involved in Proposition 9) would lead either to real cuts in public spending (and possibly real cuts in services) or to new proposals for additional taxation. To avoid such possibilities, the majority of those who had supported 13 decided to oppose 9.

In failing to approve 9, voters made it clear that they wanted to maintain the services that their tax dollars had built up over the years. However, it was equally clear that the expected exhaustion of the surplus played a key role in their decision. Yet, the growth of this surplus had been a catalyst for the overwhelming voter sentiment to approve Proposition 13. At that time, the surplus symbolized a level of taxation that voters found intolerable. By 1980, voters knew that the "obscene" surplus had been reduced to a prudent reserve fund, for unforeseen needs.

It was the voters' commitment to public services that largely accounts for the sudden electoral turnabout. The electorate had simply decided to call a halt to tax cutting in order to safeguard public services that the government warned were in danger of collapse.

MEAT-AX OR SCALPEL?

James Buchanan and Richard Wagner have set forth an excellent statement on the criteria for adopting constitutional amendments:

> There are several qualities that any such rule must possess if it is to be effective. First of all, it must be relatively simple and straightforward, capable of being understood by members of the public. Highly sophisticated rules that might be fully understood only by an economists' priesthood can hardly qualify on this count alone. Secondly, an effective rule must be capable of offering clear criteria for adherence and for violation. Both the politicians and the public must be able readily to discern when the rule is being broken. Finally, and most importantly, the fiscal rule must reflect and express values held by the citizenry, for then adherence to the precepts of the rule may, to some extent, be regarded as sacrosanct. These three basic qualities add up to a requirement that any effective budgetary rule must be understood to "make sense" to the ordinary voter.[4]

Jarvis's text of Proposition 13 resembled his four earlier measures that failed to qualify for the ballot.[5] But Proposition 13 had a number of advantages due to its overall simplicity. Among these were brevity and ease of legal enforcement. Because of this, its detractors were quick to label it the "meat ax." It was a straightforward exercise for government to compute annual assessment increases of 2 percent, and it was equally simple for property owners to multiply their current assessment by 1 percent to derive their annual property taxes. No new taxes could be levied on real property. The limitation clause on other new taxation was equally clear. New or higher taxation could be imposed only by a two-thirds vote of the legislature or by two-thirds approval of the qualified electorate in any local government district.

Some of the problem areas related to 13 were created by its terminology. In particular, it has been necessary to obtain legal rulings on the extent to which various fees and charges are to be considered a tax and thus subject to the two-thirds vote requirement. A court ruling that the increasingly prevalent fees, charges, and benefit assessments do not constitute taxes will weaken 13's restraints on government's revenue-raising powers.

Another practical problem has arisen with homes sold after July 1, 1976, which can be reassessed at full market value. Historically, the annual turnover of single-family homes in California has averaged from 10 to 15 percent of available housing. By the mid-1980s, a majority of new homeowners will be paying substantially higher property taxes than those owners who have not moved since 13 took effect. Pressure may eventually build to amend the reassessment clause in order to remedy this perceived inequity. One frequently suggested alternative to the problem is to split the assessment rolls and tax business property at higher rates than residential property. This could affect the state's business climate disastrously. Such a measure might roll back all residential assessments to their 1975–76 levels, with higher tax rates on business properties to recoup the lost revenues. This change would require a constitutional amendment, but several organizations have already expressed an interest in an initiative drive.

Comparing the effects of Proposition 13 with those of Proposition 4 has been described as comparing a meat-ax with a scalpel. Gann's Proposition 4 has, as yet, brought about no cuts in spending and no tax refunds. Any reductions have been deferred to the distant future. Yet, despite its simplicity of intent, its language and implementation have proved complex and difficult.

Proposition 4 is lengthy and open to interpretations by both the legislature and courts. Its application requires precise population data, not necessarily available in usable form, in order to prove that any given jurisdiction of local government is spending beyond its permitted increase. Proof of this is required before spending cuts can be enforced or tax rebates granted.

So far most of the measure's clauses have remained virtually inoperative. Tax receipts have not kept pace with increases in personal income or the state's Consumer Price Index, adjusted for population growth. If the carryover surplus funds remain embedded in the base-year formula, the spending limit will remain inoperative at the state level for years to come.

Legislative interpretation has helped to underline the weakness of the measure. For example, in relation to the population clause, the legislature eased the plight of San Francisco, a city with declining population, by allowing officials to use the population of the entire Bay Area to compute changes in its population growth. It also aided school districts with declining enrollments by counting the excess spending of any given district against the state limit. This made sense since the state supplies 80 percent of public education funds.

However, new fees and charges for services rendered by government do not count against the state limit. To the extent that these fees are not considered taxes and thus not subject to voter approval, the revenue from these fees imposed by government can be spent above and beyond the state limit.

Proposition 4 is less restrictive than 13 in that only a simple majority vote suffices to raise or lower spending levels, compared with the two-thirds vote required to raise new taxes under 13. But, although 4 may be more democratic than 13, it may also be less effective in limiting the growth of government. Yet it is important to note the two measures aimed at different targets. Proposition 13 rolled back and limits future increases in property taxes and requires two-thirds approval of any new tax. It says nothing about overall spending, but implies that the most effective way to curtail spending is to cut off a source of tax revenue. In contrast, Proposition 4 limits and ties increases in spending to increases in some suitable index of inflation or personal income, unless a majority votes to exceed those levels. It does not deal with the structure and level of taxation, but implies that tax collections above the appropriations limit must be returned to taxpayers within a fixed time period.

With passage of these two measures Californians set up an ongoing experiment in taxation and government. The test pits the meat ax against the scalpel, tax cuts against spending limits. Which will ultimately emerge as the better mode of manipulating the system, it is not yet possible to say. A comprehensive analysis must incorporate the evidence of other states that have adopted either or both of these two approaches and await further observation and study.

Until 1981, 13 had met its goals more effectively than had Proposition 4. However, future litigation may modify the original intent of each measure as envisioned by its sponsors. So far, the behavior of the legislature, the courts, and local governments suggests that further efforts will be made to weaken and manipulate the wording of the two amendments to lessen their effect. Barring any dramatic changes in political behavior or public opinion, the tax reduction cycle may well have run its course.

APPENDIXES

A.

TEXT OF ARTICLE XIII A (PROPOSITION 13)

Section 1. (a) The maximum amount of any ad valorem tax on real property shall not exceed One percent (1%) of the full cash value of such property. The one percent (1%) tax to be collected by the counties and apportioned according to law to the districts within the counties.

(b) The limitation provided for in subdivision (a) shall not apply to ad valorem taxes or special assessments to pay the interest and redemption charges on any indebtedness approved by the voters prior to the time this section becomes effective.

Section 2. (a) The full cash value means the County Assessors valuation of real property as shown on the 1975-76 tax bill under "full cash value," or thereafter, the appraised value of real property when purchased, newly constructed, or a change in ownership has occurred after the 1975 assessment. All real property not already assessed up to the 1975-76 tax levels may be reassessed to reflect that valuation.

(b) The fair market value base may reflect from year to year the inflationary rate not to exceed two percent (2%) for any given year or reduction as shown in the consumer price index or comparable data for the area under taxing jurisdiction.

Section 3. From and after the effective date of this article, any changes in State taxes enacted for the purpose of increasing revenues collected pursuant thereto whether by increased rates or changes in methods of computation must be imposed by an Act passed by not less than two-thirds of all members elected to each of the two houses of the Legislature, except that no new ad valorem taxes on real property, or sales or transaction taxes on the sales of real property may be imposed.

Section 4. Cities, Counties and special districts, by a two-thirds vote of the qualified electors of such district, may impose special taxes on such district, except ad valorem taxes on real property or a transaction tax or sales tax on the sale of real property within such City, County or special district.

Section 5. This article shall take effect for the tax year beginning on July 1 following the passage of this Amendment, except Section 3 which shall become effective upon the passage of this article.

Section 6. If any section, part, clause, or phrase hereof is for any reason held to be invalid or unconstitutional, the remaining sections shall not be affected but will remain in full force and effect.

B.

TEXT OF ARTICLE XIII B (PROPOSITION 4)

Section 1. The total annual appropriations subject to limitation of the state and of each local government shall not exceed the appropriations limit of such entity of government for the prior year adjusted for changes in the cost of living and population except as otherwise provided in this Article.

Section 2. Revenues received by any entity of government in excess of that amount which is appropriated by such entity in compliance with this Article during the fiscal year shall be returned by a revision of tax rates or fee schedules within the next two subsequent fiscal years.

Section 3. The appropriations limit for any fiscal year pursuant to Section 1 shall be adjusted as follows:

(a) In the event that the financial responsibility of providing services is transferred, in whole or in part, whether by annexation, incorporation or otherwise, from one entity of government to another, then for the year in which such transfer becomes effective the appropriations limit of the transferee entity shall be increased by such reasonable amount as the said entities shall mutually agree and the appropriations limit of the transferor entity shall be decreased by the same amount.

(b) In the event that the financial responsibility of providing services is transferred, in whole or in part, from an entity of government to a private entity, or the financial source for the provision of services is transferred, in whole or in part, from other revenues of an entity of government, to regulatory licenses, user charges or user fees, then for the year of such transfer the appropriations limit of such entity of government shall be decreased accordingly.

(c) In the event of an emergency, the appropriation limit may be exceeded provided that the appropriation limits in the following three years are reduced accordingly to prevent an aggregate increase in appropriations resulting from the emergency.

Section 4. The appropriations limit imposed on any new or existing entity of government by this Article may be established or changed by the electors of such entity, subject to and in conformity with constitutional and statutory voting requirements. The duration of any such change shall be as determined by said electors, but shall in no event exceed four years from the most recent vote of said electors creating or continuing such change.

Section 5. Each entity of government may establish such contingency, emergency, unemployment, reserve, retirement, sinking fund, trust, or similar funds as it shall deem reasonable and proper. Contributions to any such fund, to the extent that such contributors are derived from the proceeds of taxes, shall for purposes of this Article constitute appropriations subject to limitation in the year of contribution. Neither withdrawals from any such fund, nor expenditures of (or authorizations to expend) such withdrawals, nor transfers between or among such funds, shall for purposes of this Article constitute appropriations subject to limitation.

Section 6. Whenever the Legislature or any state agency mandates a new program or higher level of service on any local government, the state shall provide a subvention of funds to reimburse such local government for the costs of such program or increased level of service, except that the Legislature may, but need not, provide such subvention of funds for the following mandates:

(a) Legislative mandates requested by the local agency affected;

(b) Legislation defining a new crime or changing an existing definition of a crime; or

(c) Legislative mandates enacted prior to January 1, 1975, or executive orders or regulations initially implementing legislation enacted prior to January 1, 1975.

Section 7. Nothing in this Article shall be construed to impair the ability of the state or of any local government to meet its obligations with respect to existing or future bonded indebtedness.

Section 8. As used in this Article and except as otherwise expressly provided herein:

(a) "Appropriations subject to limitation" of the state shall mean any authorization to expend during a fiscal year the proceeds of taxes levied by or for the state, exclusive of state subventions for the use and operation of local government (other than subventions made pursuant to Section 6 of this Article) and further exclusive of refunds of taxes, benefit payments from retirement, unemployment insurance and disability insurance funds;

(b) "Appropriations subject to limitation" of an entity of local government shall mean any authorization to expend during a fiscal year the proceeds of taxes levied by or for that entity and the proceeds of state subventions to that entity (other than subventions made pursuant to Section 6 of this Article) exclusive of refunds of taxes;

(c) "Proceeds of taxes" shall include, but not be restricted to, all tax revenues and the proceeds to an entity of government, from (i) regulatory licenses, user charges, and user fees to the extent that such proceeds exceed the costs reasonably borne by such entity in providing the regulation, product, or service, and (ii) the investment of tax revenues. With respect to any local government, "proceeds of taxes" shall include subventions received from the state, other than pursuant to Section 6 of this Article, and, with respect to the state, proceeds of taxes shall exclude such subventions;

(d) "Local government" shall mean any city, county, city and county, school district, special district, authority, or other political subdivision of or within the state;

(e) "Cost of living" shall mean the Consumer Price Index for the United States as reported by the United States Department of Labor, or successor agency of the United States Government; provided, however, that for purposes of Section 1, the change in cost of living from the preceding year shall in no event exceed the change in California per capita personal income from said previous year;

(f) "Population" of any entity of government, other than a school district, shall be determined by a method prescribed by the Legislature, provided that such determination shall be revised, as necessary, to reflect the periodic census conducted by the United States Department of Commerce, or successor agency of the United States Government. The population of any school district shall be such school district's average daily attendance as determined by a method prescribed by the Legislature;

(g) "Debt service" shall mean appropriations required to pay the cost of interest and redemption charges, including the funding of any reserve or sinking fund required in connection therewith, on indebtedness existing or legally authorized as of January 1, 1979 or on bonded indebtedness thereafter approved according to law by a vote of the electors of the issuing entity voting in an election for such purpose.

(h) The "appropriations limit" of each entity of government for each fiscal year shall be that amount which total annual appropriations subject to limitation may not exceed under Section 1 and Section 3;

provided, however, that the "appropriations limit" of each entity of government for fiscal year 1978–79 shall be the total of the appropriations subject to limitation of such entity for that fiscal year. For fiscal year 1978–79, state subventions to local governments, exclusive of federal grants, shall be deemed to have been derived from the proceeds of state taxes.

(i) Except as otherwise provided in Section 5, "appropriations subject to limitation" shall not include local agency loan funds or indebtedness funds, investment (or authorizations to invest) funds of the state, or of an entity of local government in accounts at banks or savings and loan associations or in liquid securities.

Section 9. "Appropriations subject to limitation" for each entity of government shall not include:

(a) Debt service.

(b) Appropriations required for purposes of complying with mandates of the courts or the federal government which, without discretion, require an expenditure for additional services or which unavoidably make the providing of existing services more costly.

(c) Appropriations of any special district which existed on January 1, 1978, and which did not as of the 1977–78 fiscal year levy an ad valorem tax on property in excess of 12½ cents per $100 of assessed value; or the appropriations of any special district then existing or thereafter created by a vote of the people, which is totally funded by other than the proceeds of taxes.

Section 10. This Article shall be effective commencing with the first day of the fiscal year following its adoption.

Section 11. If any appropriation category shall be added to or removed from appropriations subject to limitation, pursuant to final judgment of any court of competent jurisdiction and any appeal therefrom, the appropriations limit shall be adjusted accordingly. If any section, part, clause or phrase in this Article is for any reason held invalid or unconstitutional, the remaining portions of this Article shall not be affected but shall remain in full force and effect.

C.

TEXT OF PROPOSITION 9

First. Section 26.5 is added to Article XIII thereof, to read:

26.5 (a) Taxes on or measured by income which are imposed under the Personal Income Tax Law or any successor thereto shall be at rates not to exceed 50 percent of those rates in effect for the 1978 taxable year.

(b) The Legislature shall provide for a system of adjusting the personal income tax brackets under the Personal Income Tax Law or any successor thereto to reflect annual changes in the California Consumer Price Index or any successor thereto.

Second. Subdivision (s) is added to Section 3 of Article XIII thereof, to read:

(a) Business inventories.*

Third. If any provision of this measure or the application thereof to any person or circumstance is held invalid, such invalidity shall not affect other provisions or applications of the measure which can be given effect without the invalid provision or application, and to this end the provisions of this measure are severable.

---

*Authors' note: That is, business inventories were to be added to a list of items exempt from taxation.

NOTES

one

1. Jeremy Main, "The Tax Revolt Takes Hold," *Money*, February 1980, p. 52; and "State Tax Prospects, 1979," *Tax Review* (Tax Foundation), 40, no. 2 (February 1979).

2. *Newsweek*, September 24, 1979, p. 45.

3. Main, "The Tax Revolt Takes Hold," pp. 54–55.

4. *Newsweek*, June 19, 1978, p. 20.

5. *Time*, June 19, 1978, p. 20.

6. John E. Petersen and Marcia Claxton, "Tax and Expenditure Limits: Proposition 13 and Its Alternatives," in Selma J. Mushkin, ed., *Proposition 13 and Its Consequences for Public Management* (Cambridge, Mass.: Abt Books, 1979), p. 35.

7. Barry N. Siegel, "Thoughts on the Tax Revolt," Original Paper 21 (Los Angeles: International Institute for Economic Research, 1979), p. 1.

8. See Mark David Menchik and Anthony H. Pascal, "The Equity Effects of Restraints on Taxing and Spending," Rand Paper Series P-6469 (Santa Monica, Calif.: Rand Corporation, May 1980), p. 1.

9. Joel Kotkin, "Once a Celebrity, Jarvis May Fade With Latest Loss," *Washington Post*, June 5, 1980.

10. Rowland Evans and Robert Novak, "The Dying Tax Revolt," *Washington Post*, May 30, 1980.

11. These figures are computed from California, Department of Fi-

nance, Financial Research Section, *California Statistical Abstract, 1979,* Table D-10, p. 49.

12. Everett Carll Ladd, Jr., and Seymour Martin Lipset, "Public Opinion and Public Policy," in Peter Duignan and Alvin Rabushka, eds., *The United States in the 1980s* (Stanford: Hoover Institution Press, 1980), pp. 59, 63–71.

13. *Monthly Tax Features* (Tax Foundation), June–July 1980, based on U.S., Treasury Department, *Statistics of Income, Individual Income Tax Returns, 1973* and (preliminary) 1978.

14. U.S., Advisory Commission on Intergovernmental Relations, *Inflation and Federal and State Income Taxes,* A–63 (Washington, D.C., November 1976), pp. 13–15.

15. William H. Oakland, "Proposition 13: Genesis and Consequences," *Economic Review* (Quarterly Journal of the Federal Reserve Bank of San Francisco), Special Issue on "Proposition 13 and Financial Markets," Winter 1979, p. 12.

16. U.S., Advisory Commission on Intergovernmental Relations, *Significant Features of Fiscal Federalism, 1978–1979 Edition* (Washington, D.C., 1979), cited in Menchik and Pascal, "Equity Effects," p. 7.

17. Conrad C. Jamison, *California Tax Study: An Analysis of Taxes and Expenditures of State and Local Government in California* (Los Angeles: Security Pacific National Bank, February 1979), table entitled "Total Tax Revenue of State and Local Government in California from Fiscal Year 1966–67 to Fiscal Year 1978–79," n.p.

18. Oakland, "Proposition 13," p. 9. See also Stephen J. DeCanio, "Proposition 13 and the Failure of Economic Politics," *National Tax Journal* (Proceedings of a Conference on Tax and Expenditure Limitations), 32, no. 2 (June 1979): 57; DeCanio plots the change in tax rates and home equity increases, showing that gains in wealth far offset the higher cash flow requirements of increasing property taxes.

19. Computed from *California Statistical Abstract, 1979,* Table D-9 ("Disposable Income per Capita, 1958–1978"), p. 49, and Table D-10 ("Consumer Price Index"), p. 49.

20. Tables prepared by Conrad C. Jamison, Security Pacific National Bank, October 19, 1979 (mimeo.).

21. California, State Board of Equalization, *Annual Report, 1978–1979* (for fiscal year ending June 30, 1979), Table A: "General Property Tax: Assessed Value of Tangible Property, Tangible Property Tax Levies, and Average Tangible Property Tax Rates, 1969–70 to 1979–80," p. 22.

22. See, for example, Bernard Frieden, *The Environmental Protection Hustle* (Cambridge, Mass.: MIT Press, 1979).

23. Ladd and Lipset, "Public Opinion and Public Policy," pp. 64–65.

24. U.S., Bureau of Economic Analysis, *The National Income and Product Accounts of the United States*, and *Survey of Current Business* (July 1979), cited in Menchik and Pascal, "Equity Effects," p. 9.

25. U.S., Bureau of the Census, *Statistical Abstract*, cited in Menchik and Pascal, "Equity Effects," p. 5.

26. See *California Poll*, News release dated June 16, 1978 (62 percent of the respondents want to cut welfare spending), and the *Los Angeles Times*, July 9, 1978 (54 percent want to cut welfare).

27. See Roger A. Freeman, *The Wayward Welfare State* (Stanford: Hoover Institution Press, 1981), especially pp. 181–209.

28. Maureen S. Fitzgerald, "Computer Democracy: An Analysis of California's New Love Affair with the Initiative Process," *California Journal* 11, no. 6 (June 1980): 1–15 (special report inside).

two

1. *Cal-Tax News*, June 15–30, 1980. For statistics on the total number of propositions submitted to the voters between 1912 and 1980, see Winston W. Crouch, John C. Bollens, and Stanley Scott, *California Government and Politics*, 7th ed. (Englewood Cliffs, N.J.: Prentice-Hall, 1981), p. 150.

2. Comprehensive treatments of the events leading up to the passage of Proposition 13 can be found in Frank Levy, "On Understanding Proposition 13," *Public Interest*, no. 56 (Summer 1979): 66–89; and Howard Jarvis, *I'm Mad as Hell* (New York: Times Books, 1979), pp. 15–157.

3. See Diane B. Paul, *The Politics of the Property Tax* (Lexington, Mass.: Lexington Books, 1975), pp. 34–35, 93–97.

4. Mervin Field, "Sending a Message: Californians Strike Back," *Public Opinion*, July/August 1978, p. 5.

5. George Skelton, "Support for 13 Still Growing," *Los Angeles Times*, September 1, 1978.

6. Jarvis, *I'm Mad as Hell*, pp. 89–90; and *San Francisco Chronicle*, August 4, 1978. The full list of contributors can be obtained from the state's Fair Political Practices Commission.

7. Jarvis, *I'm Mad as Hell*, pp. 89–90; and *San Francisco Chronicle*, August 4, 1978.

8. *Cal-Tax News*, February 15, 1978.

9. *Sacramento Bee*, June 2, 1978.

10. Ibid., May 30, 1978.

11. Ibid., May 18, 1978.

12. *Cal-Tax News*, November 1, 1978.

13. *Los Angeles Times*, July 24, 1978.

14. Ibid., July 15, 1978.

15. This story is beautifully told in Robert Kuttner, *Revolt of the Haves* (New York: Simon and Schuster, 1980), pp. 74–76.

16. Mervin Field, "Sending a Message," p. 5.

17. Ibid., p. 6.

18. William Schneider, "Punching Through the Jarvis Myth," *Los Angeles Times*, Opinion Page, Part VI, June 11, 1978.

19. We thank the *Los Angeles Times* for providing us with a copy of the *Los Angeles Times* Poll no. 6, the follow-up survey taken three weeks after election day.

20. Richard A. Brody, "Who Voted For Proposition 13?" *Taxing & Spending*, February 1979, pp. 26–28.

21. Multiple regression techniques permit the exclusion of those factors that are statistically insignificant in the final explanation of the vote. Several regression analyses were performed, and the results are summarized in the text.

22. A cross-sectional study of voting results in the 58 counties of California tested how potential gainers (the elderly and homeowners) and potential losers (government employees and low-income households) voted. The study concluded that the coalition of bureaucrats constituted the major opposition to Proposition 13. The group with the most to gain from a simple redistribution of a fixed tax bill—homeowners—was not a significant factor in the election outcome. Proposition 13 was seen as a broadly based vote against growing government spending. (J. P. Magaddino, Eugenie Froedge Toma, and Mark Toma, "Proposition 13: A Public Choice Appraisal," *Public Finance Quarterly* 8, no. 2 [April 1980]: 223–35.)

23. *Newsweek*, June 19, 1978, p. 22.

24. CBS/*New York Times* Poll, Release, June 27, 1978; *New York Times*, June 28, 1978. See also Everett Ladd, "Opinion Roundup: The

Tax Revolt!" *Public Opinion,* July/August 1978, p. 32.

25. Harris Survey, Release, June 29, 1978, ISSN 0046–6875.

three

1. *Sacramento Bee,* May 31, 1978.

2. *Kansas City Times,* October 17, 1978.

3. Quoted in Rick Atkinson, "Brown Perfects the Prop. 13 Twirl," *Kansas City Times,* October 17, 1978.

4. Ed Salzman, *Jerry Brown: High Priest and Low Politician* (Sacramento: California Journal Press, 1976), p. 44.

5. Ibid., p. 45.

6. Ibid., p. 48.

7. Ibid., p. 107.

8. *Los Angeles Times,* September 7, 1978.

9. Ibid., September 6, 1978.

10. *San Francisco Chronicle,* September 11, 1978.

11. *Los Angeles Times,* September 5, 1978.

12. *Wall Street Journal,* October 10, 1978.

13. Ibid.

14. Edward K. Hamilton, "The Greening of California," *Taxing & Spending,* October/November 1978, p. 23.

15. Albert J. Lipson, "Political and Legal Responses to Proposition 13 in California," R-2483-DOJ (Santa Monica, Calif.: Rand Corporation, January 1980).

16. *Eureka Times-Standard,* June 27, 1978.

17. Details about full funding of protective services are chronicled in Lipson, "Responses to Proposition 13," pp. 23–24, 26–27, and 48–49.

18. Hamilton, "Greening of California," p. 22.

19. Ibid.

20. Ibid.

21. *Eureka Times-Standard,* July 25, 1978.

22. Ibid., August 1, 1978.

23. *Los Angeles Times,* December 31, 1978.

24. Ibid., June 29, 1978.

25. This information was compiled from news releases of the Of-

fice of the Controller in Sacramento and detailed tables printed in the *Los Angeles Times,* July 14, 1978, and the *San Francisco Chronicle,* July 13, 1978.

26. *San Diego Union,* June 24, 1978.

27. Ibid.

28. Ibid.

29. Ibid.

30. *San Francisco Chronicle,* November 22, 1978.

31. Ibid.

32. *San Diego Union,* June 25, 1978.

33. See *Tax Revolt Digest,* March 1979, for a comprehensive analysis of the Post Commission's activities and report.

34. Ibid.

35. Ibid.

36. Ibid.

37. Ibid.

38. Ibid.

39. *San Francisco Chronicle,* August 12, 1978.

40. Ibid.

41. *Los Angeles Times,* August 12, 1978.

42. Ibid.

43. Ibid.

44. Ibid.

45. The Supreme Court's vote was unanimous save for Chief Justice Rose Bird's dissent on one of the seven issues raised by the petitioners. In a separate but concurring opinion, Bird argued that differential assessments, and thus tax benefits, for owners of identical properties (i.e., of equal worth) purchased before and after 1975 violated the equal protection clause of the United States Constitution. (See *Prop. 13 Impact Reporter,* no. 7 [October 19,1978]).

46. California School Boards Association, *Proposition 13 Information Service,* February 16, 1979.

47. Ibid.

48. California's constitution authorizes any city or county to adopt a home-rule charter. Ten counties and 87 cities have made use of this opportunity. Once a charter has been drafted and approved by a majority of the registered voters of a city or county, its provisions take precedence over state laws with respect to municipal affairs, though the State Su-

preme Court has to interpret the term "municipal affairs" under new and changing circumstances. Cities and counties without charters conduct their affairs under the authority of general laws, which consist of state statutes applying uniformly to all nonchartered localities. (See Winston W. Crouch, John C. Bollens, and Stanley Scott, *California Government and Politics*, 7th ed. [Englewood Cliffs, N.J.: Prentice-Hall, 1981], pp. 45–46.)

49. California School Boards Association, *Proposition 13 Information Service*, February 16, 1979.

50. *Prop. 13 Impact Reporter*, no. 6 (September 26, 1978).

51. *Los Angeles Times*, September 12, 1978.

52. "The Proposition 13 Court Calendar," *Cal-Tax News*, July 15–31, 1979.

53. *San Francisco Chronicle*, July 26, 1978.

54. Ibid.

55. *Cal-Tax News*, February 1–14, 1979.

56. A survey of nine counties in the San Francisco Bay area showed widespread, often substantial, increases in local impact fees imposed on new construction. Local development fees became an important source of replacement revenues for reduced property taxes. Between 1976 and 1979, the average fee for a standard single-family home in the region rose from $1,121 to $1,505, an increase of 34 percent in real terms (figures expressed in constant 1979 dollars). Changes in fee levels reflect increases in existing fees and the imposition of new fees. About three-fourths of the cities surveyed said that fee increases were a direct response to 13. However, not all of the fee changes are attributable to Proposition 13, reflecting, instead, local attitudes toward growth, quality of local amenities, and an unprecedented demand for housing. Several of the new fees were imposed in 1977 and early 1978 before passage of 13. But Proposition 13 has intensified the trend toward greater reliance on fees and charges. (See Stuart Gabriel, Lawrence Katz, and Jennifer Wolch, "Local Land-Use Regulation and Proposition 13," *Taxing & Spending*, Spring 1980, pp. 73–81. For the results of a more comprehensive survey, see "Local Government Profile," *Cal-Tax Research Bulletin*, November 1978, p. 3; its calculations reveal an increase in total city and county fees of $101.5 million alone between June 1, 1978, and November 1, 1978.)

57. *Tax Revolt Digest*, September 1979.

58. Ibid.

59. Among the more important of these statutes are AB 108, Ch.

133; AB 549, Ch. 261; AB 618, Ch. 397; SB 785, Ch. 903; AB 2066, Ch. 88; and AB 2345, Ch. 672. Results of elections based on these statutes are presented in Chapter 5.

four

1. Interview with William Hamm, November 14, 1978.
2. Interview with Kirk West, November 13, 1978.
3. *Sacramento Bee*, May 30, 1978.
4. Ibid., May 18, 1978.
5. *Business Week*, June 5, 1978.
6. *Sacramento Bee*, June 2, 1978.
7. Ibid., May 17, 1978.
8. *San Francisco Examiner-Chronicle*, July 16, 1978.
9. *Sacramento Bee*, June 11, 1978.
10. *San Francisco Examiner-Chronicle*, July 16, 1978.
11. Ibid.
12. Release of the quarterly economic forecast of the UCLA Graduate School of Management's Business Forecasting Project, dated June 15, 1978.
13. *Wall Street Journal*, June 15, 1978, editorial page.
14. UCLA, quarterly forecast, December 1978.
15. *San Francisco Chronicle*, July 6, 1978.
16. Ibid., July 13, 1978.
17. *EDD Layoff Report News Release*, no. 176 (October 6, 1978).
18. Ibid., no. 178, November 3, 1978.
19. Ibid., no. 181, December 8, 1978.
20. *Los Angeles Times*, July 1, 1978.
21. Ibid., January 1, 1979.
22. *Taxing & Spending*, October/November 1978.
23. U.S., Congress, Congressional Budget Office, *Proposition 13: Its Impact on the Nation's Economy, Federal Revenues, and Federal Expenditures* (Washington, D.C.: Government Printing Office, 1978).
24. California, Employment Development Department, *Annual Report on Job Growth in California, 1978* (Sacramento, 1978).
25. *Peninsula Times-Tribune*, October 24, 1979, p. E–3.
26. Arthur P. Solomon, "The Cost of Housing: An Analysis of

Trends, Incidence, and Causes," in *The Cost of Housing* (Proceedings of the Third Annual Conference, Federal Home Loan Bank of San Francisco, December 6–7, 1977), p. 33.

27. Richard F. Muth, "National Housing Policy," in Peter Duignan and Alvin Rabushka, eds., *The United States in the 1980s* (Stanford: Hoover Institution Press, 1980), p. 351.

28. *California Construction Trends* (Los Angeles: Security Pacific National Bank), April 1980, p. 3, and June 1980, p. 3.

29. These facts are reported in Jack Flanigan, "Apartments," in Cal-Tax Conference, ed., *Construction Activity Post–Proposition 13* (Sacramento, 1979), pp. 36–38. Information on the incidence and status of rent control deliberations or initiatives is periodically published in memorandums of the California Association of Realtors.

five

1. As of January 1982, no single unified source on state and local revenues existed for any period later than fiscal 1979–80. The numbers in the text include federal transfers. Overall estimates are derived by adding together totals for local agencies and the state government, excluding state subventions to local agencies. This information is typically assembled from state controller's reports, analyses issued by the legislative analyst, and the State Department of Finance. The 1980–81 numbers presented in the text are taken from a report issued by Security Pacific National Bank, "Taxes and Other Revenue of State and Local Government in California," January 1982, p. B-2.

Compared with fiscal year 1979–80, county revenues grew 13.5 percent and city revenues 11 percent in fiscal year 1980–81. The state's local bailout aid in fiscal year 1981–82 (the fourth year under 13) was sufficient to allow overall revenues to grow 7.9 percent for cities and 7.5 percent for counties, or approximately that period's likely inflation rate.

2. *Tax Revolt Digest*, August 1979.

3. California, State Board of Equalization, *1979–80 Annual Report* (Sacramento, 1980), p. 28.

4. *Peninsula Times-Tribune*, July 24, 1979.

5. *Tax Revolt Digest*, August 1979.

6. *Peninsula Times-Tribune*, July 24, 1979.

7. *San Francisco Chronicle*, July 21, 1979.

8. The legislature rejected efforts by Governor Brown to change

Bailout II by shifting property tax money from cities, counties, and special districts to schools in the 1981–82 state budget.

9. Werner Z. Hirsch, "Lessons for the Era of Fiscal-Limitation Movements," *Taxing & Spending*, Fall 1980, pp. 59–64.

10. Legislative Analyst, *An Analysis of the Effect of Proposition 13 on Local Governments*, 79–19 (Sacramento, 1979), p. 32.

11. See Roger A. Freeman, *The Wayward Welfare State* (Stanford: Hoover Institution Press, 1981), pp. 12–33. See also Anthony H. Pascal et al., "Fiscal Containment of Local and State Government," Rand/R-2494-FF/RC (Santa Monica, Calif.: Rand Corporation, September 1979), pp. 36–37.

12. Robert W. Poole, Jr., *Fiscal Watchdog*, column 22, August 22, 1978.

13. Cited in ibid., p. 2.

14. Cited in Don Kates, "Can We Arrest Police Budgets?" *Taxing & Spending*, April 1979, p. 25.

15. *Tax Revolt Digest*, June 1979, p. 4.

16. "Sheriffs Workload," *Cal-Tax Research Bulletin*, May 1979.

17. Ibid.

18. Computed from State Controller's "Annual Reports on Counties."

19. Computed from State Controller's "Annual Reports on Cities."

20. State Controller's "Annual Reports on Cities."

21. See *Tax Revolt Digest*, May 1979, for a full description of this plan.

22. *Cal-Tax News*, November 15–30, 1980.

23. Governmental Research Council of San Mateo County, "Analysis of the Fire Services System in San Mateo County," mimeo. (Redwood City, Calif., November 1979), p. ix.

24. Ibid., p. xi.

25. Ibid., p. xii.

26. *San Francisco Chronicle*, June 16, 1981. For a detailed examination of city and county finances in the two years following passage of Proposition 13, see Kevin M. Bacon, "City and County Finances in the Post–Proposition 13 Era: An Analysis of Changes in the Fiscal Condition of California Cities and Counties During the 1977–78 to 1979–80 Fiscal Years," mimeo. (Sacramento: Assembly Office of Research, June 1981), vols. 1–2.

27. *California Journal*, November 1978, p. 349. See also 1977–78 State Controller's "Report on School Districts."

28. *California Journal*, November 1978, p. 349.

29. Ibid.

30. *San Diego Union*, July 16, 1978.

31. *Phi Delta Kappan*, September 1978, p. 11.

32. To the opposition, this was "not very reassuring, since the state is only obligated to provide a flat grant of $120 per student" (ibid.).

33. In a landmark case, *Serrano v. Priest*, the state Supreme Court ruled that the California public school finance system, which largely depended on local property taxes, was unfair to children in poor school districts. Differences in local property wealth per pupil among districts gave children in rich districts disproportionate educational resources, thereby violating the equal protection provisions in the state constitution.

This decision gave the legislature until September 1980 to develop a more equitable means of financing public schools. The key measure, AB 65, provided additional state assistance to increase per pupil expenditures in low-wealth districts and impose limits on the growth of expenditures in high-wealth districts. Bailout II, which made schools more dependent on state funds, facilitated court compliance since under the terms of bailout, allocations to rich and poor school districts could vary.

34. *Phi Delta Kappan*, September 1978, p. 2.

35. Legislative Analyst, *An Analysis of Proposition 13, The Jarvis-Gann Property Tax Initiative* (Sacramento, 1978), pp. 125, 131.

36. The study noted that this alternative might be illegal since it appeared to run counter to the *Serrano v. Priest* decision (see ibid., p. 141).

37. See ibid., p. 146.

38. *Wall Street Journal*, June 28, 1978.

39. *Sacramento Bee*, May 16, 1978.

40. *Phi Delta Kappan*, September 1978, p. 12.

41. *San Francisco Examiner-Chronicle,* September 3, 1978.

42. *Los Angeles Times*, July 30, 1978.

43. Legislative Analyst, *An Analysis of the Effect of Proposition 13 on Local Governments* (Sacramento, 1979), p. 77.

44. State Controller's "Annual Report on School Districts for 1978–79."

45. *Tax Revolt Digest*, December 1978, p. 1.

46. *Wall Street Journal*, July 26, 1978.

47. State Controller's "Annual Report on School Districts for 1978–79."

48. Gregory Jackson, "Community Colleges and Budget Reduction," mimeo. (Stanford: Institute for Research on Educational Finance and Governance, Stanford University, 1978).

49. *San Mateo Times*, March 14, 1979.

50. *Tax Revolt Digest*, October 1979, p. 2.

51. State Controller's "Annual Report on School Districts for 1979–80."

52. *Cal-Tax News*, June 15–30, 1979.

53. *Tax Revolt Digest*, January 1979, pp. 1–2.

54. Ibid.

55. Ibid., p. 2.

56. Ibid.

57. State Controller's "Annual Reports on Cities."

58. Ibid.

59. State Controller's "Annual Reports on Counties."

60. Ibid.

61. *Tax Revolt Digest*, December 1978, p. 4.

62. "Results of the C.P.R.S. Post–Prop. 13 Park and Recreation Survey," mimeo. (November–December 1978).

63. Pascal et al., *Fiscal Containment*.

seven

1. Ed Salzman, "Power to the Controller Under the New Gann Plan," *California Journal*, January 1979, pp. 17–18.

2. For a copy and detailed analysis of the text of Proposition 4, see *Cal-Tax News*, August 1–14, 1979.

3. Details of the campaign appear in *Wall Street Journal*, October 12, 1979; Robert Kuttner, *Revolt of the Haves* (New York: Simon and Schuster, 1980), pp. 304–6; and *Cal-Tax News*, November 15–30, 1978, and March 15–31, 1979.

4. See *Wall Street Journal*, October 12, 1979.

5. California Poll, Field Institute Release 1032, June 21, 1979, and Release 1042, September 19, 1979.

6. We thank the *Los Angeles Times* for providing us with a copy of the *Los Angeles Times* Poll no. 19, the pre-election survey taken October 15–21, 1979.

7. Multiple regression techniques permit the exclusion of those factors that are statistically insignificant in the final explanation of the vote. These analyses were performed, and the main findings are reported in the text.

8. *San Francisco Chronicle*, November 8, 1979.

9. *Tax Revolt Digest*, July 1979.

10. Interview with Professor William Craig Stubblebine, November 13, 1980.

eight

1. *San Francisco Examiner*, May 22, 1980. For an in-depth treatment of the initiative process during the 1980 election, see Maureen S. Fitzgerald, "Computer Democracy: An Analysis of California's New Love Affair with the Initiative Process," *California Journal*, June 1980, pp. 229–44.

2. California Poll, Release 1063, April 14, 1980.

3. In sharp contrast to previous years, the Department of Finance's May 1981 revision of the January revenue estimates for the 1981–82 fiscal year contained no major upward adjustments (*Cal-Tax News*, May 15–31, 1981).

4. Ibid., March 15–31, 1980.

5. *California Finance Report*, March 1980, pp. 1–2.

6. *Cal-Tax News*, May 15–31, 1980.

7. *Peninsula Times-Tribune*, January 9, 1980.

8. *Oakland Tribune*, May 28, 1980.

9. *San Francisco Chronicle*, January 30, 1980; and *Los Angeles Times*, March 12, 1980.

10. *Oakland Tribune*, May 8, 1980.

11. *Sacramento Bee*, May 8, 1980. During 1977–78, California received $7.63 billion in federal funds. In the three years following Proposition 13, receipts of federal funds first fell to $7.56 billion, then rose in successive years to $8.16 billion and $10.45 billion, respectively. See the 1978–79 State Controller's "Annual Report on the State" and the *1981–82 Governor's Budget*, p. A–4.

12. *Los Angeles Times*, March 28, 1980.

13. *California Finance Report*, March 1980, pp. 8–9. Hamm used sharper shears on the 1981–82 budget, recommending $1.23 billion in reductions. The legislature and Governor Brown disregarded these as well since spending cuts are typically unpopular. (*Cal-Tax News*, June 1–14, 1981.)

14. *Berkeley Gazette*, January 26, 1980, and February 19, 1980; *Los Angeles Times*, March 22, 1980, and March 29, 1980; and *San Francisco Examiner*, April 21, 1980.

15. *Daily Guardian* (University of California, San Diego), February 4, 1980.

16. *Santa Ana Register*, February 16, 1980.

17. *Sacramento Bee*, March 6, 1980.

18. *San Francisco Chronicle*, May 30, 1980.

19. *Sacramento Union*, March 21, 1980.

20. *San Francisco Chronicle*, March 21, 1980; and *Sacramento Union*, March 21, 1980.

21. *Sacramento Union*, May 21, 1980.

22. Milton Friedman, *Tax Limitation, Inflation and the Role of Government* (Dallas: Fisher Institute, 1978), p. 19.

23. *Los Angeles Times*, May 2, 1980.

24. *Los Angeles Times*, May 28, 1980.

25. We thank the *Los Angeles Times* for providing us with a copy of the raw data from their Poll no. 29, the May 1980 survey on Proposition 9.

26. Multiple regression techniques permit the exclusion of those variables that are statistically insignificant in the final explanation of the vote. Several regressions were performed, and the final results are summarized in the text of the chapter.

27. These terms are borrowed from Seymour Martin Lipset and William Schneider, "Is the Tax Revolt Over?" *Taxing & Spending*, Summer 1980.

nine

1. National Association of State Budget Officers, "Limitations on State Deficits: Text of Constitutional and Statutory Provisions" (Lexington, Ky.: Council of State Governments, 1976).

2. U.S., Department of Commerce, Bureau of Economic Analysis, *Survey of Current Business* (Washington, D.C., December 1980).

3. Ibid., September 1979.

4. This section follows Alvin Rabushka, "Tax and Spending Limits," in Peter Duignan and Alvin Rabushka, eds., *The United States in the 1980s* (Stanford: Hoover Institution Press, 1980), pp. 93–97.

5. See Jeremy Main, "The Tax Revolt Takes Hold," *Money*, February 1980, pp. 49–55, and *Congressional Quarterly*, August 25, 1979, pp. 1762–818. See also Winnifred M. Austermann and Daniel E. Pilcher, "The Tax Revolt Transformed," *State Legislatures*, July/August 1980, pp. 25–33.

6. *Tax Revolt Digest*, May and June 1979.

7. *State Tax Review*, November 11, 1980, pp. 1–7.

8. *Newsweek*, December 8, 1980, p. 33.

9. *Forbes*, November 24, 1980, pp. 34–35.

10. For a detailed account, see Susanne Tompkins, "Proposition 2½: Massachusetts and the Tax Revolt," *Journal of the Institute for Socioeconomic Studies* 4, no. 1 (Spring 1981): 21–32.

11. *San Francisco Sunday Examiner & Chronicle*, January 18, 1981.

12. *Wall Street Journal*, June 23 and 25, 1981.

13. Several unobtrusive indicators reflect the general waning of the tax revolt. *Taxing & Spending*, established in 1978 to publish articles on the causes and consequences of the tax revolt, quietly changed its name in early 1981 to *Journal of Contemporary Studies*, beginning with vol. 4. Other important outlets on tax limitation issues, such as *Tax Revolt Digest*, *Prop. 13 Impact Reporter*, and the California School Boards Association's newsletter, *Proposition 13 Information Service*, ceased publication.

14. Rabushka, "Tax and Spending Limits," pp. 95–98.

15. Robert Kuttner, *Revolt of the Haves* (New York: Simon and Schuster, 1980), pp. 281–87.

16. See Attiat F. Ott and Ludwig O. Dittrich, *The Federal Income Tax Burden on Households: The Effects of Tax Law Changes* (Washington, D.C.: American Enterprise Institute, 1981).

17. Larry J. Kimbell, "Economic Forecast," *Top Priority*, Winter 1981, pp. 6–7.

18. See Alvin Rabushka, "The Attractions of a Flat-Rate Tax System," *Wall Street Journal*, March 25, 1981.

ten

1. One example is split rolls, which would impose higher assessments and taxes on business property than on residential property.

Were it not for Jerry Brown's past inconsistent record of opposition, support, and then opposition for the various tax and spending limitation measures that have structured California public finances since 1978, we might be tempted to call him "conservative" and the state legislature "profligate." In January 1981, Brown proposed a budget for fiscal year 1981–82 of $24.5 billion, an increase of 2 percent over his request for 1980–81. The legislature approved a $25.6 billion budget, almost 5 percent above his request (though only 2 percent above the actual level of spending for 1980–81). Although the legislature increased Brown's request by more than $1 billion, he chose not to exercise the governor's right to veto specific items, missing an opportunity to reduce spending.

2. Total property tax levies of $10.28 billion in fiscal year 1977–78 fell in 1978–79 to $5.04 billion, a sharp reduction of 50.9 percent. Had Proposition 13 not passed, however, property taxes would have risen more than another billion dollars. Thus the actual cut from the projected 1978–79 levies came to about $7 billion. Proposition 13 reduced the nominal tax rate on property from $10.68 per $100 of assessed valuation (or an effective tax rate of 2.67 percent on full cash or market value) to a nominal rate of $4.79 (or just over 1 percent of market value). See California, State Board of Equalization, *1978–79 Annual Report* (Sacramento, 1979), Table A, p. 22.

3. Conventional wisdom has it that Proposition 13 will cause homeowners to bear a larger and larger share of the total property tax burden and business a diminishing share. It is assumed this shift will occur because of higher turnover rates among residential properties than among commercial and industrial properties, which will occasion full-market-value reappraisals.

A study released by the State Board of Equalization on October 23, 1979, documents that a shift to homeowners had begun in 1975, arising from rapidly inflating market values on single-family homes compared with nonresidential properties. Jeff Reynolds, research director for the state board, calculated that the residential component would have grown from 36 percent of the total property tax roll in 1975–76 to 62 percent in 1988–89. However, against the conventional wisdom, Reynolds stated that Proposition 13 slowed the shift to homeowners. The reason is the 2 percent cap on annual assessment increases in the measure, which slows the estimated increase in the residential property tax burden to 58 percent in 1988–89, some four percentage points less than without Proposition 13. (See *Cal-Tax News*, November 1–14, 1979.)

To everyone's surprise, homeowner values as a percentage of assessments continued to decline all through the 1979–80 and 1980–81 fiscal years. See ibid., November 1–14, 1981.

4. James M. Buchanan and Richard E. Wagner, *Democracy in Deficit: The Political Legacy of Lord Keynes* (New York: Academic Press, 1977), p. 176.

5. Howard Jarvis, *I'm Mad as Hell* (New York: Times Books, 1979), p. 47.

BIBLIOGRAPHY

BOOKS

Borcherding, Thomas E., ed. *Budget and Bureaucrats: The Sources of Government Growth.* Durham, N.C.: Duke University Press, 1977.

Crouch, Winston W.; John C. Bollens; and Stanley Scott. *California Government and Politics.* 7th ed. Englewood Cliffs, N.J.: Prentice-Hall, 1981.

Dvorin, Eugene Petral. *Introduction to California Government.* Menlo Park, Calif.: Addison-Wesley Publishing Company, 1969.

Jarvis, Howard. *I'm Mad as Hell.* New York: Times Books, 1979.

Kaufman, George G., and Kenneth T. Rosen, eds. *The Property Tax Revolt: The Case of Propositon 13.* Cambridge, Mass.: Ballinger, 1981.

Kuttner, Robert. *Revolt of the Haves.* New York: Simon and Schuster, 1980.

Mayer, Martin. *The Builders.* New York: W. W. Norton and Company, 1978.

Mushkin, Selma J., ed. *Proposition 13 and Its Consequences for Public Management.* Cambridge, Mass.: Abt Books, 1979.

Ott, Attiat F., and Ludwig O. Dittrich. *The Federal Income Tax Burden on Households: The Effects of Tax Law Changes.* Washington, D.C.: American Enterprise Institute, 1981.

Ott, David J., et al. *State-Local Finances in the Last Half of the 1970's.* Washington, D.C.: American Enterprise Institute, 1975.

Paul, Diane B. *The Politics of the Property Tax.* Lexington, Mass.: Lexington Books, 1975.

Salzman, Ed. *Jerry Brown: High Priest and Low Politician.* Sacramento: California Journal Press, 1976.

Singer, Ethan A., et al. *California Government in Transition: Challenges, Analyses and Strategies.* San Francisco: Canfield Press, 1975.

ARTICLES

Adams, James R. "Coping with Proposition 13." *Wall Street Journal,* October 10, 1978.

Agran, Larry. "Revolt of the Homeowners: How Long Can Brown Avoid the Tax Reform Issue?" *California Journal,* November 1976, pp. 379–80.

Allan, John H. "California Tax Vote Will Affect Its Bonds." *New York Times,* June 5, 1978, p. 3.

Allman, T. D. "Jerry Brown: Nothing to Everyone." *Harper's,* July 1979, pp. 13–20.

Arizona Tax Research Association. "Arizona Will Be Effected [*sic*] by June Ballot Measure Limiting California Taxes." *Arizona Tax Research Association Newsletter* 6 (May 1978): 1–2.

Attiyeh, Richard, and Robert F. Engle. "Testing Some Propositions About Proposition 13." *National Tax Journal,* Supplement, 32, no. 2 (June 1979): 131–46.

Austermann, Winnifred M., and Daniel E. Pilcher. "A Legislator's Guide to State Tax and Spending Limits." N.p.: National Conference of State Legislatures, March 1979.

—— and ——. "The Tax Revolt Transformed." *State Legislatures,* July/August 1980, pp. 25–33.

Balderston, Frederick, et al. "Proposition 13, Property Transfers and the Real Estate Markets." Mimeographed. Commission on Government Reform Research Report 79–1. Berkeley, Calif.: Institute of Governmental Studies, 1979.

Bank of America. "Phase One of Our Proposition 13 Action Plan Producing Results." *Management Newsletter* 8, no. 35 (August 24, 1978).

Barkume, A. J. "Criteria for Voting Judgments on a Property Tax Initiative: An Analysis of the Watson Amendment." *National Tax Journal* 29 (December 1976): 448–60.

——. "Empirical Studies on Voting Behavior on Fiscal Referenda." Ph.D. dissertation. University of California at Santa Barbara, 1974.

Barnett, Mary. "How California Cities Are Curbing Residential Growth." *California Journal*, December 1980, pp. 475–77.

Barone, Michael. "What the Voters Were Saying." *Wall Street Journal*, November 22, 1978.

Bartell, Ken. "Unemployment Insurance and Jarvis-Gann." *Western City* 53 (May 1978): 10.

Bartlett, Bruce. "Kemp-Roth Revolution of 1978." *National Review*, October 27, 1978, pp. 1333–336.

———. "Whatever Happened to the Tax Revolt." *National Review*, December 7, 1979, pp. 1546–549.

Beebe, Jack H. "The Effect of Proposition 13 on California Municipal Debt." *Federal Reserve Bank of San Francisco Economic Review*, Winter 1979, pp. 25–38.

———. "Limiting Property Taxes." *Federal Reserve Bank of San Francisco Weekly Letter*, May 26, 1978, pp. 1–3.

———. "Proposition 13 and the Cost of California Debt." *National Tax Journal*, Supplement, 32, no. 2 (June 1979): 243–60.

Bevilacqua, N. D., and T. M. Larson. "Proposition 13 Research Inventory." Mimeographed. Berkeley, Calif.: Institute of Local Governmental Studies, 1978.

"The Big Tax Revolt." *Newsweek*, June 19, 1978.

Blackburn, Daniel J. "The Man Who Stole the Behr Bill." *New West*, May 8, 1978, pp. 79–81.

Blaustein, Arthur I. "Proposition 13 = Catch 22." *Harper's*, November 1978, pp. 18–22.

Borys, Michael J., and John F. Santoro. "An Analysis of the California Bond Market in 1978." *Municipal Market Developments* (Public Securities Association, New York City), November 9, 1978.

Boskin, Michael J. "So Where Do We Go from Here? The Recent Performance of the U.S. Economy and Its Prospects for the 80's." *Taxing & Spending*, Summer 1980, pp. 5–16.

———. "Some Neglected Economic Factors Behind Recent Tax and Spending Limitation Movements." *National Tax Journal*, Supplement, 32, no. 2 (June 1979): 37–42.

Bowen, Frank M., and Eugene C. Lee. "Limiting State Spending: The Legislature, the Electorate." Mimeographed. Commission on Government Reform Research Report 79–4. Berkeley, Calif.: Institute of Governmental Studies, 1979.

Break, George F. "After Proposition 13—the Deluge?" *Challenge,* January/February 1979, pp. 54–56.

————. "Interpreting Proposition 13: A Comment." *National Tax Journal,* Supplement, 32, no. 2 (June 1979): 43–46.

————. "State and Local Finance in the 80s." *Taxing & Spending,* Summer 1980, pp. 25–38.

Brennan, Geoffrey, and James M. Buchanan. "Tax Instruments as Constraints on the Disposition of Public Revenues." *Journal of Public Economics,* 9 (June 1978): 301–18.

Brody, Richard A. "Who Voted for Proposition 13?" *Taxing & Spending,* February 1979, pp. 26–28.

Burgess, Philip. "Political Implications of the Taxing and Expenditure Limitation Movement." In Selma J. Mushkin, ed., *Proposition 13 and Its Consequences for Public Management.* Cambridge, Mass.: Abt Books, 1979.

California Association of Realtors. "Directors Vote for Property Tax Relief." *California Real Estate* 58 (April 1978): 29–30.

California Council for Environmental and Economic Balance. "The Fiscal Impact of New Residential Development After Proposition 13." San Francisco, August 1979.

California Taxpayers' Association. "Law Enforcement Workload: A Comprehensive Survey of Sheriff and Police Budgets, Personnel, Workloads and Service." *Cal-Tax Study,* June 1979.

————. "Survey of Workloads in the Sheriff's Department of California Counties, 1967–68." Sacramento, *Cal-Tax Survey,* April 1968.

California Tax Reform Association. "Jarvis-Gann and the Behr Bill at a Glance: A Comparison." *Tax Back Talk* 4 (May 1978): 4–5.

————. "Tax Reform and School Finance for the Children." Mimeographed. Sacramento: California Tax Reform Association Foundation, February 14 and 15, 1979.

"California: Will It Choke Off Its Boom?" *Business Week,* July 17, 1978, pp. 54–60.

Cal-Tax Conference. "Construction Activity Post–Proposition 13." Mimeographed. Sacramento, Calif.: Cal-Tax, November 8, 1978.

Chaiken, Jan M., and Warren E. Walker. "Fiscal Limitation in California: Design for a Study of Effects on the Criminal Justice System." Santa Monica, Calif.: Rand Corporation, December 1978.

———— and ————. "Growth in Municipal Expenditures: A Case Study of Los Angeles." Santa Monica, Calif.: Rand Corporation, June 1979.

Chambers, Jay G. "Educational Cost Differentials Across School Districts in California." Mimeographed. Sacramento: School Finance Equalization Project, California State Department of Education, September 1978.

Champion, Hale. "Husbanding the Public Dollar." In Selma J. Mushkin, ed., *Proposition 13 and Its Consequences for Public Management*. Cambridge, Mass.: Abt Books, 1979.

Chapman, Jeffrey I., and John S. Kirlin. "Changes in Government Land Use Policies—An Unforeseen Response to the Jarvis-Gann Initiative." *Urban Interest*, Spring 1979, pp. 81–86.

Children's Rights Groups. "A Preliminary Analysis of the Effects of Proposition 13 on Services for Children in California." San Francisco, December 1978.

Citrin, Jacob. "Do People Want Something for Nothing: Public Opinion on Taxes and Spending." Working Paper no. 16. Mimeographed. Berkeley: University of California, 1978.

———. "The Alienated Voter." *Taxing & Spending*, October/November 1978, pp. 7–11.

Cochran, Dena. "The Rising Cost of Justice Compliments of Proposition 13." *California Journal*, January 1981, pp. 30–31.

Cohen, Richard E. "The Political System Attempts to Cope with Public Loss of Faith in Government." *National Journal* 3 (January 19, 1980): 110–16.

Congressional Quarterly Staff. "Congress Reacts to California Tax Revolt." In *Urban America*, Washington, D.C.: *Congressional Quarterly*, August 1978.

Connerly and Associates, Inc. "Fiscal Impact Analysis: A Broader Context." Mimeographed. N.p.: California Building Industry Association, April 1979.

Cook, Louise. "Voters Order Cities, States to Trim Budgets." *Palo Alto Times*, November 10, 1978.

Cooley, Thomas F., and C. J. LaCivita. "Allocative Efficiency and Distribution Equity in Water Pricing and Finance: A Post–Proposition 13 Analysis." *National Tax Journal*, Supplement, 32, no. 2 (June 1979): 215–28.

Coons, John E., and Josef Kul. "Schools: What's Happening to Local Control?" *Taxing & Spending*, October/November 1978, pp. 37–39.

Costa, Alan (California Assembly Office of Research). "Report on the Status of Redevelopment Agency Bonds and Notes as of June 30, 1978." Mimeographed. Sacramento, August 18, 1978.

Courant, Paul N., et al. "Public Employee Market Power and the Level of Government Spending." *American Economic Review,* forthcoming.

—— et al. "Why Voters Support Tax Limitation Amendments: The Michigan Case." *National Tax Journal,* 32, no. 1 (March 1980): 1–20.

Cox, Gail Diane. "The GOP Secret Weapon: Howard Jarvis's Signature." *California Journal,* January 1979, pp. 7–9.

Curtis, Ellen. "Analysis and Projections of Law Enforcement in Palo Alto." Mimeographed. Palo Alto, Calif.: Palo Alto Police Department, January 18, 1977.

Danziger, James N. "Rebellion on Fiscal Policy: Assessing the Effects of California's Proposition 13." *Urban Interest,* Spring 1979, pp. 59–67.

Danziger, James N., and Julius Margolis. "Research on Proposition 13: Report from Two Workshops." Mimeographed. Irvine: University of California, Irvine, Public Policy Research Organization, 1978.

Davis, Richard J. "Proposition 13 and Its Consequences for Public Management." In Selma J. Mushkin, ed., *Proposition 13 and Its Consequences for Public Management.* Cambridge, Mass.: Abt Books, 1979.

DeCanio, Stephen J. "Proposition 13 and the Failure of Economic Politics." *National Tax Journal,* Supplement, 32, no. 2 (June 1979): 55–66.

Dent, James. "Report of the State Advisory Committee on School Finance Equalization." Mimeographed. Sacramento: School Finance Equalization Project, California Department of Education, October 18, 1978.

Divoky, Diana. "Running Scared." *Inquiry,* September 18, 1978, pp. 6–8.

Donner, Al. "Balancing the Federal Budget." *Tax Revolt Digest,* August 1979, pp. 1–6.

Elias, Thomas D. "Initiative Loss Pattern Continues in California." *Santa Barbara News-Press,* November 17, 1978.

Federal Reserve Bank of San Francisco. "Proposition 13 and Financial Markets." *Economic Review,* Winter 1979.

Field, Mervin. "Sending a Message: Californians Strike Back." *Public Opinion,* July/August 1978, p. 5.

Fitzgerald, Maureen S. "California's Future Under Proposition 13." *California Journal,* Special Report, 1980, pp. 1–4.

——. "Computer Democracy: An Analysis of California's New Love

Affair with the Initiative Process." *California Journal*, June 1980, 1–15.

———. "The New Gann Plan: Is it Loaded With Loopholes?" *California Journal*, August 1979, pp. 284–85.

———. "What Went Wrong with the Post Commission?" *California Journal*, March 1979, pp. 87–90.

Fletcher, Thomas. "Anticipation and Uncertainty." In Selma J. Mushkin, ed., *Proposition 13 and Its Consequences for Public Management*. Cambridge, Mass.: Abt Books, 1979.

——— et al. "Allocating the One Percent Local Property Tax in California: An Analysis." Commission on Government Reform, Research Report 79–4. Berkeley, Calif.: Institute of Governmental Studies, 1979.

Foldvary, Fred E. "Public to Private." *Reason*, November 1978, pp. 20–23.

Foran, John F. "Proposition 13: Despite Its Appeal, It Isn't What the Doctor Ordered!" *California Savings and Loan Journal* 51 (May 1978): 12, 28–29.

Forrest, Lisa. "District Recreation Programs Go Private." Mimeographed. Redwood City, Calif.: Governmental Research Council of San Mateo County, 1979.

Freedman, Elisha C. "A Poorman's Guide to Restricting Local Government Taxes." In Selma J. Mushkin, ed., *Proposition 13 and Its Consequences for Public Management*. Cambridge, Mass.: Abt Books, 1979.

Freeman, Roger A. "Uncle Sam's Heavy Hand in Education." *National Review*, August 4, 1978, pp. 947–57.

Friedlander, George D. "The Jarvis-Gann Initiative, A Taxpayer Revolt in California: Implications for Municipal Bonds." N.p.: Smith Barney, Harris Upham and Co., February 3, 1978.

———. "The Jarvis-Gann Initiative, the 'Behr Bill' and the Investment Climate for California Municipal Securities." N.p.: Smith Barney, Harris Upham and Co., April 4, 1978.

Friedman, Milton. "A Progress Report." *Newsweek*, April 10, 1978, p. 90.

Gabriel, Stuart; Lawrence Katz; and Jennifer Wolch. "Local Land-Use Regulation and Proposition 13." *Taxing & Spending*, Spring 1980, pp. 73–81.

Gaffney, Mason. "Proposition 13: The California Model of the Taxpayer's Revolt." *Center Magazine*, November/December 1978, pp. 18–19.

Gelfand, M. David. "Seeking Local Government Financial Integrity Through Debt Ceilings, Tax Limits, and Expenditure Limits: The New York City Fiscal Crisis, The Taypayers Revolt and Beyond." *Minnesota Law Review* 63, no. 4 (April 1979): 545–608.

Genetski, Robert J., and Young D. Chin. "The Impact of State and Local Taxes on Economic Growth." *Harris Economic Research Office Service*, November 3, 1978.

Gerber, Edward R. "Life After Jarvis: The New Political Climate and the Changing Government Structure." *California Journal*, September 1978, pp. 291–93.

Giertz, J. Fred. "An Economic Approach to the Allocation of Police Resources." Evanston, Ill.: Northwestern University, June 1970.

Goetz, C. J. "Fiscal Illusion in State and Local Finance." In T. E. Borcherding, ed., *Budgets and Bureaucrats: The Sources of Government Growth*, Durham, N.C.: Duke University Press, 1977.

Goldwater, Barry. "Limiting Taxation in California: A Message to the Nation." *Congressional Record*, May 22, 1978, p. H4404.

Governmental Research Council of San Mateo County. "Analysis of the Fire Services Systems in San Mateo County." Mimeographed. Redwood City, Calif., November 1979.

———. "The San Mateo County Fire Services System in Perspective." Draft. Mimeographed. Redwood City, Calif., April 11, 1979.

Gramlich, E. M. "State and Local Budget Surpluses and Federal Grant Policies." In U.S., Congress, Joint Economic Committee, and House, Committee on Banking, Finance, and Urban Affairs, Subcommittee on the City, *Local Distress, State Surpluses, Proposition 13: Prelude to Fiscal Crisis or New Opportunities. Hearings*, 95th Cong., 2d sess., Washington, D.C.: Government Printing Office, July 25–26, 1978.

Green, Larry, and William C. Rempel. "Many States Make Severe Budget Cuts." *Los Angeles Times*, November 16, 1980.

Greene, Richard. "The Second Boston Tea Party." *Forbes*, November 24, 1980.

Gregory, Kristiana. "Emotion Building Over Jarvis-Gann." *Southern California Business* 42 (March 22, 1978): 1.

Greytak, David. "The Increasing Costs of Local Government: Underlying Causes and Policy Considerations." In U.S., Congress, Joint Economic Committee, and House, Committee on Banking, Finance, and Urban Affairs, Subcommittee on the City, *Local Distress, State*

Surpluses, Proposition 13: Prelude to Fiscal Crisis or New Opportunities. Hearings, 95th Cong., 2d Sess., Washington, D.C.: Government Printing Office, July 25–26, 1978.

Guthrie, James W. "Proposition 13 and the Future of California's Schools." *Phi Delta Kappan*, September 1978, pp. 12–15.

—— et al. "Proposition 13 and the Pursuit of Equality and Efficiency for California's Schools." Mimeographed. Berkeley, Calif.: School Finance Project, School of Education, University of California, July 1978.

Hagman, Donald G. "Life After Jarvis: How to End 'Coordimeetparalysis' and Reorganize Local Government." *California Journal*, October 1978, 336–37.

Halpern, Johnathan, et al. "The Relationship Between Response Time and Property Losses in Residential Fires." In *The Analysis of the Response Operations of a Municipal Fire Department.* Mimeographed. City of Calgary, Alberta, 1979.

Hamilton, Bruce W. "Capitalization of Intrajurisdictional Differences in Local Tax Prices." *American Economic Review* 66 (December 1976): 743–53.

Hamilton, Edward K. "The Greening of California." *Taxing & Spending*, October/November 1978, pp. 20–23.

——. "Ongoing Developments in California." In Selma J. Mushkin, ed., *Proposition 13 and Its Consequences for Public Management.* Cambridge, Mass.: Abt Books, 1979.

Hanna, Paul R. "The Instructional Dilemma Today: One Educator's Perspective." Mimeographed. Paper delivered before California County Superintendents of Schools and Staffs Annual Convention, January 20, 1977.

Hannan, J. Richard. "Tax Initiative: A Closer Look. Jarvis Dream Raises Questions, Could Turn into a Nightmare for All." *Southern California Business* 42 (February 22): 1, 14.

Harris, C. Lowell. "Property Taxation After the California Vote." *Tax Review* 39, no. 8 (August 1978): 35–38.

Haug Associates. "Public Attitudes Toward Taxation." Mimeographed. 3 volumes. Claremont, Calif.: Center for the Study of Law Structures, 1979.

Hechinger, Fred M. "Schoolyard Blues; The Decline of Public Education." *School Report*, January 20, 1979, pp. 20–21.

Heller, Walter. "Meat Axe Radicalism in California." *Wall Street Journal*, June 5, 1978, p. 20.

Hing, Mel. "Time or Surgery: A Local View." *California Journal*, February 1981, pp. 49–50.

Hirsch, Werner Z. "Lessons for the Era of Fiscal-Limitations Movements." *Taxing & Spending*, Fall 1980, pp. 59–64.

Hughes, Heiss and Associates. "Analysis of Performance Measurement in Local and State Governments." San Mateo, Calif., 1976.

———. "Analysis of the Fire Services System in Northern Monterey County." Mimeographed. San Mateo, Calif., 1980.

Inan, Michele. "Savior of the Cities: Would You Believe, Howard Jarvis?" *California Journal*, April 1979, 138–39.

Institute for Local Self-Government. "Alternatives to Traditional Public Safety Delivery Systems: Municipal Fire Insurance." Berkeley, Calif., 1977.

Irving, Carl. "Prop. 13 Casts Shadow Over State's Election." *San Francisco Sunday Examiner and Chronicle*, June 4, 1978.

Jackson, Gregory A. "Community Colleges and Budget Reduction." Mimeographed. Stanford: Institute for Research on Educational Finance and Governance, Stanford University, 1978.

Jacoby, Neil H. "A Case for Legal Limits on Government Spending." *Taxing & Spending*, October/November 1978, pp. 28–31.

Kasindorf, Jeanie. "Big Business Fights Jarvis." *New West*, May 22, 1978, p. 21.

———. "One More Vote for Proposition 13." *New West*, June 5, 1978, p. 72.

Kates, Don. "Can We Arrest Police Budgets?" *Taxing & Spending*, April 1979, p. 25.

Kemp, Jack. "Jarvis-Gann Is a Warning to Governments Everywhere That High Taxes Will Not Be Tolerated." *Congressional Record*, May 24, 1978, pp. H4567–569.

Kerper, M. "The California Tea Party." *American Educator* 2 (Winter 1978): 54–57.

Kimbell, Larry J. "Deciphering the Messages Behind California's Proposition 13." Mimeographed. Los Angeles: Office of Communications, Graduate School of Management, University of California, Los Angeles, July 24, 1978.

———. "Economic Forecast." *Top Priority*, Winter 1981, pp. 6–7.

Kimbell, Larry J., et al. "A Framework for Investigating the Tax Incidence Effects of Proposition 13." *National Tax Journal*, Supplement, 32, no. 2 (June 1979): 313–24.

Kirlin, John J. "Proposition 13 and the Financing of Public Services." In Selma J. Mushkin, ed., *Proposition 13 and Its Consequences for Public Management*, Cambridge, Mass.: Abt Books, 1979.

Kirlin, John J., and Jeffrey I. Chapman. "California State Finance and Proposition 13." *National Tax Journal*, Supplement, 32, no. 2 (June 1979): 269–76.

Kirst, Michael W. "The New Politics of State Education Finance." *Phi Delta Kappan*, February 1979, pp. 427–32.

———. "Research Issues Arising from Proposition 13." Mimeographed. Paper prepared for the Ford Foundation Conference on "Education Finance After Propostion 13," San Francisco, Calif., June 1978.

———. "Spenders Versus Tax Cutters: A Tale of Two Networks." Mimeographed. Stanford, Calif., n.d.

Kuzela, Lad. "Taxpayers Revolt Is Starting to Happen." *Industry Week* 197 (May 29, 1978): 17–19.

Ladd, Everett Carll. "Opinion Roundup: The Tax Revolt." *Public Opinion*, July/August 1978, p. 32.

———. "What Voters Really Want." *Fortune*, December 18, 1978, pp. 40–48.

——— et al. "The Polls: Taxing and Spending." *Public Opinion Quarterly* 43, no. 1 (Spring 1979): 126–35.

Ladd, Helen F. "An Economic Evaluation of State Limitations on Local Taxing and Spending Powers." *National Tax Journal*, March 1978, pp. 1–18.

League of California Cities. "Effect of Proposition 13 on Police and Fire Services." Sacramento: League of California Cities, April 1978.

Leary, Mary Ellen. "California: The Property Tax War." *Atlantic*, May 1978, pp. 20–25.

Lee, Mordecai. "Personnel Management in Wisconsin." In Selma J. Mushkin, ed., *Proposition 13 and Its Consequences for Public Management*. Cambridge, Mass.: Abt Books, 1979.

Leff, Donna Rosene. "States Follow California's Lead." *Taxing & Spending*, October/November 1978, pp. 26–27.

Leischuck, Gerald. "A Discouraging Summer: A Calamitous Future?" *Phi Delta Kappan*, September 1978, pp. 2–11.

Lekachman, Robert. "Proposition 13 and the New Conservatism." *Change*, September 1978, pp. 22–27.

Levin, David S. "Receipts and Expenditures of State Governments and of Local Governments, 1959–76." *Survey of Current Business*, May 1978, pp. 15–21.

Levy, Elaine I. "Can Public-Employee Unions Rebound After Proposition 13?" *California Journal,* December 1978, pp. 398–99.

Levy, Frank. "On Understanding Proposition 13." *Public Interest,* no. 56 (Summer 1979): 66–89.

Levy, Frank, and Paul Zamolo. "The Preconditions of Proposition 13." Mimeographed. Working Paper 1105–01. Washington, D.C.: Urban Institute, October 1978.

Levy, M. "Voting on California's Tax and Expenditure Initiative." *National Tax Journal,* 28, no. 4 (1975): 426–35.

Lewis, Charles R. "The Effects of Proposition 13 on the City of El Cerrito." *Urban Interest,* Spring 1979, pp. 68–74.

Lewis, I. A. "Tax Revolt: The California Data." Paper for 34th Annual Conference of the American Association for Public Opinion Research, Buck Hill Falls, Pennsylvania, May 31–June 3, 1979.

Liebert, Larry. "The Brown Campaign: Jostling Among the Big Six." *California Journal,* September 1978, pp. 286–88.

Likert, Rensis, and Charles T. Araki. "Improving the Performance of a Governmental Agency." In Selma J. Mushkin, ed., *Proposition 13 and Its Consequences for Public Management.* Cambridge, Mass.: Abt Books, 1979.

Lindsey, Robert. "California Tax Revolt: Lesson for Legislators." *New York Times,* June 12, 1978.

———. "California to Vote on Plan to Limit Property Taxes: Schools and Local Governments Fear Revenue Losses." *New York Times,* January 5, 1978, p. 14.

———. "Few Cutbacks in Service." *Sacramento Bee,* November 7, 1978.

Lipset, Seymour Martin. "The Public Pulse." *Taxing & Spending,* April 1979, pp. 32–33.

Lipset, Seymour Martin, and Earl Raab. "The Message of Proposition 13." *Commentary,* September 1978, pp. 42–46.

Lipset, Seymour Martin, and William Schneider. "Is the Tax Revolt Over?" *Taxing & Spending,* Summer 1980, pp. 73–78.

Lipson, Albert J. "Political and Legal Responses to Proposition 13 in California." R-2483-DOJ. Santa Monica, Calif.: Rand Corporation, January 1980.

Luttgens, Leslie L. "Proposition 13: The Implications for Philanthropy." *Grants Magazine,* 2, no. 1 (March 1979): 23–30.

Magaddino, J. P.; Eugenie Froedge Toma; and Mark Toma. "Proposition

13: A Public Choice Appraisal." *Public Finance Quarterly* 8, no. 2 (April 1980): 223–35.

Magstadt, Thomas M. "Using Proposition 13 to Introduce Students to Political Science." *News* 22 (Summer 1979): 5–8.

Main, Jeremy. "The Tax Revolt Takes Hold." *Money*, February 1980, pp. 49–55.

Margolis, Julius. "Benefits-Costs, Government Behavior and Tax Limitations." Paper for Conference on Tax Limitations at the University of California, Santa Barbara. University of California, Irvine: December 14–15, 1978.

Martin, Rich. "Prop. 13 Threatens Pay." *California State Employee* 49 (May 24, 1978): 1.

McDiarmid, Hugh. "The Tax Packages All Wrapped Up In Tisch." *Detroit Free Press*, November 2, 1980.

McWatters, Ann R. "Financing Local Government Capital Formation Under Proposition 13." *Urban Interest*, Spring 1979, pp. 87–92.

"Measuring Education." *Cal-Tax Research Bulletin*, August 1–14, 1981.

Meier, Marcia. "State Employees: Both Underpaid and Overpaid." *California Journal*, January 1979, pp. 22–24.

Meltsner, Arnold J. "Earthquakes and Proposition 9." *Taxing & Spending*, Summer 1980, pp. 87–94.

Menchik, Mark David, and Anthony H. Pascal. "The Equity Effects of Restraints on Taxing and Spending." Rand Paper Series P-6469. Santa Monica, Calif.: Rand Corporation, May 1980.

Merry, George B. "Proposition 13–Type Measures on Ballots in Nine States." *Christian Science Monitor*, September 11, 1980.

Mieszkowski, P. "The Property Tax: An Excise Tax or a Profits Tax?" *Journal of Public Economics* 1, no. 1 (April 1972): 72–96.

Mitchell, Laura Remson. "Life After Jarvis: How Proposition 13 Changed Assessment Practices." *California Journal*, December 1978, pp. 400–402.

———. "The Science of Serendipity." *California Journal*, February 1981, pp. 51–52.

Mitofsky, Warren, et al. "An Exchange on the Public's View of Proposition 13." In Selma J. Mushkin, ed., *Proposition 13 and Its Consequences for Public Management*. Cambridge, Mass.: Abt Books, 1979.

Mulrooney, Keith F. "Tax Restriction: A Public Administrator's View." In Selma J. Mushkin, ed., *Proposition 13 and Its Consequences for*

Public Management. Cambridge, Mass.: Abt Books, 1979.

Mushkin, Selma J. "The Case for User Fees." *Taxing & Spending,* April 1979, pp. 16–19.

Mushkin, Selma J., et al. "The Taxpayer Revolt: An Opportunity to Make Positive Changes in Local Government." In Selma J. Mushkin, ed., *Proposition 13 and Its Consequences for Public Management.* Cambridge, Mass.: Abt Books, 1979.

Nakao, Annie. "What's Wrong with Our Public Schools and What Can We Do to Make Them Better?" *California Journal,* November 1978, pp. 348–50.

Neufeld, John. "Taxrate Referenda and the Property Taxpayers' Revolt." *National Tax Journal* 30, no. 4 (December 1977): 441–56.

Nigro, Peter D. "Proposition 13 and the Subterranean Income." *USA Today,* January 1980, pp. 20–22.

Oakland, William H. "Proposition XIII: Genesis and Consequences." *National Tax Journal,* Supplement, 32, no. 2 (June 1979): 387–409.

————. "Proposition 13: Genesis and Consequences." *Economic Review* (Quarterly Journal of the Federal Reserve Bank of San Francisco), Special Issue on "Proposition 13 and Financial Markets," Winter 1979, p. 12.

Orr, Daniel. "Proposition 13: Tax Reform's Lexington Bridge?" *Policy Review,* Fall 1978, pp. 57–67.

Paddock, Brian. "Taxes: Which is Better, Sales or Income?" *Palo Alto Times,* November 15, 1978.

Parrott, J. B. "Proposition 13: What It Does, Why It Passed in California." *California School Boards* 37, no. 6 (July/August 1978): 27.

Pascal, Anthony H., and Mark David Menchik. "Fiscal Containment: Who Gains? Who Loses?" Santa Monica, Calif.: Rand Corporation, September 1979.

Pascal, Anthony H., et al. "Fiscal Containment of Local and State Government." Rand/R-2494-FF/RC. Santa Monica, Calif.: Rand Corporation, September 1979.

Paschall, Glenn. "Life with Jarvis: The First Two Months." Mimeographed. Research Council Report, August 15, 1978.

Paschall, Robert H. "The Unknown World of Proposition 13." Mimeographed. Unpublished paper, June 1978.

Petersen, John E., and Marcia Claxton. "Tax Expenditure Limits: Proposition 13 and Its Alternatives." In Selma J. Mushkin, ed., *Proposition 13 and Its Consequences for Public Management,* Cambridge, Mass.: Abt Books, 1979.

Peterson, George E., and Arthur P. Solomon. "Property Taxes and Populist Reform." *Public Interest,* Winter 1973, pp. 60–75.

Pollard, Vic. "The Post-13 Legislature: Beautiful For Business." *California Journal,* January 1980, pp. 32–34.

Poole, Robert W., Jr. "Fees vs. User Charges." *Fiscal Watchdog,* Column 35 (September 1979).

———. "User Fees Sweep California." *Fiscal Watchdog,* Column 21 (July 1978).

———. "Whither Public Libraries?" *Fiscal Watchdog,* Column 36 (October 1979).

Posner, Paul L. "Proposition 13 and the Federal Grant System." In Selma J. Mushkin, ed., *Proposition 13 and Its Consequences for Public Management,* Cambridge, Mass.: Abt Books, 1979.

Post, A. Alan. "California's Fiscal Future." *Tax Revolt Digest,* July 1979, pp. 1–4.

———. "Effects of Proposition 13 on the State of California." *National Tax Journal,* Supplement, 32, no. 2 (June 1979): 381–86.

Prothro, Laurie. "Tax Revolt Round-Up." *Taxing & Spending,* Summer 1980, pp. 79–81.

Purnell, Dan. "Wounding the Culprit That Created the 'Obscene' Surplus." *California Journal,* November 1978, pp. 373–75.

Quinn, Tony. "The Specter of 'Black Wednesday': How the Establishment Destroys Unwanted Initiatives Like Jarvis." *California Journal,* May 1978, pp. 153–54.

Rabinovitz, Francine F., and Edward K. Hamilton. "On Piper-Payers and Tune Callers: Proposition 13 and the Financing of the Los Angeles Unified School District." *National Tax Journal,* Supplement, 32, no. 2 (June 1979): 355–70.

Rabushka, Alvin. "The Attractions of a Flat-Rate Tax System." *Wall Street Journal,* March 25, 1981.

———. "Tax and Spending Limits." In Peter Duignan and Alvin Rabushka, eds., *The United States in the 1980s,* Stanford: Hoover Institution Press, 1980, pp. 85–108.

Rafuse, Robert W. "Proposition 13: Initial Impacts on the Finances of Four County Governments." *National Tax Journal,* Supplement, 32, no. 2 (June 1979): 229–42.

Ranney, Austin. "The Year of the Referendum." *Public Opinion,* November/December 1978, pp. 26–27.

Reid, Joseph D. "Tax Revolts in Historical Perspective." *National Tax Journal,* Supplement, 32, no. 2 (June 1979): 67–74.

Reischauer, Robert D. "Intergovernmental Responsibility for Meeting the Equity Considerations of Proposition 13: The Federal Role." In Selma J. Mushkin, ed., *Proposition 13 and Its Consequences for Public Management*, Cambridge, Mass.: Abt Books, 1979.

Rennert, Leo. "Jarvis-Gann Along the Potomac." *California Journal*, March 1978, p. 167.

Reston, James. "Uniquack on Prop. 13." *New York Times*, June 9, 1978, p. A27.

"Revolt Against Property Taxes: Outcries from Householders, Call for Reform, New Legislation." *U.S. News & World Report*, January 17, 1977, pp. 81–83.

Ricardo-Campbell, Rita. "Proposition 13 and National Health Policy." *Forum on Medicine*, April 1979, pp. 274–77.

Romans, Thomas, and Ganti Subrahmanyam. "State and Local Taxes, Transfers and Regional Economic Growth." *Southern Economic Journal* 46, no. 2 (October 1979): 435–43.

Roscow, James P. "Municipals Under Attack." *Financial World*, May 15, 1978, pp. 35–38.

Rousselot, John H. "High Tax Burdens." *Congressional Record*, April 27, 1978, pp. E2186–187.

———. "Property Tax Limitation in California." *Congressional Record*, April 4, 1978, pp. E1650–651.

Salzman, Ed. "Brown's Austerity Plan." *California Journal*, February 1981, pp. 46–48.

———. "Brown's Shaky Budget, Even Without Jarvis II." *California Journal*, February 1980, pp. 59–60.

———. "Dear Landlord: You Have a Friend in Howard Jarvis." *New West*, February 27, 1978, pp. 68–69.

———. "Do Liberals Dare Challenge Brown's Republican Budget?" *California Journal*, February 1979, pp. 50–51.

———. "The Facts of Life in a Post Proposition 13 World." *California Journal*, May 1979, pp. 169–71.

———. "Power to the Controller Under the New Gann Plan." *California Journal*, January 1979, pp. 17–19.

———. "The Reagan Model for Brown's Political Future." *California Journal*, June 1980, pp. 216–18.

———. "What Happened to the Rules in the Brown-Younger Race." *California Journal*, September 1978, pp. 283–85.

Sansweet, Stephen J. "Catch 13 Californians Discover Tax-Cut Mania

Has a Corollary: Fee Fever." *Wall Street Journal*, June 1, 1979.

———. "Companies' Big Saving From Proposition 13 Is Slow to Reach Public." *Wall Street Journal*, February 13, 1979.

Sapp, Terry F. "Perspective Reconciling Jarvis." *E. F. Hutton Fixed Income Research*, June 23, 1978, pp. 1–3.

Savarese, James M. "Tax Reform and Proposition 13." In Selma J. Mushkin, ed., *Proposition 13 and Its Consequences for Public Management*, Cambridge, Mass.: Abt Books, 1979.

Schneider, William. "Punching Through the Jarvis Myth." *Los Angeles Times*, Opinion Page, Part VI, June 11, 1978.

Sears, D. O. "The Jarvis Amendment: Self-Interest or Symbolic Politics?" Unpublished paper, University of California at Los Angeles.

Security Pacific National Bank. "California Construction Trends." Monthly bulletin. Los Angeles: Security Pacific National Bank, Research Department, April 1980.

———. "California Construction Trends." Monthly bulletin. Los Angeles: Security Pacific National Bank, Research Department, June 1980.

Settle, Allen K. "California State Legislative Efforts Towards School District and Property Tax Reform." Mimeographed. San Luis Obispo, Calif.: Polytechnic State University, 1978.

Seward, Davis K. "Property Tax Reform: A Game of Chance?" *Critique* 3 (Winter 1978): 5–11.

Shalala, Donna. "The Early Referenda and Federal Response." In Selma J. Mushkin, ed., *Proposition 13 and Its Consequences for Public Management*, Cambridge, Mass.: Abt Books, 1979.

——— et al. "The Property Tax and the Voters: An Analysis of State Constitutional Referenda in 1972–3." New York: Institute of Philosophy and Politics of Education, Columbia University, 1973.

Shannon, John, and Carol S. Weissert. "After Jarvis: Tough Questions for Fiscal Policymakers." *Intergovernmental Perspective* 4 (Summer 1979): 8–12.

Shapiro, Perry, and W. Douglas Morgan. "The General Revenue Effects of the California Property Tax Limitation Amendment." *National Tax Journal*, 31, no. 2 (June 1978): 119–28.

Shedd, Margaret. "Shift to Fees Poses Seven Key Questions." *Cal-Tax News*, May 1–14, 1979, pp. 1–6.

Shulman, Davis. "For Land's Sake, What's Prop. 13 Done?" *Los Angeles Times*, July 23, 1978, Part 4, p. 5.

Siegel, Barry N. "Thoughts on the Tax Revolt." *International Institute for Economic Research Original Paper* 21. Los Angeles, Calif., June 1979.

Simpson, Richard P. "The Five Key Provisions of SB1." *Cal-Tax News,* March 1, 1978, pp. 3–4.

————. "Jarvis-Gann: How 'Bad' Do You Want Tax Relief?" *Cal-Tax News,* October 1, 1977, p. 1.

————. "Spotlight on Proposition 13." *Western City* 53 (April 1978): 9–12.

Solomon, Arthur P. "The Cost of Housing: An Analysis of Trends, Incidence, and Causes." In *The Cost of Housing,* Proceedings of the Third Annual Conference, Federal Home Loan Bank of San Francisco, December 6–7, 1977.

Sonstelie, Jon. "Should Businesses Pay More Taxes Than Individuals?" *Taxing & Spending,* October/November 1978, pp. 16–19.

Spindel, Ervin. "Potholes and Prayers." *Western City* 53 (May 1978): 12.

Stanfield, Rochelle L. "Less Than a Full-Scale Rebellion." *National Journal,* no. 45 (December 11, 1978): 1820–821.

Stanton, John. "Business Climate Improved by '13.' " *Peninsula Times-Tribune,* November 24, 1979.

"State of Health." *Cal-Tax Research Bulletin,* May 1979, pp. 1–8.

Steiger, Paul E. "Study Predicts Short-Lived Economic Upturn." *Los Angeles Times,* June 14, 1979.

Stern, David, et al. "From Both Sides, How California Teachers and School District Representatives View Collective Bargaining Under SB160 of 1975." Mimeographed. Berkeley: Field Service Center, School of Education, University of California, June 1978.

Stumpf, Jack, and Paul Terrell. "Proposition 13 and California Human Services." Mimeographed. California, National Association of Social Workers, February 1979.

Sussman, Barry. "Waste Angers Taxpayers, Poll Shows." *Los Angeles Times,* October 15, 1978.

Teilhet, Paul. "Proposition 13 (Jarvis-Gann Initiative)." Burbank: California Federation of Teachers, March 15, 1978.

Thomas, William V. "Property Tax Relief." *Editorial Research Reports* 1 (May 19, 1978): 363–80.

Tobin, Charles A. "Proposition 13 and Intergovernmental Relations." Unpublished paper, 1979.

Tompkins, Susanne. "Proposition 2½: Massachusetts and the Tax Revolt." *Journal of the Institute for Socioeconomic Studies* 4, no. 1 (Spring 1981): 21–32.

Tracy, Phil. "The Jarvis Revolt: Rallying 'Round an Old Man's Obsession." *New West*, May 22, 1978, pp. 17–21.

Tullock, Gordon. "Why Politicians Won't Cut Taxes." *Taxing & Spending*, October/November 1978, pp. 12–14.

Turk, Herman. "Public Portrayals of Electoral Mandate and Governmental Response." Photocopied. Los Angeles, 1978.

Turner, Wallace. "Next Weeks Vote on a Tax Limit Has California Officials in Turmoil." *New York Times*, May 30, 1978, p. 2.

———. "Proposal to Limit Tax Dominates G.O.P. Campaign in California." *New York Times*, April 30, 1978, p. 26.

———. "Tax Limit Becomes Key Issue in Coast G.O.P. Primary." *New York Times*, May 19, 1978, p. 13.

———. "Tax Question Divides Voters in California: Opponents of Proposal to Limit Local Revenue Open Drive as Poll Shows Plan Lagging." *New York Times*, April 13, 1978, p. 24.

University of California, Los Angeles. Business Forecasting Project. "Additional Impacts of Proposition 13 Not Quantified in the Model Run." Los Angeles, May 11, 1978.

———. "The Impacts of Proposition 8 and 13 on the California Economy." Los Angeles, May 11, 1978.

———. "Initial Fiscal Impacts of Proposition 8 on the California Economy." Los Angeles, May 11, 1978.

———. "Initial Fiscal Impacts of Proposition 13 on the California Economy." Los Angeles, May 11, 1978.

———. "The UCLA Business Forecast for California Forecasts: 3rd Quarter 1978, 4th Quarter 1983." Los Angeles, September 1978.

Van Slambrouck, Paul. "Tax Outlook to Year 2000: Lighter Load." *Christian Science Monitor*, January 18, 1980, p. 3.

Vincent, Phillip E. "Alternative Measures of Fiscal Capacity of School Districts in California." Mimeographed. Denver: Education Finance Center, January 1979.

Vincent, Phillip E., and Raymond M. Reinhard. "Tax Burden Distribution and Property Tax Capitalization in School Districts in California." Mimeographed. Denver: Education Finance Center, March 1979.

Wagman, Robert. "Tax-Slashing Measures Fail at Polls in 5 States." *Peninsula Times-Tribune*, November 14, 1980.

Walker, D. B. "Proposition 13 and California's System of Governance." *Intergovernmental Perspective* 4 (Summer 1978): 13–15.

Walker, Warren E., et al. "The Impact of Proposition 13 on Local Criminal Justice Agencies: Emerging Patterns." Santa Monica, Calif.: Rand Corporation, June 1980.

Weber, Christopher P. "The Great Tax Cutters: From Napoleon to Indira Gandhi." *Conservative Digest*, January 1979, pp. 32–34.

———. "Slashing Taxes Is Good for What Ails Us." *Reason*, November 1978, pp. 17–24.

White, Michelle J. "Renters and Proposition 13: What Went Wrong?" *Taxing & Spending*, October/November 1978, pp. 24–27.

Wildavsky, Aaron. "The Reverse Pogo Principle: Constitutional Expenditure Limitation Is Not Worthwhile for Anyone Unless Everyone Does It." Unpublished paper. Fels Lectures, 1979.

Winkler, Donald. "Fiscal Limitations in the Provision of Local Public Services: The Case of Education." *National Tax Journal*, Supplement, 32, no. 2 (June 1979): 329–42.

Wong, William. "California Property-Tax Cut Jeopardizes Universal Access to College in the State." *Wall Street Journal*, July 26, 1978.

———. "Year of the Ax." *Wall Street Journal*, November 30, 1978.

Zion, William R. "Special Districts: A Special Tax Limitation Problem." *Urban Interest*, Spring 1979, pp. 75–80.

GOVERNMENT PUBLICATIONS

Atherton [Calif.]. Police Department. "Yearly Report, 1978." Mimeographed. Atherton, 1979.

California. Department of Education. "California Schools Beyond Serrano." Mimeographed. Sacramento, 1978.

———.———. "Profiles of School District Performance, 1977–78: A Guide to Interpretation." Mimeographed. Sacramento, 1978.

———.———. State Advisory Committee on School Facilities. "Report: A Recommended Plan for Statewide Financing of School Facilities." Mimeographed. Sacramento, 1976.

———. Department of Finance. Financial Research Section. *California Statistical Abstract*. Selected issues. Sacramento.

———. Department of Justice. Division of Law Enforcement. Bureau of Criminal Statistics. *County Criminal Justice Agency Data in California by Fiscal Year*. Selected years. Sacramento.

———. Employment Development Department. *Annual Report on Job Growth in California, 1977.* Sacramento, 1977.

———.———. *Annual Report on Job Growth in California, 1978.* Sacramento, 1978.

———.———. "EED News Release." Mimeographed. Sacramento, 1978–1981.

———.———. "Wage and Salary Employment by Industry: California, 1972–1977." Mimeographed. Sacramento.

———. Fair Political Practices Commission. *Campaign Contribution and Spending Report.* Sacramento, 1978.

———. Legislature. Assembly. Committee on Local Government. "Current Financial Status of Special Districts." Mimeographed. Sacramento: Assembly, Office of Research, September 1978.

———.———.———.———. "The Impact of Proposition 13 (The Jarvis-Gann Property Tax Initiative) on Local Government Programs and Services." Mimeographed. Sacramento, May 1978.

———.———.———.———. and Committee on Revenue and Taxation: Staff. *The Impact of Proposition 13 on Local Government Programs and Services.* Sacramento, May 1978.

———.———.———. Committee on Revenue and Taxation. "Facts About Proposition 13, the Jarvis-Gann Initiative." Rev. ed. Mimeographed. Sacramento, February 21, 1978.

———.———.———.———. "Legislative Hearings on Property Tax Reform and Relief, Analysis of Current Legislation with Supporting Materials, February 28–March 2, 1977." Mimeographed. Sacramento, 1977.

———.———.———. Office of Research. "An Analysis of the AB 8 Deflator: Statement to the Assembly Ways and Means Committee." Mimeographed. Sacramento, January 14, 1981.

———.———.———.———. "City and County Finances in the Post-Proposition 13 Era: An Analysis of Changes in the Fiscal Condition of California Cities and Counties During the 1977–78 to 1979–80 Fiscal Years." Mimeographed. 2 vols. Sacramento, June 1981.

———.———.———.———. "Local Government Finance: Statement to the Assembly Committee on Ways and Means." Mimeographed. Sacramento, January 14, 1981.

———.———. Joint Budget Committee. "An Analysis of Proposition 13, the Jarvis-Gann Property Tax Initiative." Mimeographed. Sacramento, May 1978.

———.———.———. and Legislative Analyst's Office. *Analysis of the*

Budget Bill of the State of California, Fiscal Year, July 1, 1979, to June 30, 1980, and other selected years. Sacramento.

——.——. Legislative Analyst's Office. "Impact of Inflation on the State Budget Growth. Statement to the Assembly Ways and Means Committee." Mimeographed. Sacramento, November 17, 1980.

——.——. Senate. Office of Research. "Jarvis-Gann Initiative." Mimeographed. Sacramento, December 13, 1977.

——. Secretary of State. *Statement of Vote, June 8, 1976, Primary Election.* Sacramento, 1976.

——.——. "Thirteen: Tax Limitation-Initiative Constitutional Amendment." In *California Voters Pamphlet (June 6, 1978),* Sacramento, 1978, pp. 56–60.

——. State Board of Equalization. *Annual Report, 1978–79.* Sacramento, 1979.

——.——. *California Property Tax Laws.* Sacramento, 1977.

——. State Controller. *Annual Report of Financial Transactions Concerning Cities of California.* Selected issues. Sacramento.

——.——. *Annual Report of Financial Transactions Concerning Counties of California.* Selected issues. Sacramento.

——.——. *Annual Report of Financial Transactions Concerning School Districts of California.* Selected issues. Sacramento.

——.——. *Annual Report of Financial Transactions Concerning Special Districts of California.* Selected issues. Sacramento.

——.——. *Annual Report of the State of California.* Selected issues. Sacramento.

——. Supreme Court. Concurring and dissenting opinions: *Amador Valley Joint Union High School District et al.* v. *State Board of Equalization et al. County of Alameda et al.* v. *SBC City and County of San Francisco et al.* v. *Joseph E. Tinney as Tax Assessor.* Filed September 22, 1978. Mimeographed.

California School Boards Association. "Cutting the Fat." Special issue of *California School Boards,* 37, no. 6 (July/August 1978).

——. *Proposition 13 Information Service.* 2 vols. Sacramento, October 16, 1978–August 21, 1979.

California Fire Chiefs Association. Workshop. "California Fire Services Post Proposition 13." Mimeographed. Sacramento, February 1979.

California Community Colleges. Chancellor's Office. "Impact of Proposition 13, Chancellor's Office Survey, Part 1." Mimeographed. October 1978.

Council of State Governments. "Limiting State Taxes and Expenditures." Lexington, Ky., n.d.

County Supervisors Association of California. *California County Fact Book.* Annual report. Sacramento.

––––. "Special County Report on the Effects of Proposition 13 (Jarvis-Gann and Proposition 8/Senate Bill 1)." Mimeographed. Sacramento, n.d.

Mill Valley [Calif.]. Task Force on Municipal Fire Insurance. "Report." Mimeographed. November 20, 1978.

Mountain View [Calif.]. Police Department. "Activity Report." Annual report. Mimeographed. 1974–1978.

National Association of State Budget Officers. "Limitations on State Deficits." Mimeographed. Lexington, Ky.: Council of State Governments, April 1976.

––––. "Limitations on State Deficits: Text of Constitutional and Statutory Provisions." Lexington, Ky.: Council of State Governments, 1976.

Palo Alto [Calif.]. Police Department. "Annual Report." Mimeographed. 1968–1975/76.

San Mateo [Calif.]. Local Agency Formation Commission. "General Policies and Criteria for the Development and Determination of Spheres of Influence." Mimeographed. Adopted September 18, 1974; revised June 18, 1975.

U.S. Advisory Commission on Intergovernmental Relations. *State Limitations on Local Taxes and Expenditures.* Washington, D.C., 1977.

––––. Comptroller General. "Will Federal Assistance to California Be Affected by Proposition 13?" Washington, D.C.: General Accounting Office, August 10, 1978.

––––. Congress. Congressional Budget Office. *Proposition 13: Its Impact on the Nation's Economy, Federal Revenues, and Federal Expenditures.* Washington, D.C.: Government Printing Office, 1978.

––––. Department of the Interior. Heritage Conservation and Recreation Service. *Fees and Charges Handbook.* Washington, D.C., March 1979.

––––. President. *Economic Report* (transmitted to the Congress, January 1981). Washington, D.C.: Government Printing Office, 1981.

INDEX

A